# The Hawke Battalion of the Royal Naval Division

Lieutenant-Colonel Sir Leslie Wilson, K.C.I.E., C.M.G.

# The Hawke Battalion of the Royal Naval Division

During the First World War at Gallipoli and on the Western Front

Douglas Jerrold

**LEONAUR**

*The Hawke Battalion of the Royal Naval Division*
*During the First World War at Gallipoli and on the Western Front*
by Douglas Jerrold

First published under the title
*The Hawke Battalion*

Leonaur is an imprint of Oakpast Ltd

Copyright in this form © 2014 Oakpast Ltd

ISBN: 978-1-78282-413-8 (hardcover)
ISBN: 978-1-78282-414-5 (softcover)

http://www.leonaur.com

Publisher's Notes

# Contents

# Introduction

This record lays no claim to be a work of art. It is, however, a straightforward story, based largely on contemporary documents, and always on the impressions of the principal actors in the different scenes, of the doings of one of those predominantly civilian units whose successes were in some ways the most unexpected military feature of the war.

As far as has been possible for me, I have set down not what we afterwards imagined our feelings to have been, still less what appeared afterwards as the military significance of our small achievements, but our actual day to day experiences as they came to us and as we reacted to them.

Regarded as military history, the narrative shows a certain lack of proportion, and on the human side it concerns itself too greatly, though inevitably, with the doings of the officers. I can only excuse these defects by putting this forward largely as a personal narrative. I have written elsewhere what I believe to be a reasonably critical history of the military achievement of the Royal Naval Division; here I have written of what, within my personal experience and that of my many collaborators, was seen and known, from the front line or thereabouts, of some of the more romantic as well as of many of the routine incidents of a great historical event.

We shall not see again with the eyes of youth the magic waters of the Dardanelles, or hear for the first time the thunder of the guns from the sea. If we revisit the dust-swept plains of Gallipoli, where we spent such ardent hours, it will not be under the shadow of a hostile and implacable Achibaba. We cannot experience again the disillusion which the barren austerity of the Somme battlefields brought down on us as we crossed them for the first time in October, 1916. Certainly we shall not see it a second time on the horizon the signs of such a victory as seemed possible before the promise of the autumn of 1918 was forgotten in the corridors of Versailles.

Yet these vivid sensations were as real in our experience then as those faint impressions which are all that we retain of that experience today. Rather, they are infinitely truer in relation to the events which gave rise to them, and if that fact is forgotten, the events themselves will be distorted in the mind of posterity.

This is the justification for such works as the present one, and if the pages which follow can here and there kindle once again the fires of recollection, they will not have been written in vain.

My best thanks for much help and advice and for the loan of documents and maps are due to Lieutenant-Colonel Sir Leslie Wilson, K.C.I.E., C.M.G., D.S.O., Commander W. G. Ramsay Fairfax, C.M.G., D.S.O., R.N., Lieutenant-Commander R. Blackmore, M.C., Commander E. M. Lockwood, D.S.O., Commander R. H. Shelton, D.S.O., Lieutenant Stephenson, R.N.V.R., Lieutenant H. W. Dickins, R.N.V.R., and many other former officers of the battalion.

Particular thanks are due to Mr. Charles Ker for his kindness in allowing me to publish so many extracts from the letters of his son, Lieutenant William Ker, R.N.V.R., which give an interest and value to portions of this record far above any which I could have supplied.

Douglas Jerrold.
Hastings.

CHAPTER 1

# A False Dawn

The origin and early activities of the Hawke Battalion have an interest rather remote from this story. Yet the reasons for the formation by the Admiralty in August, 1914, of the Royal Naval Division must be touched upon. The Naval Division, and therefore the Hawke Battalion, had its beginning in a pre-war decision of the Committee of Imperial Defence authorizing the organisation by the Admiralty of a land force (to be formed from the Royal Marine Light Infantry and Artillery), to be used on the outbreak of war for the seizure, fortification, or protection of any temporary naval bases which might be required overseas.

The Great War, opening with the German threat to the Channel ports, gave a new and perhaps unexpected relevance to this decision, and the peace-time establishment of the Royal Marines provided no basis from which any substantial military force could be improvised. It was in these circumstances that some eight thousand naval reservists were sent to Walmer and Bettysanger to construct their own camps, and turn themselves into eight infantry battalions to form the two Naval Brigades of what was to be known as the Royal Naval Division.

These reservists were officered by a few retired naval officers, a few officers lent from the brigade of Guards, one or two Indian Army officers on leave, and a great number of officers of the Royal Naval Volunteer Reserve. The rank and file consisted of a R.N.V.R. ratings from the different R.N.V.R. divisions, R.F.R. stokers, a number of fishermen from the Hebrides belonging to the R.N.R., a few active service naval ratings (mostly senior N.C.O.'s), and thirty-two retired Marine Sergeants. This heterogeneous collection of enthusiastic amateur soldiers were hurriedly organised into eight battalions within a day or two of their arrival in camp, and it was one of these rather empirical formations which took the name of the Hawke Battalion, to become forthwith the 2nd Battalion of the 1st Royal Naval Brigade.

The first commanding officer of the Hawke was a retired naval officer, Commander Beadle, R.N., and their first Adjutant Major Fletcher of the Scots Guards. Beyond these, and their allowance of Marine Sergeants naval ratings, the battalion consisted, even before the arrival of wholly untrained recruits, mainly of civilians with a scanty training as naval reservists.

It is fair to say that the material was more than promising. The achievements of Anson, Hood, Howe, Nelson, and Drake Battalions in Gallipoli prove it. But the facilities for intensive military training were lacking. Few of the officers knew the rudiments of drill; none except the Adjutant knew anything at all about tactics, or the handling of troops in the field. An adequate training staff was not available for a division as yet unrecognized by the War Office, looked at askance by the official Admiralty, not within the cognizance of the Marine officer, and without even a divisional commander.

Commander Shelton (then a leading seaman, R.N.V.R., in "A" company of the Hawke), writes:

> The four marine sergeants were practically the only instructors we had. The one attached to my company ('A' company) had been a postman for the last twelve years; he was a thundering good fellow, with a vast sense of humour, and a wonderfully philosophical outlook.
>
> Our C.O., Commander Beadle, a retired naval officer, naturally found himself very much 'up against it' through being given command of a battalion with no experience whatever. He was, however, splendid, and always ready to listen to complaints even from the humblest.
>
> The training was primitive—a good deal of old-fashioned arm-drill, some rather comic platoon and company drill, a great deal of route marching (which, however, turned out to be of infinite value later !), and, towards the end of our time, one or two battalion and brigade field days—glorious picnics.
>
> Our shooting instruction consisted of about ten rounds per man at a miniature range—and that was all.
>
> About ten days before our departure a vast number of Kitchener's Army, mostly North Country miners, arrived to join the division. These had been hustled about from pillar to post for a considerable time, and some of them had hardly a rag to their backs. They were immediately given a sea-bath and some kit, elementary necessities which the army at that time could not supply! This accident was, indeed, fateful in our history,

for it solved a really serious difficulty for the War Office, who were threatened with the gravest trouble from thousands of recruits whom they could neither clothe nor feed. Mr. Winston Churchill came to the rescue, and the War Office showed their gratitude by a modified recognition of the Naval Division as a fighting force. The navy were, indeed, generous to profusion with their stores at this time.

If any member of the tent required crockery, blankets, and such-like, a raid was immediately made on the stores, and we took what was required. There is a perfectly true story of a hardened old stoker who, when boots were being handed out, went in his stockinged feet no less than twelve times to be fitted, and sold the surplus pairs in Deal! Most of the local poor were comfortably supplied with blankets as well as boots, owing to our generosity!

The sequel to these first weeks of enthusiastic soldiering is well known. It is no longer imagined in the Carlton Club that the then First Lord of the Admiralty mistook the hurried aggregations of re-servists at Walmer and Bettysanger for trained troops. It is, on the contrary, realized now that Mr. Winston Churchill had merely seen at once what General Joffre refused to see till much later—namely, the vital character of the struggle which was impending for the control of the Channel ports, and that the dispatch of the untrained Naval Brigades, following the earlier dispatch of the Marines, into Antwerp was a brilliant improvisation designed to gain a few vital hours at a small risk.

The risk was certainly small enough compared to the gain. If Ant-werp had fallen five days earlier, as it would have done but for the arrival of the Naval and Marine Brigades, we might never have held even the line of the Yser. And the actual loss fell far short of the po-tential, owing to the firmness with which a most difficult task was handled by General Paris, who took command for the first time of the three brigades actually in Antwerp itself. Even the losses which occurred were due more to mischance than to the ordinary hazards of war. Among these losses, however, must be reckoned the intern-ment of all but one officer and two men of the first Hawke Battalion. Only the three who escaped—the late Commander C. S. West, D.S.O. (then commanding "A" company, later second in command of the Collingwood, and, later still, in command of the Howe Battalion), Commander Shelton, D.S.O. (then a Leading Seaman), and C.P.O. Stewart (then a petty officer)—returned to the Crystal Palace to serve that other Hawke Battalion, which is the real subject of these pages.

11

Some measure of continuity, however, there was, for Antwerp not only gave the new battalion their first adjutant (Commander Shelton) and their first Regimental Sergeant-Major (C.P.O. Stewart), but also the first faint trace of a battalion tradition, and so I make no apology for quoting here from two very vivid and contemporary accounts of the Antwerp expedition written, the one by Commander Shelton himself, and the other by Commander Lockwood, then serving in the ranks of the Benbow Battalion. These accounts tell in some detail the first incidents of the Odyssey.

Commander Lockwood writes:

On Sunday morning, October 5th, 1914, I woke up about 5.30 a.m. and thought with joy of the extra hour in bed. But it wasn't to be. At 5.45 a stentorious voice shouted at the outside of our tent: 'Get up show-a-leg,' and, what is more, continued to shout. We answered back in none too polite language, telling the unknown visitor to take his unwelcome presence elsewhere. He then began to undo the tent ropes; we resisted, till, recognizing the voice as that of some superior, we let him in. It was no less a person than Commander Fargus himself. He ordered us to get up without delay, and proceed at once to the parade ground. Everyone was fairly buzzing with excitement, and we dressed in record time, doubling up to the parade ground, finishing our hurried toilet as we ran.

In about five minutes the whole battalion was on parade, and Commander Fargus told us that in a very few hours we were to embark for France. He couldn't tell us where we were going to, or what we were going for. We were to be ready to fall in at 11 a.m.

This was a regular bombshell to us. Mad with excitement, we rushed back to our tents and packed our gear, sending back as much as possible. One kit-bag between two men was allowed— most of us took a whole one to ourselves.

Then to the Y.M.C.A. tent to write farewells. It sounded magnificent to be able to actually say with truth that we were off to France. That morning was nothing more or less than hectic'

At 11 we were ready hanging about the parade ground in little groups. What were we going to do? Where? Dunkirk was almost certain. One 'buzz' was that we were being sent over to take charge of a large number of German prisoners at Lille. A thousand and one guesses were made. Not one was near the truth.

My platoon commander, C. R. Ingleby, was on leave in London, going to get married this very day. We missed him, and hoped he would get down in time to go with us, but doubted it.

In the meantime, the town of Deal had got the rumour that we were off, and came up to the camp in hundreds.

We were hanging about altogether for about three hours. I think it was just about 1 p.m. when the 'fall-in' was given, and the battalion formed up on the parade ground for the last time in its very short existence.

The neighbouring battalions were also lined up. And a really fine show they were. All the blue uniforms—the smart upstanding of the men (for we had learnt to drill in our short training, and drill well, too)—the various bands playing. A sharp order of command, and the head of the column swung out towards the Dover road, everyone in the crowd cheering and waving handkerchiefs. Old women weeping—the yearning sad look of the wives—and we marched at attention through them. I have never felt such a thrill before—to be actually one of these men—to be actually going to France; it made one thank Heaven to be alive at that moment.

Words cannot express that march; it was about seven or eight miles, I think, and the road was lined with people the whole way, wishing us God-speed.

Nearly all of us had been inoculated the previous day, and we were very sore and weary when we swung into the old town.

The tasks of the Benbow and Hawke Battalions differed from now onward, and the remainder of the Antwerp story is taken from Commander Shelton's account.

We reached Dover at about 5 p.m., and there waited on the pier until, at last, we embarked at 11 p.m. We arrived at Dunkirk towards 10 o'clock the following morning, after a very cold and uncomfortable but, luckily, fairly smooth passage. The Hawke, together with the rest of the 1st Brigade, spent the whole of the day unloading ship. Up to this time our destination had been a well-kept secret, so far as the rank and file were concerned. At about 7 p.m., when we entrained, we were for the first time told that we were going to Antwerp. Thirty rounds of ammunition were handed out to each man—a highly dangerous proceeding, as a certain percentage of the men had not fired a rifle for years. The fear was, we were told, that there should be firing at the train *en route*. If there had been, the casualties would certainly have been very heavy, but not among the enemy, I fear.

We reached Antwerp at 5 a.m. after a night of extreme discomfort, packed like sardines in a wretched Belgian train. Our kit was dumped at the station; we had, incidentally, taken everything we had with us.

The people received us with ecstasy, and we marched about five miles through cheering crowds, being looked on as saviours of the town. Cigars and wine were lavished on us. On arriving somewhere at the outskirts we were sent into billets, and had just comfortably settled ourselves when the order came that we were immediately to parade in the market square. There we were told by Commodore Henderson that we were to go into the line at once, and 300 rounds of ammunition were served out to each man.

We were also told that the Germans in front of us were of very inferior quality, and that the appearance of the well-trained Naval Brigades would be quite sufficient to induce them to retire! These remarks of the Commodore were received with cheers, and off we went in high fettle. Unfortunately we lost our way, and after wandering through the outskirts of Antwerp (where, incidentally, we saw Winston Churchill in a car looking very worried) we were halted on a country road, and told to 'pipe down' for the night. This I, for one, did in a ditch, which, luckily, was fairly dry.

At 3 a.m. whispered orders were passed down the line that we were to 'march away' immediately. . . . Apparently we had wandered near the German lines! After marching away most of the night, we eventually reached our position, Forts 3 and 4, about 8 a.m., only to be told to complete the trenches. This was rather difficult, as we had no entrenching tools whatsoever ; however, we managed to borrow a few picks and shovels from a neighbouring farmhouse, and, more or less, completed some kind of a trench. Meanwhile, our marine sergeant went round instructing the men how to fill their magazines with clip ammunition, as some of us had never seen this modern device
before!

The only redeeming feature was provided by some remarkably

14

fine wire entanglements in front of us to a depth of 50 yards; these made us feel very safe.

Nothing happened during the day, but at 12 o'clock, midnight, the Germans fired the first 11-inch shell into Antwerp, about four miles away. This was repeated through the night at two-minute intervals. The following morning heavy shelling stopped, but we were visited with a few shells of smaller variety, which did little or no damage—to the Hawke, at any rate.

During the preceding night there was a heavy fusillade from one of the battalions on our left. Report has it that they saw movement behind the wire. When dawn broke, it was discovered there had been three cows grazing. . . . They were still grazing! During the day imaginary *Uhlans* were continually seen in the woods behind the entanglements, but personally, as far as I am concerned, I never saw one. Later on the trenches were shelled a good deal, but the Hawke escaped with very little damage.

When dusk fell the enemy started again bombarding Antwerp very heavily, and fires sprang up in many directions. These— together with a heavy pall of smoke caused by the firing of the petrol tanks in the town—formed a very eerie spectacle.

At about 9.30 that night orders were received for us to retire.[1] Certain British detachments had been sent to various forts to try and cheer up the Belgian gunners, who were on the verge of chucking their hands in. Lieutenant West called me up, and gave me a note to the officer in command of Fort 4 (Lieutenant Grant, D.S.C.), in case no order to retire had been given him. This proved to be the case; he had heard nothing. On leaving him I fell in with the major part of the Benbow Battalion, and we spent most of that night wandering up and down different roads, trying to find our way to the River Scheldt. This was most unpleasant, as the Germans were bombarding some aeroplane sheds near by with 11-inch. Again we were very lucky, having no casualties, as far as I know.

Eventually we reached the Scheldt—only to find that the bridge of boats had been blown up!

After waiting for what seemed an unconscionable time, a river

---

1. The orders should have reached at 5 p.m. and should have instructed an immediate retirement. Owing to a mistake by a staff officer, since identified, the orders did not reach Commodore Henderson till 9 p.m., and then in an incorrect form.

tug was commandeered, and we were taken over in batches.

The following morning, to my great joy, I discovered the Hawke resting in a field—this after hearing wild rumours to the effect that they had been annihilated.

Then started our weary march, and, as map-reading was not a strong point, we successfully lost our way. At one period we marched at least 6 kilometres along a straight, dusty road, only to have to turn back. During the afternoon a report was received from the scouts in front that a party of mounted Uhlans were barring our way. The whole battalion promptly lined a turnip-field two deep, and started to blaze away, the rear ranks firing in very unpleasant proximity to the front rank's heads. Commander Beadle dashed out in front (how he escaped being shot, the Lord only knows!), and shouted out orders to stop fire. It was then discovered that we were firing at some Belgian cavalry, who had returned our fire hotly. No damage was done to either side !

We eventually reached St. Gilles-Waes at about 4 p.m.—and the last train had gone.

By this time the battalion was sadly attenuated, many men having dropped by the wayside. The Marine Sergeant (ex-postman) attached to our company was a tower of strength, and endeavoured to cheer the men up with scurrilous songs.

It was at St. Gilles-Waes that we were told that the Dutch frontier was only five miles away, and that, so long as we managed to get through Holland in twenty-four hours, we should be able to get home to England. (This was an unfortunate mix-up between the naval and military laws of war.) On we staggered; march discipline had long since ceased, and we were just a straggling mob, footsore, weary, and utterly dejected.

On arriving at La Clinge, on the frontier, we discovered our mistake—and that, if we entered Holland, we should be interned!

Through losing our way we had trudged over forty miles on empty stomachs, and had had practically no sleep since leaving England. The officers consulted one with another for two or three hours, while we men lay down in the road, and didn't care a damn what happened. Luckily there was food of a kind in some of the shops, so we managed a sort of a meal.

At length orders came that the battalion would march into

Holland.

Lieutenant West came up to me, and said that he would not go across, further suggesting we should get as many men as possible to stay on the Belgian side. About forty men decided to stay with us. During the night there was a lot of firing at the back of the village; one by one the men went across, and when dawn broke there were three of us left—West, Petty Officer Stewart, and myself. We were too tired and too cold to sleep. Poor West was practically delirious throughout the night, but still undaunted.

In the circumstances Commander Beadle could have done nothing other than he did; the battalion consisted merely of a mass of hopelessly weary, crippled men, with no resisting power left, and it would have been a physical impossibility for it to have made its way along the frontier. It must have been an appalling situation for Commander Beadle to face.

Early that morning we three exhausted wretches came across about a dozen men of the Benbow Battalion who, after arriving at the village the previous afternoon, had spent the night in the local church, where they had been lucky enough to snatch a good sleep. We tried to keep up with them for a bit, but as they were comparatively fresh we soon had to drop behind. This party eventually found its way to Ostend.

Left to ourselves, the three of us managed to get about half a mile along the frontier, and were then taken pity on by some kindly women at a Belgian farmhouse, who took us in, gave us food, and wrapped up our feet in oily rags.

After a much-needed rest we prepared to start off again, but were informed that a few miles farther up the enemy had arrived at the frontier, thus cutting off our line of retreat. This was probably untrue, but we decided that the only thing to do was to disguise ourselves, and go across the frontier into Holland. To this end we borrowed some peasants' old clothing, which we put on over our uniforms. Then the question arose as to what we were to call ourselves; this was decided by our coming across a little Belgian and his wife, who told us they were employed at the Anglo-Continental Gas Association at Antwerp. On being asked whether they employed any British workmen, they told us there had been twenty gas-fitters there. So we decided to be three of them.

17

In about two days' time, after many adventures, we reached the town of Terneuzen on the Scheldt, and there ran into a Dutch sentry-post. The officer in charge suggested we were English soldiers, which we strenuously denied. As he seemed rather unfriendly and wished to arrest us, we demanded to see the English representative. He told off a sentry to take us to his house. On arriving there we found he was out, but expected at the quay-side very shortly. Off we went down to the river with the wretched sentry still in tow. Luckily he could speak English, so when we reached the quay we told him we did not require his services any longer—and he, evidently a peace-loving individual, very kindly absented himself. I may add that at this time we three were not exactly pretty to look at, not having had a bath or a shave for the best part of a week . . . also the Belgian peasants' discarded clothing was not particularly attractive.

We stormed the harbour-master, and, by much eloquence, persuaded him to give us three tickets for a boat which was shortly leaving for Flushing. We got to Flushing in about two hours' time, and, as the quay was very crowded and not particularly friendly, we boarded a tram-car, being still comparatively wealthy—we had at least three-ha'pence between us!

On the tram-car were two English Red Cross nurses, who quietly came and sat beside us, and asked if they could do anything for us. We told them our plight, and they took us to the vice-consul, giving us strict instructions not to tell him who we really were. So we stuck to our gas-fitters' yarn. He did not believe us, but the nurses persuaded him to let us have three tickets (paid for by them) for a boat sailing to England the following morning. Then they gave us some more money, and we went off and had an enormous meal.

Having arranged to meet the nurses on the quay at 8 o'clock that evening, we spent the afternoon in a cinema in order to avoid unpleasant risks. At night we went down to the quay, and were just boarding the boat when a Dutch officer came up and demanded our credentials. The nurses, however, were equal to the occasion, and, telling him that we were their stretcher-bearers, they bundled us on board. We spent the night in the coal-bunkers in case of accident, but the following morning we sailed for England.

Apart from these three adventurers, none of the original Hawke

Battalion escaped internment. With them, as is known, were interned the Collingwood and Benbow Battalions, in identical circumstances, and for the same reasons. Quite a number, however, of those who suffered this fate escaped in the autumn of 1914, and four of them—Lockwood, Boot, and Sawyer of the Benbow (all at that date Able Seamen), and Sub-Lieutenant the Hon. Vere Harmsworth (on the staff of the 1st Brigade)—joined the new Hawke Battalion as platoon commanders at the Crystal Palace in January, 1915.

How the new battalion was formed, and of what manner of men, we must now tell. This time the foundation was to be more solid, and the superstructure was to last until March, 1919, when on Horse Guards Parade, before H.R.H. the Prince of Wales, the Hawke Battalion paraded for the last time, and, incidentally, paraded under the command of the Leading Seaman whose escape from Antwerp we have told in this chapter.

CHAPTER 2

# Playing at Soldiers

The result of the Antwerp expedition was, as we have seen, that the Hawke Battalion had to be fashioned afresh. With its merits and defects the original battalion had disappeared. A very different battalion, the real subject of this record, was now to be formed.

The task fell to the staff of the Crystal Palace Depot, and under the joint patronage, as it were, of the late Prince Consort and Mr. Winston Churchill, the new Hawke Battalion was brought to birth, and tenderly nourished under glass through the stormy autumn of 1914.

The depot had come into being in September, while the original Naval Brigades were still with irrelevant optimism practising the advance on the Walmer downs. The first inmates of the depot were not selected uniformly on grounds of merit. But during September and October recruits from the R.N.V.R. Divisions, new army recruits transferred from a War Office suffering from acute indigestion to an acquisitive Admiralty, and civilians inadequately disguised as officers, swelled alike the numerical strength and the importance of the new organisation.

To emphasize its significance in the official hierarchy, the depot had been placed under the command of a Commodore—Sir Richard Williams Bulkeley, R.N.R.—and Lieutenant-Colonel Ramsden was appointed Chief Military Instructor. An administrative staff, consisting at the outset of Lieutenant-Commander Roberts Wray, and on its completion of Depot Staff Commander Roberts Wray, shared with the Commodore and Colonel Ramsden the burden of administrative responsibility, while a number of retired naval officers and some senior officers of the R.N.V.R. took over the executive command of the miscellaneous recruits, whose numbers rose rapidly from 1,000 on September 15th to five times that number six weeks later.

Under these auspices the organisation of reserve battalions had been only a matter of hours, and they had multiplied with an astonishing rapidity. Where to train them, how to discipline them, what to teach them, were subjects for legitimate discussion, but, at least, the improvised staff could, and did, form battalions as readily as the recruits themselves could form fours. With the permutations and combinations of these battalions we are happily not concerned; all that matters is that the three most efficient were those commanded by Captain Hunter, R.N., Commander Spearman, R.N., and Commander the Hon. Rupert Guinness, R.N.V.R., and that, when the major part of the 1st R.N. Brigade got itself interned in Holland, these became the new Hawke, Collingwood, and Benbow battalions.

To the veterans of Antwerp these new battalions were, for divers reasons, very inferior substitutes for their predecessors. The interned battalions had consisted mainly of pre-war reservists with an exclusively naval tradition. The new battalions, civilians with a smattering of orthodox military training, seemed a fresh element in the Naval Division. The antithesis between military drill and naval *esprit de corps* was, of course, absurd and unnecessary. The Crystal Palace battalions acquired the latter as quickly as the Antwerp legionaries (when they wished) learnt the former. The fact remains—and it is not unimportant—that the depot and its battalions remained indefinitely detached from the rest of the division till that tragic 4th of June on Gallipoli, when so many of the survivors of the amateur strategies of Antwerp met their end in a pitched battle operated by a trained staff.

To realise the atmosphere in which the new Hawke Battalion was to live and move and have its being we must understand this. Those officers and men who grew into companies and battalions at the Crystal Palace in October, November, and December, 1915, had for a time a place apart.

The Marine Brigade were the aristocracy of blood. They had battle honours; they had traditions; they had experience; above all, they had regular officers ready to emphasize by precept, as well as example, the extreme irregularity of those who enjoyed none of their advantages, even though they ranked in their own world in no way below them.

In the case of the five naval battalions who had returned from Antwerp, the aristocracy was one of time, pure and simple—and of a matter of a few days at that. The fact remained that these veterans of Antwerp went round the country as independent self-supporting units, learning, if not of men and cities at any rate of staffs and camps and barracks, and grew efficient.

It was very different with the Hawke and other battalions at the Crystal Palace, who found themselves things of no importance in an organisation which boasted of a commodore, a chief military instructor, a depot staff commander, a drafting commander, and any number of lesser lights resplendent in blue and gold, who consumed their whiskies and soda in silence, but burst upon the noisy arena which passed for a parade ground with a publicity which demanded prompt and continuous salutes.

For they were giants in those days.

Indeed, the only relief which the novice in war experienced at the Crystal Palace came from the disputes which raged as to the true interpretation of Napoleon's maxim that land warfare was too serious an affair to be left in the hands of professionals. This view was not shared in any degree by the chief military instructor—a man of considerable weight, and a lieutenant-colonel in the Royal Marines. His Adjutant, Captain Levey—once a warrant officer in the brigade of Guards, never again anything but an extremely accomplished officer—was less confident, and would certainly have applied the doctrine to naval officers, and possibly, if the impiety may be hinted at, to the Marines. The sea captains themselves, on the other hand, interpreted the doctrine in its literal significance. Most decidedly these soldiers must not be given a free hand.

The result was an atmosphere of compromises and professional rivalry, amid which the untutored amateurs who comprised the officers as well as the rank and file of the growing battalions had to pick a careful path. In matters of military training the chief military instructor and his staff were clearly the fountain-head of wisdom, and their approval was the passport without which no permanent appointment, whether as an officer or as an N.C.O., in one of the new battalions could be secured. Once, however, past the preliminary stages of instruction and within the pale, the acute strategist must effect a certain mistrust of purely soldierly qualities, and acquire, if only at second hand, from some retired third officer of the Merchant Service or enthusiastic petty officer of the Volunteers the technique of the quarter-deck.

The supreme test for the young officer came when the round of duties made him orderly officer for the depot. On these occasions a naval sword had to be borrowed and worn, and the guard had to be changed at sunset (the sun always set at 6 o'clock at the Crystal Palace) with full naval ceremonial, to which even Captain Levey's lectures provided no clue. The guide, philosopher, and friend of the junior officer on these occasions was, if I recollect aright, the Master-at-Arms, a sort of Captain Kettle turned stage doorkeeper, whose *staccato* whispers prompted the faltering lips of the orderly officer, otherwise in very truth at sea on the quarter-deck under the eyes of the soldiers and sailors for once united by a common interest. Ceremonial drill is, of course, common to both services, but the method by which the desired result is reached differs fundamentally. The military school hold that any direct reference to arms in the ritual words of command is subversive of discipline, which must, as all good soldiers know, be independent of any appeal to mere reason. Those, therefore, who looked to military favour for naval promotion would exhort their guard to slope, present, and once more slope their "*hyp*," "*hup*," or "*hip*." Those who in the same context aspired to the favour of the naval element made frank, open, and sailorly reference to "*Arms*." The guard themselves, having been drilled by the Master-at-Arms in secret into a mood of complete indifference to any word of command given by a mere officer, and taken their orders in deaf-and-dumb language from that worthy himself, were totally indifferent to the controversy, but the spectators concealed the intensity of their feelings with difficulty, and paid up their bets on this great daily event with but an ill grace.

This controversy gained in bitterness because it followed on the great "Form fours" dispute, in which the military party had scored a signal victory, the naval view that a diagonal step backward, reducing the manoeuvre to a mere two movements, was compatible with strict discipline having been set aside almost brusquely by the very highest authority.

Amid these scenes the Hawke Battalion was hardened to the discipline of conflict. The battalion as it was first formed at the depot after the Antwerp *débâcle* consisted solely of R.N.V.R. officers and men who had taken commissions in, had been recruited by, or had rejoined the R.N.V.R. in the belief that they were signing on for service afloat. As at Walmer and Bettysanger, the former were even less satisfied with their metamorphosis into soldiers than were the latter. They were not newly commissioned officers, but were either serving officers at the outbreak of war, or retired R.N. or R.N.V.R. officers who had rejoined for service afloat. And so, while the men grumbled a little, and remembered with a faint longing those posters of windswept decks in the North Sea which had seemed to mirror for them a future of novel but exhilarating adventure, the R.N.V.R. officers drafted to the Crystal Palace took more active steps, and disappeared one by one into the silence of the naval shore establishment.

The men were less fortunate. But they, too, were a fluctuating quantity, since numbers of them left for Bettysanger, Walmer, and, later, Blandford, as reinforcements for the older battalions, while a few landsmen went to sea. The result was that, of these R.N.V.R. ratings, only two companies remained in Commander Hunter's battalion by January, 1915, and of the original complement of officers hardly any. Only one, Lieutenant Peckitt, R.N.V.R., actually accompanied the Hawke Battalion overseas. The balance of the officers of these

OFFICERS OF THE HAWKE BATTALION, MAY, 1915.

*Top Row:* Sub-Lieut. Southon, Pay.-Lieut. Paton, Lieut. Cotter, Sub-Lieut. Marvin, Lieut. Harmsworth, Sub-Lieut. Boot, Lieut. Brereton, Lieut. Rush, Lieut. Nicholson, Lieut. Jerrold, Lieut. Peckitt, Lieut. Ker, Sub-Lieut. Gibson, Lieut. Peckham, Lieut. Horsfield.
*Middle Row:* Sub-Lieut. Tremayne, Surgeon Bradbury, Lieut. Shelton, Lieut.-Com. Ramsay-Fairfax, Lieut.-Col. Leslie Wilson, Lieut. Morgan, Lieut. Price, Lieut. Wolfe Barry, Lieut. Stevenson.
*Bottom Row:* Sub-Lieut. Milvaine, Sub-Lieut. Little, Sub-Lieut. Sawyer, Sub-Lieut. Farrow, Sub-Lieut. Venn, Sub-Lieut. Herbert.

companies ("A" and "B" companies, as they eventually became) were drawn from the civilian officers as they were passed out of Colonel Ramsden's training school; there were two important exceptions in Lieutenant Vere Harmsworth and Lieutenant E. M. Lockwood, who escaped from Holland in the autumn of 1914, and were eventually posted to "A" and "B" companies respectively. The final complement of these two companies was as follows:

*"A" Company.*
Lieutenant W. W. Morgan, R.N.V.R. (in command).
Lieutenant Horsfield, R.N.V.R. (second in command).
Sub-Lieutenant Rush (No. 1 Platoon).
Sub-Lieutenant Little (No. 2 Platoon).
Sub-Lieutenant Boot (No. 3 Platoon).
Lieutenant E. M. Lockwood (No. 4 Platoon).

*"B" Company.*
Lieutenant G. U. Price, R.N.V.R. (in command).
Lieutenant Peckitt, R.N.V.R. (second in command).
Sub-Lieutenant Sawyer (5th Platoon).
Sub-Lieutenant La Fontaine (6th Platoon).
Lieutenant Harmsworth (7th Platoon).
Sub-Lieutenant Brereton (8th Platoon).

These companies were led with one or two exceptions by officers of no naval or military experience whatever, and in this were on a footing with the two new companies which were added to complete the battalion establishment. A very large proportion, however, of the N.C.O.'s had peace-time volunteer training, and two of the Chief Petty Officers—C.P.O. Gillard (Company Sergeant-Major of "B" company), and C.P.O. Price (Company Q.M.S. of "A" company)— were active service naval ratings. In the result these companies, who were, in the main, London men, conformed in type and quality more to the London Territorials than to the new armies as a whole. They disciplined themselves, for the most part. They learnt quickly, and they acquired easily the appearance of smartness and efficiency. Like all town-bred troops, they yielded nothing in courage to any other formation, but were more mercurial in temperament, and required leadership of a traditional kind rather than discipline to make them fighting troops.

The other two companies were widely different, alike from "A" and "B" companies and from each other. "C" company was composed almost to a man of North Country miners, volunteers of August, 1914, who had joined the Army, and had been transferred to the Naval Division in September and October, because food, uniforms, and sleeping quarters for Army recruits were at the time a monopoly of the Admiralty. These miners were many of them miners only in name, being mere boys, but they came from mining villages, and had inherited a tradition of self-reliance and of endurance, and a natural aptitude for exertion which never became laborious to them if it often became irksome. They appeared to respect what they evidently disliked—namely, a strict discipline, though this had to rest less on traditional authority than on personal efficiency, or at least the attempt at it. This company wanted a strong commander, and found one in Lieutenant A. F. Stevenson, R.N.V.R., who brought to bear on a fine body of men, who had not been too well handled, the fruits of many years' service in the Artists Rifles, including some months in the trenches in France. The other postings to the company were as follows:

> Lieutenant D. F. Jerrold, R.N.V.R. (second in command).
> Sub-Lieutenant W. Ker, R.N.V.R. (9th Platoon).
> Lieutenant A. V. W. Cotter, R.N.V.R. (10th Platoon).
> Sub-Lieutenant A. P. Herbert (11th Platoon).
> Sub-Lieutenant Southon (12th Platoon).

The fourth ("D") company of the new battalion provided yet another element, for it was formed from the visible remains of a perhaps too empirical battalion of public school men (and boys) raised by the late Commander Victor Gibson, R.N.V.R., in the early days of the war. This battalion first saw the light of day in Bond Street, and ended its career in the equally appropriate atmosphere of Epsom. But the magnificent enthusiasm of its promoters found a more responsive welcome at the Admiralty Headquarters, and such of the officers as wished, and those of. the rank and file as had resisted or escaped the deluge of commissions which heralded the breaking-up of the organisation as a military formation, were transferred *en masse* to the navy for service with the Naval Division.

The army's loss was the Naval Division's, and in particular the Hawke Battalion's, gain. This miscellaneous, cheerful, enthusiastic, and wholly undisciplined collection of babes, bookmakers, and beachcombers became known for purposes of official returns as "D" company, and was the life, even if it was not the soul, of the battalion. Its second in command, Lieutenant G. Russell Peckham, R.N.V.R., known to all for so long as he served with the division as the embodiment of the peculiar, unorthodox, but by no means unamusing, traditions of the battalion (and he served with it without a day's absence till he was severely wounded on the Somme in 1916), was perhaps its representative figure, but even this claim might be disputed in a company where even the licensed lunatic was an old Etonian.

The final complement of "D "company was as follows:
Lieutenant S. Wolfe Barry, R.N.V.R. (in command).
Lieutenant G. R. Peckham, R.N.V.R. (second in command).
Sub-Lieutenant Nicholson, R.N.V.R. (13th Platoon).
Sub-Lieutenant Marvin, R.N.V.R. (14th Platoon).
Sub-Lieutenant Venn, R.N.V.R. (15th Platoon).
Sub-Lieutenant Farrow, R.N.V.R. (16th Platoon).

In the ranks of the company, however, were many others destined to equally long and, indeed, in some cases longer, service as officers of the Hawke Battalion. Among these were (to give them their future ranks) Lieutenant-Commander R. Blackmore, M.C., Lieutenant C. S. Codner, M.C., Lieutenant Bessel, M.C., Sub-Lieutenant Henderson, Sub-Lieutenant Tompkins, Sub-Lieutenant S. G. Poole, Sub-Lieutenant Aron, and Sub-Lieutenant H. A. Burr. But for these officers, one and all promoted during the Gallipoli campaign, the battalion would have been hard pressed indeed in the everlasting summer and autumn of 1915.

"D" company was, indeed, a unique company, even in a unique division. It contained many "characters." G. Tomson,[2] petty officer of machine-gun section, tall, handsome, a hard taskmaster, and therefore not always popular. He was nearly killed in Gallipoli by the Senegalese, who mistook him for a Turk. Daily in the line, so he alleged, he was asked by the Colonel: "Well, Tomson, got a good field of fire," and daily he reported a new and more audacious reply, which, however, came to be taken with a grain of salt. A fine soldier withal! F. S. Firmstone, a solicitor, known as the String King by virtue of the fact that he went about in Gallipoli with all sorts of oddities tied to his equipment. S———, our German spy—put under arrest both at the Crystal Palace and Gallipoli.

E. d'A. Barnard, noted for his "turn" at the "D" company concert at Blandford when they were isolated for measles, and in particular for his drawing of a young blood as an officer entitled "The blue blood of England; or, by Christ, I've got a commission," which much amused the H.Q. officers present. C. B. C———, of the machine-gun section, a fine old fellow whom Tomson delighted to run off his feet, till one day someone protested. For a week or so afterwards Tomson gave his orders in this strain: "Would you mind, my dear, hurrying a little more." E. G. E———, a Cambridge man, who took such great pride in his work as company sanitary man! F. T. B. L———, a somewhat heavy-drinking Irishman, when hit by a shrapnel bullet in a latrine in Gallipoli, complained bitterly of the tactlessness of the Turk.

---

2. Subsequently commissioned to become Battalion M.G. Officer in Gallipoli.

Charles Waterer, a member of the Stock Exchange, and such a delightful romancer. L. D. Sewell, known as the "Silent Knight," because he so frequently took his chief petty officer into Blandford on the back of his motorcycle; and an old Etonian, whose name I omit, who, when found after July 13th in a lice-infested Turk machine-gun emplacement with several dead, said he preferred to be there than with the rest of "D" company. These were only a few among the many strange personalities in a strange unit.

I print here some notes sent me by Lieutenant-Commander Blackmore, who joined the R.N. Division as a recruit in the autumn of 1914, to find himself in a few weeks a Chief Petty Officer in "D" company. The notes serve a doubly valuable purpose: they give many details of the origin and formation of an important section of the Hawke Battalion, and the particulars they give us of life in the ranks may be read as applying, with few exceptions, to the men of all companies.

Commander Blackmore writes:

On the outbreak of war, I presented myself at the R.N.V.R. Headquarters, and was promptly rejected as medically unfit. In October I was seeking a unit that *would* take me, and was advised to try for the Public School Unit of the R.N.V.R., then being formed. The next day I called at Bond Street, and there made the acquaintance of George Peckham. (I also met then 'long' Nicholson, a sergeant of the U.P.S., waiting for his commission.) George, of course, told me he didn't care what the doctors said; he would get me in. Again I went to the R.N.V.R. Headquarters, avoided the fleet surgeon of the London Division, and, after some trouble with a civilian doctor, became a member of the R.N.D.

The fleet surgeon, I remember, very much impressed most of the new-comers by ordering them to 'toe that line on the deck'; we had already been told, of course, that we should not be required for sea service. After being enrolled and sworn, we were ordered to report in the morning, which disappointed me, I know, as I had expected to be imprisoned immediately; being allowed to go home seemed to me to minimize the importance of the occasion. This was on the 6th November.

The recruits were handed over to a petty officer, Whisking, who in private life was Commander Rupert Guinness's servant, Commander Guinness at that time being the commander of the London R.N.V.R. We had quite a lot to thank Whisking for. He had the happy knack of instilling quite severe discipline in the recruits in a very kindly way, always with a touch of humour. The recruiting marches through the heart of London, pulling the old seven-pounder, were enjoyed by most of us. We had a week of this, during which time those of us who wished returned home each evening.

Our draft to the Crystal Palace was quite a small one. On arrival we were attached to the nucleus of the Public School Battalion, and were quartered for sleeping in the old Art Gallery. At this time the weather became bitterly cold for a long space. In hammocks you have to keep as warm *under* as *over*, and as the supply of blankets was quite insufficient, few of us slept at all that first night. Later, we 'roughed it' with the aid of eiderdowns and extra blankets from home! One came to like hammocks, which are very comfortable when you get used to them. They were certainly quite the best way of sleeping large numbers of men, and it was undoubtedly much more healthy to be off the floor.

All things considered, one's time at the palace was quite enjoyable. The routine was pleasant, and the food, supplied by Lyons and, naturally, rather roughly served, tolerably good, though it may have been the run before breakfast which enabled us to enjoy that particular meal as much as we did. For the rest, it is arguable that one's civilian meal in the evenings made a certain difference to the feeling of sufficiency which I, at least, enjoyed.

The grounds were beautiful and quite ideal for preliminary training, while the palace, despite its coldness, afforded sheltered and convenient places for musketry, etc., though naturally we failed to appreciate all its advantages till we got to Blandford. The nautical atmosphere fostered at the palace with the naval ranks, 'leave boats,' 'sick bay,' etc., was attractive, and I am confident that this peculiarity, common only to the Naval Division, was the foundation of that wonderful spirit which pervaded the whole division later on. One soon felt at home with the old naval instructors (good fellows, most of them), and we were often grateful to them (especially when they sheltered us from Levey!), but one must admit their shortcomings at drill.

In time one became acquainted with those who were afterwards to share with us, in a greater or less degree, the strange life we had embarked upon: Nicholson, Peckham, Wolfe Barry, Shelton, Farrow, Venn, Marvin, and others; and on one rare occasion we even discovered Commander Gibson under an enormous cap. I found myself in Nicholson's squad, and though of a somewhat retiring disposition, I had the temerity a little later to step out of the ranks to ask if I might be made a Leading Seaman. (Even then I felt that without the responsibility of rank, commissioned or non-commissioned, one must suffer mentally from a prolonged period of obedience to orders.)

Perhaps Nicholson was, as he suggested, 'not impressed,' but he certainly put me forward, and I soon 'shipped a killick' and took charge of a section. My platoon P.O. was Marvin, the others being Farrow, Venn, and Martel, and when the first three took commissions I became the P.O. This meant a great deal. There were certain privileges attached to the rank (an extra hour at night, for instance), but the principal advantage was the P.O.'s mess, which was really excellent.

By this time we had a full company, and training then became more interesting. In turn many of us suffered, with very good effect, at Levey's hands. At any rate, we came from his class keen soldiers with at least sufficient knowledge to give us confidence, and to take a certain pride in the efficiency of our platoons or companies. But then we had our first disappointment. Sir R. Williams Bulkeley had very properly condemned the inclusion in the ranks of one unit so many men who would obviously make good officers, and a great number were persuaded to take commissions.

It was soon apparent that it would not be possible to raise a P.S. Battalion, and though for a moment I regretted I had resisted the temptation, I was very glad afterwards that I had remained with the company. Commander Gibson ' evaporated,' and the company came under the orders of Commander (Joey) Hunter, R.N., a name to conjure with! It was at this time that it was decided that we should form the fourth company of the Hawke Battalion, then at Blandford, only two companies strong. And so we became 'Hawkes.'

The addition of "D" company to the Hawke Battalion was one of the determining facts in its career. Another was the selection of Lieutenant-Colonel Leslie Wilson, D.S.O., M.P., to the command of the battalions in the field. This selection was made early in February, 1915, when the composition of the battalion had at last been determined. "A" and "B" companies had completed their recruit training, had got their full complement of officers, and had done their musketry course at one of the naval ranges. They were thus ready for company training at Blandford, the camp on the Wiltshire Downs where the rest of the Naval Division was by now, for the first time since Antwerp, being gathered together. "C" and "D" companies had still to do their musketry, and some of their officers had not passed through the officers' school of instruction.

But this was only a small matter, and on February 20th Colonel Wilson, with "A" and "B" companies and the nucleus of a headquarters staff, left the Crystal Palace for good. The Hawke Battalion, incomplete, untrained, but remarkably cheerful under their buoyant and optimistic commander, took the field. On March 7th "C" and "D" companies—Lieutenant Wolfe Barry in command—followed the main body, and the next day saw the new Hawke Battalion paraded for the first time as a living entity decently disguised as an orthodox military formation.

The fortnight which had elapsed between the arrival of the first and the second two companies of the Hawke had seen the departure of the other nine battalions of the division for the dawning campaign at the Dardanelles. The Hawke, Benbow, and Collingwood Battalions, and one field company of Engineers, alone remained in the vast camp, where a few days before there had been so fervent an activity. To those who had known it in the days of brigade and divisional field-days, it wore an air of unreality. The silence before the storm. And in very truth the period of training which lay before the Hawke Battalion depended on no academic reckoning of the time which was necessary for the purpose, but on the issue of certain events in the Eastern Mediterranean.

Yet these days of spring were only the gayer because they might be few. There was no dead hand of tradition resting over Blandford Camp, and the Hawke Battalion thrived in the freer atmosphere. Incidentally, set to solve its own problems, it began to learn something, if not of war, at any rate of the art of life under conditions where self-reliance is the main secret of success.

The battalion, as it took final shape, had certainly a character of its own, which it was to retain through vicissitudes quite unusually exacting. Distrustful of authority, indifferent to the appearances of efficiency, it cannot have been an easy battalion to command; the strong belief of its officers that they held concealed from any vulgar publicity the secret key to that efficiency which others displayed in brazen fashion on public parade grounds can hardly have been as fully justified as we imagined; but we were perhaps not too difficult a battalion to lead.

The officers' mess was not Spartan in its tone. I remember, indeed, George Peckham's description of an ideally cheerful evening as oblivion after the soup, which strikes rather a different note, and sentiments of innumerable French generals, that the war would not be won by any reckless sacrifice of the indispensable after-dinner liqueur, would have found a hearty echo had the conversation ever turned on winning the war. But I doubt if it did.

It is often said that one battalion's training is much like another, and that the incidents and amusements of this period of incubation are of no possible interest. This is in one sense perfectly true. The wanderings of platoons and companies round Tarrant Monkton and Tarrant Hinton, over Cranborne Chase, or round Wimborne, live in the memory, but the old stratagems that seemed so new, the alarms and excursions that preceded the inevitable attack, even the issue of the long-drawn-out and keenly contested battles, are forgotten. But what remains is the memory of the confidence which was born of these now remote experiences, the feeling, slowly dawning, that at a pinch one could move one's men across unknown country in the dark and reach the right rendezvous at the right time, that compasses did not necessarily lie even in a shaky hand, that the choice of the right position to entrench was not a task beyond civilian potentialities, and that miners could dig rather better than the most regular of soldiers.

The Hawke Battalion must have been almost the last battalion to be trained on the old rough-and-ready system which brought this all-important, if sometimes misplaced, confidence in its train. The day of specialists had not dawned, and the battalion was still regarded as a genuinely communal organisation, not as a mere aggregation of individuals and groups existing mainly for disciplinary purposes. The why and wherefore of our long field-days may have been ostensibly the capture of Hill 365, or the consolidation of the "P" in Pimperne, but in reality their purpose was to give sections, platoons, and companies the realization of their responsibilities to themselves and to each other, to break down the artificial barriers which separated man from man, officer from officer, platoon from platoon, and company from company in the early days of individual training.

As the days went, the process brought in its wake the acceptance of a fact hard for Englishmen to learn, that individual characteristics are no bar to effectual co-operation, or even to the warmest intimacy. Officers and men made their friends at the Crystal Palace, but at Blandford they came to know and often to like their enemies.

True to the tradition of its origin, the public schools company developed measles at an early stage of the Blandford training, and its isolation was the occasion for one of the best concerts ever given in the camp. But these entertainments were only farcical interludes in a continuous comedy. For the Hawke Battalion could be serious about everything except itself.

The mere fact that "A" company posed as the partisans of the orthodox tradition, expert in drill and the formalities of war, developed in "B" company a contempt for these same formalities, which they ignored in resolute defiance of all military precepts. Meanwhile, "C" company, late arrivals with a questionable discipline, could take their stand neither on formality nor its absence, for the one was impossible to achieve, and the other too easy to provide even a *succès de scandal*. Efficiency was, therefore their motto, and their own opinion of what they could do out of sight of the parade ground was a high one indeed.

"D" company had, it might be thought, a ready-made tradition of "playing the game," but the adjutant had made the phrase synonymous with the punctual and correct fulfilment of orders which had never been issued, or had been issued in a sense opposite to that intended; besides, the company represented, on the whole, the less orthodox side of public school life. "*It will be all right on the night,*" was their final and justified commentary on their own share in these mock serious rehearsals of the impending tragi-comedy.

Perhaps I should have written "tragedy," but in this almost personal record to do so would involve a loss of perspective. For this peculiar, tolerably sane, but pre-eminently light-hearted battalion did not see its entry into the war in any sombre light. That the Hawke Battalion should take the field in a serious—perhaps, actually in a critical—campaign was surely one of humours of a time not over-burdened with humour. And it was up to the battalion not to miss the point. The attempt to combine a sense of duty with a sense of humour was a hazardous one. But it was, or so it seemed, at least worth making. In the slang of the period, "*no stunting*" was the accepted motto. Translated into terms appropriate to inspections by highly gilt-edged generals, it meant "*no eyewash*"; into terms of the trenches, it was to mean no superfluous activities in no-man's-land and much smoking in the front line; into terms of domestic economy and discipline, it meant the rigorous restriction of the formalities to the parade ground, and a compendious disregard for impracticable regulations. Above all, it meant the whole-hearted enjoyment of every possible moment of leisure.

Without the genial and enterprising leadership of Colonel Wilson, the battalion must either have been much duller or much less efficient. As it was, he fought the battalion's battles with unswerving loyalty, and when it came to serious training and the routine of war the battalion at least tried to show its gratitude.

The headquarters staff of the battalion consisted, in addition, of Lieutenant-Commander Ramsay Fairfax, R.N., as second in command, Surgeon Bradbury, R.N., Lieutenant R. H. Shelton, R.N.V.R. (Adjutant), Hon. Lieutenant Pitman, R.M. (Quartermaster), Sub-Lieutenant Tremayne, R.N.V.R. (Machine-Gun Officer), Sub-Lieutenant Brereton, R.N.V.R. (Transport Officer), C.P.O. Stewart (Regimental Sergeant-Major), C.P.O. Hawker (Battalion Quartermaster-Sergeant), and Sergeant-Major Lydiard, whose exact position in the hierarchy in these early days I never exactly determined. He was, however, a serving soldier on the outbreak of the war, and as the only representative of this not unimportant body of men, he enjoyed with the battalion a prestige which outweighed a lack of official status so complete that he had to be smuggled out of the country to the front in the disguise of an officer's servant.

A peculiar feature of the Hawke Battalion Headquarters was that there were blended there, in so far as blending was possible, an infinite variety of traditions. Colonel Wilson himself was at once a regular soldier, a Territorial gunner, a country gentleman, and a Member of Parliament, and was as courageous in defending his battalion against the machinations of the staff as he was in defending his trenches against the enemy. Reserving, however, his military experience for his dealings with the enemy, he turned on hostile staff officers that armoury of tact, suavity, and determination, which was to carry him later to high political office, so that his mainly civilian subordinates recognized in him their ideal of the amateur defeating the professionals at their own game. Commander Ramsay Fairfax brought to the serious work of fighting the varied and adaptable genius of the naval officer, but since the days of his fleet service he had been a Yeomanry captain and an explorer, while his outside interests ranged from divorce law reform to company finance.

It was really inevitable in the circumstances that the unfortunate junior officers, who could not even air their civilian acquirements with any convincing effect in the ears of the two senior officers of the battalion, should have concentrated on the unfortunate adjutant their share of that outraged dignity which every competent barrister, stockbroker, or journalist turned subaltern concealed somewhere beneath his as yet unconvincing khaki in those nursery days of 1914. Yet this history cannot go out without some juster measure of appreciation of our first adjutant's unfailing energy and good nature than our ribald fusillade of back-chat conveyed by word of mouth in those days of light-hearted training. What anyone else would have done if turned by a stroke of the pen from a leading seaman of Naval Volunteers into the adjutant of an infantry battalion cannot be imagined. Shelton succeeded, despite, it was even alleged, a deep-seated belief in the philosophy of Ian Hay,[3] in keeping the battalion machine running, despite the worst blunders of recalcitrant company commanders and subalterns, and all this without even the assistance of a trained regimental sergeant-major or orderly-room sergeant. And he achieved this sensational result without making an enemy—not even among the Turks.

The quartet of senior officers was completed by Surgeon Bradbury—a naval surgeon on the permanent establishment, with many years' service to his credit. As things turned out, his was to be the hardest task of all, and no one could have been better equipped for it. But at Blandford we knew him best when we saw him most, in the mess. No festive evening was complete in his absence, but his unfailing high spirits never allowed him to be absent. If they had, we should certainly have raised a protest.

Yet with all these varied experiences, Battalion Headquarters were at one with the rest of the battalion in this: that they came fresh to the task of training an infantry battalion. There was thus combined with experience of war and the habit of command an understanding of lay doubts and difficulties, a readiness to allow of experiment, a broadminded tolerance of the characteristic attitude to war as a novel, rather quaint, dangerous, but not overwhelmingly complex adventure. No one on the Hawke Battalion Headquarters was ever heard to voice the complaint, so familiar elsewhere, that he had served fifteen years in a regular battalion before he became a company commander, or to draw the logical inference that any independent thinking by anyone who had served a less time would be an action insolent to the point of insubordination, and foolish to the point of certifiable lunacy. The Hawke Battalion, in short, was led by senior officers who might have been thought ideally suited to a peculiar task, and who, in the event, were found to be so suited. Whatever faults there may have been rested with their juniors.

Yet it is impossible to think that the light-hearted spirit of those days, which remained as a living tradition of the battalion to the day of its final disbandment in 1919, was anything but good. It permeated all ranks, and could be upset only by a gratuitous display of authority, or the substitution of empty rhetoric for competent leading. These men, so different in their origins and their beliefs that the old Etonian, fighting side by side in the ranks of the Tyneside miner, had to master a new (or rather an older) idiom before he could exchange conversa-

---

3. *Doing Our 'Bit'* by Ian Hay is also published by Leonaur.

tional pleasantries, were united in one thing. They would not tolerate cant. They were not, and did not, mean to be unnecessarily like other battalions. They would not sacrifice themselves to mere appearances. Why should they? They would rather "get on with the war" than "play the game." This characteristic would sometimes arouse grave doubts in the minds of the adjutant, but it existed. The Hawke Battalion never sang "Tipperary" or "Keep the Home Fires Burning." It had too much common sense to take a return ticket for the front. But it went there all the same.

The Hawke had no mascots and no traditions; it had no past and no future. It was of the present; and in a world of turmoil its officers and men were no more than light-hearted spectators, who had become actively involved through an excess of enthusiasm which has, perhaps, in retrospect a faintly ironic significance. When, on an ever-memorable 7th of May (but how many of us remember that date?), the orders for overseas, so long expected that they were hardly credited, actually arrived, there were, I think, no regrets. The confusion that followed the receipt of the orders was immense. Even at this eleventh hour not all the men had got the right kind of rifle (one forgets at this interval of time what the right kind was, or what was wrong with the other kind), and in any case the art of moving men and baggage is, if not the greatest, certainly the last of military arts. It was not made easier in the present case by the natural desire, amounting to positive determination, of the men to leave camp at the earliest possible moment for a farewell visit to Blandford.

Virtually, only Friday afternoon and Saturday morning were available for the final preparations. True, it was easier to prepare for a campaign in May, 1915, than to prepare for a raid in 1918, but the comparison, if it had been possible, would not have helped in the replacement of lost kit, the repacking of incorrectly packed packs, or the simulation of a superficial sobriety. Still less would it have facilitated the harnessing of mules and their direction by unskilled hands, which was a necessary preliminary to the entrainment of the battalion transport, which, if my memory serves me correctly, was only drawn from store (or was it from stable?) an hour or two before.

In the circumstances, there was nothing solemn about the final parades of the Hawke Battalion. Nevertheless, headquarters and "A" and "B" companies moved off at 10 p.m. on Saturday the 8th, and "C" and "D" companies at 3.30 a.m. on Sunday morning, without any serious *contretemps*; by breakfast-time their place on those sunlit downs knew the Hawke Battalion no more.

Forever! There might have been a certain solemnity in such a thought, but not until one had revisited alone those once familiar lanes with their accumulated memories, or walked across the parade ground peopled with ghosts, could any significance attach to those gay and fleeting moments which were actually at the time, and for all of us, neither grave nor regretful.

The night of surprises had a fitting climax. We caught the train.

CHAPTER 3

# Active Service

The destination of the Hawke Battalion was, of course, the Gallipoli Peninsula. The political and military origins of that now almost legendary campaign are fully set out elsewhere. To the Hawke, however, the origin, and even the prospects of a campaign, were things of little relevance. A successful campaign may see the annihilation of a battalion which may come scathless through a disaster leaving its mark on history. An isolated battalion can only play a decisive part in an operation so small that it cannot have more than a local significance, and its doubts and anxieties are necessarily of a local kind. So we must not imagine the officers and men of this battalion—so especially personal in its characteristics—swarming on to the two transports which lay waiting for them on the Avonmouth quay-side in the brilliant morning sunshine of May 10th with eager arguments on their lips as to the strategic merits of Easterners and Westerners. But they had in their hands morning papers which, nevertheless, took their minds forwards to their Eastern battlefield, for, as chance had it, that morning's papers contained the first casualty list of the Naval Division at Gallipoli.

The Hawke Battalion was divided between the two transports, headquarters and "A" and "B" companies on the *Ascania* (with Colonel Wilson as O.C. troops), and "C" and "D" companies with the Collingwood on the *Ivernia*.

The voyage of these two transports marked an epoch in the life of more than the Hawke Battalion, since, for the first time, there were serious fears of submarines in the Mediterranean. The rumours were founded on fact, but it was curious to mark, as we proceeded on our way, the different attitudes of dawning realization. The naval authorities in home waters provided an escort for some twelve hours, and were superbly confident that nothing more was required in the face of an idle rumour. At Gibraltar the rumour itself was only a rumour, and the blandest indifference was displayed when the transports anchored outside the harbour and enquired quite vainly for information. At Malta the rumour was in process of confirmation, with the result (paradoxical to mere civilians) that ships which, before the panic, sailed straight into the harbour now waited for several hours outside, so vast and compendious were the precautions round about the harbour mouth. Twenty-four hours' steaming farther east, the *Ivernia* (a day and a half ahead of the *Ascania* at this point) spoke to the first boat (a French transport) which had actually seen a submarine, and her Captain sailed across the bows of the *Ivernia* and shouted the information through a megaphone. To the logical Frenchman a torpedo was clearly a thing to be avoided. At Mudros, however, when the *Ivemia* came to anchor on the 17th May (followed two days later by the *Ascania*), the submarine, torpedoes and all, was a *fait accompli*. The *Majestic* had been torpedoed the day before, and the submarine "panic" was over.

The Hawke Battalion had, indeed, arrived on the scene at a moment of reaction. Mudros Harbour, to a landsman's eye one of the finest natural harbours in Europe, though not without some serious defects as a naval base, had been the inevitable point of assembly not only for the fleet, but for the army and administrative services, throughout January, February, and March. From there the fleet had sailed out on the 17th March to the last of the great naval attacks on the Straits. From there the transports, carrying the troops destined for the landing, had sailed to their appointed rendezvous off the coast on April 24th. For the first and last time in the history of the war the scenes on this second occasion, so rich in significance, broke through the almost impregnable reserve of the British temperament, and the transports, passing one by one out of the harbour to their desperate adventure, had evoked from the scores of ships waiting at anchor a display of spontaneous and uncontrollable enthusiasm.

No malignancy of fate, no human improvidence, can rob that scene of its dignity. Henry Nevinson and John Masefield have each written, in memorable passages which stand out eminent amid the desert of post-war literature, accounts of this historic occasion which are themselves history. But by May 17th those brilliant feats of arms which had accompanied the landing and made it possible had also, as it turned out, committed us to a serious and exhausting campaign against entrenched positions. The situation now called for resolute organisation and endurance on behalf of what were, in effect, both at Anzac and Cape Helles, beleaguered garrisons, and officers of the administrative staff, who, three weeks before, had been issuing maps of Constantinople to an invading army, came aboard the *Ivernia* begging for looking-glass to make periscopes for the harassed defenders of the trenches at the edge of the cliffs.

The Hawke Battalion had had a foretaste of anticlimax at Malta, where both transports, on their separate occasions, had stayed for twenty-four hours, and where officers and men going ashore had met some of the doctors from the first hospital ships to leave the Peninsula after the landing. The news came from sources notoriously unreliable; but the inexperienced battalion had not yet learnt that truth, a tender plant at the best, withers quickly in the *hinterland* of a battlefield, and perishes in the malicious atmosphere of a base. So the Hawke Battalion was prepared to postpone its march to Constantinople at quite an early stage of its active service career. Mudros and its staff officers— more ignorant, though more enthusiastic, than they showed themselves later in the campaign—only hastened the return to the region of the expected, from which the spring air and the excitement of our Mediterranean odyssey had temporarily estranged us.

Above all was this true of the men, who found that, as they had suspected all along, war was, after all, mainly an affair of hard work, fatigues, and disappointments, experiences already familiar to men whose daily bread had had to be won by personal effort over long periods of time. It was thus with an equable temper that the Hawke Battalion set out in the drifters *Immingham* and *Brighton* in the evening of the 27th May to join General Mercer's 1st Naval Brigade at Cape Helles.

Stealing over the waters, the battalion came in sight of the Peninsula for the first time a little before midnight on the same evening; within half an hour they were noiselessly anchored alongside the improvised pier, and to the sound of rifle fire, which seemed very close at hand, the work of disembarkation began. It was an impressive moment, and a sad one, since the first news to reach the headquarters of the battalion was of the death of Colonel Wilson's brother, Major Frank Wilson, R.M.L.I., who had been acting as Brigade Major to General Mercer's 1st Naval Brigade, to which the Hawke Battalion was to be attached.

The scene was a strange one. The persistent rifle fire was the source of countless rumours, which were soon raised by the more imaginative to the level of confidential information, and in this way gained more rapid circulation as they were repeated in hurried whispers. The Turks were attacking; the British line was being pushed back; we were going straight into the trenches, which were, in our eager imagination, only a few yards away. There was little in our surroundings to dispel the gathering excitement. The air we breathed was poisonous with the corruption of death, and the moon, which would have revealed the comparative order of the beaches and the methodical arrangements of the embarkation staffs, was hidden behind a bank of clouds. We only saw in vague outline the towering cliffs on either side, and the gully immediately to our front peopled with furtive shadows, honey-combed with dug-outs and the remains of trenches. It is true enough that the landing of new formations had become by the middle of May almost a matter of routine to the naval and military embarkation staffs. But the landing of the Hawke Battalion was our first military experience. We had landed straight from the dining saloon of a Cunard liner on the very edge of a battlefield where history was still in the making. With no interval of acclimatization, by the mere act of setting foot on shore, we found ourselves on the edge of the fighting line.

It was, as I have written elsewhere, this sudden change, unparalleled in any other campaign of the present war, a change singularly dramatic, which so heightened the impression left by the first night on the Peninsula. On the very edge of the indifferent waters of the Straits there remained still the wreckage of boats and stores; the once-green slopes of the gully which closed the view were scarred with shell-holes, and worn to the colour and substance of dust by the ceaseless passage of men. Here and there were gathered in pitiful heaps rifles and equipment, salvage from the wounded and the dead, and amid this wreckage, across the sand still strewn here and there with the remains of rusted entanglements, men moved about with a brisk solemnity. Almost every night, for the first four months of the campaign, one heard on the beaches the ceaseless rifle fire of the Turks, and, occasionally, the sound of artillery bombardment, brought very close by the proximity of our heavy guns.

Of the extent of ground which, in fact, separated the beach from the firing line, nothing could be guessed by newly arrived troops. No wonder that, at the first glance, the narrow beach seemed the embodiment of desolation.

The night of the Hawke Battalion's landing on the Peninsula was not in reality the occasion for any unwanted activity on the part of the enemy, and our front line, at least two miles inland, was secure by this time from all attack. The battalion was drawn up in conventional formation on the beach (the Tyneside miners a little perturbed to find that they might be called on to parade in an orthodox fashion even at midnight on the shores. of the Dardanelles), and marched inland for a distance of a mile and a half. Here, on an open space of ground just to the left of the one recognizable road on the Peninsula (from Sedd-el-bahr to Krithia), and partly hidden from sight of the Turkish trenches on the slopes of Achibaba by scattered trees and shrubs, the battalion was set down to dig. By morning, we were told, all the men must be below ground, as our positions were exposed, and the enemy were able to shell the "rest camps."

With that, the battalion got down to work with more energy than experience, and in those few hours laid strange but irrevocable foundations for the camp which was to house their household goods for more than four months.

The sunrise found them still digging. But for a moment or two it may be well imagined that, in the brief half-light before the dawn, they paused to take stock of their surroundings. Before them, closing the northern horizon, was the domed forehead of Achibaba. To their immediate front, and to their right amid the scattered clumps of shrub and olive trees, were the rest camps of the other battalions of the Naval Divisions, veterans already of several desperate battles, but in their camps looking hardly as professional as might have been feared. To the left, across the Krithia road, was an expanse of sandy waste which concealed in its numerous though invisible folds other camps, and notably those of the 29th and 42nd Divisions. Behind the Hawke resting-place the ground was open on the west to the cliff's edge, and the eye could pick out to the west the sandy track running down to the opening in the line of the cliffs which marked Lancashire Landing as being the path which the battalion had taken the evening before. To the east the country was more wooded and broken, but amid the trees and in the pockets were to be seen horses, mules, Indians, and guns half concealed. In the distance the ground sloped away to the village of Sedd-el-bahr, the base of the French corps, whose lines lay on the east of the Peninsula.

This was the first rough outline of the country as it presented itself to the unseeing eyes of inexperienced troops, cautioned time and again to get on with their digging and let the campaign take care of itself. Then about 7 a.m. came breakfast, and the battalion disappeared into its half-completed dugouts, and the routine life of the Peninsula had begun.

It was a queer, quick start, in which everything had to be taken for granted. Rations arrived and were eaten, and the officers and men sat in little holes in the ground and waited for orders. The first great lesson of war was being learnt—that for the infantryman the greater part of war is to sit about and wait for orders, the smaller part is to dig, and the least part is to execute the orders which come but seldom, and which for so many individuals and for some units come but once.

Whether the waiting be in a rest camp, billet, or a trench is a great matter at the time, and there may well be more danger in one than in the other, but the danger is incidental, and the quality of the rations a matter of far greater moment. On Gallipoli in May these consisted of biscuits, tea without milk or sugar, and bully beef. This was active service indeed, and, as such, accepted, in those days of our enthusiasm, without demur.

LIEUT. MORGAN AND LIEUT. COM. RAMSAY-FAIRFAX
IN "A" COMPANY'S HEADQUARTERS, 1ST REST CAMP, 1915

The military position at Gallipoli at the end of May was fairly clearly defined. The first landings had taken Sir Ian Hamilton's force both at Anzac and at Cape Helles (where the Hawke Battalion now were) on to the edge of the cliffs. At Anzac, virtually, no further progress had been made after the first three days' fighting, and the position held was only three-quarters of a mile in depth at the utmost extent, and, being in the form, roughly, of a semicircle, was in most places much less than that. At Cape Helles, however, there had been four distinct engagements. On April 25th and 26th the beaches, and the heights commanding them, had been won (except for "Y" beach, which by an incalculable mistake, for which the responsibility will never be fixed, had been abandoned). On April 27th an unopposed advance of about a mile and a half was carried out by the 29th Division and the French; this advance had carried our line over the open ground behind the Hawke Battalion rest camp, and, roughly, hardly any farther.

The Turks had had no defended position here, but the country farther ahead was (especially in the French sector and where the Naval Division rest camps now were) sufficiently wooded to afford him good cover for his rear-guards, while in the centre of the Peninsula and on the left were two gullies (Krithia Nullah and Gully ravine), which lent themselves to secure defence, and were, in fact, defended. To carry our line forward across these gullies and well into the belt of wooded country in front of the right of our line had been an immediate and desperately essential task.

On April 28th the next advance was made, and won a mile on either side of Gully ravine. Elsewhere it failed. To complete the task was, however, vital if our troops were to have any cover for their rest camps and communications, and if any positions were to be won for the scanty complement of guns. Fighting on, we should, moreover, come in touch with the main Turkish positions this side of Achibaba (only two miles ahead), and if we could carry them the campaign would rapidly enter a new phase. With these objects the fourth advance and the third general engagement south of Cape Helles had been fought on May 6th to 8th. The immediate object was secured, and our line had been carried up the *nullahs* for a distance of nearly a mile, and, generally, to within assaulting distance of the Turkish entrenched positions from sea to sea. Here and there there were gaps and re-entrants in the line won on the evening of May 8th, but, in the next few nights, advances by the naval and other divisions had completed this stage of the campaign. At great loss, with a dangerous expenditure of time and energy, but still with ultimate success, the army had won:

> A sort of security, failing which we must, without a doubt, have withdrawn. It would have been impossible to keep an army

corps indefinitely in an area so exposed as that occupied by us on the 28th April. Now, though our advance had been at the most three-quarters of a mile, and in places less, we had got astride of the different *nullahs*, and had won a considerable belt of country, whose occasional trees provided a substantial measure of protection. The result was cover from view for our infantry and guns, and reasonably safe communication with our front-line positions.[4]

It will be seen from this that the stubborn fighting had been on the beaches and the very edge of the cliff, and over what, to the newly arrived battalion, was the *terra incognita* between the rest camps and the trenches. By May 28th the fruits of this fighting had been reaped in the landing of stores and guns, the digging of communication trenches from the rest camp to the line, and the general organisation of ration dumps, water supply, and medical arrangements. Everything was on a rough scale which easily passed for inefficiency, but the administrative services were by no means necessarily responsible, and certainly the Hawke Battalion had dug its own rest camp and could not complain that it had to stay there. Nor did it.

Ker.[5] in a letter home ,dated May 30th, wrote:

It is really very jolly here. These are what they call the ' rest trenches.' No work to speak of . . . and a shirt-sleeve climate. It is pretty hot during the day, but mornings and evenings are perfect. . . . Our food is largely corned beef in various forms, but it is good. There is a difficulty about water, which is not. The beverage which keeps us alive is tea, of which we drink incredible quantities. There is no milk.

The place is littered with camps like this. You never saw such a conglomeration of strange troops. You should have seen me and A. P. Herbert the other evening bathing in the Dardanelles near some Frenchmen and Senegalese, with the Turkish lines (or, rather, the place where they were) in sight on a ridge to our left beside some dismantled forts, the Plain of Troy before us on the other side, some guns on the Asiatic side sending an occasional shrapnel shell over on our right, and a French battery immediately behind us having shots at them. . . . I took a bathing party down to the beach yesterday. The scene was a cross

---

4. *The Royal Naval Division.*
5. Lieutenant William Ker, R.N.V.R. (commanding at this time the 9th Platoon of "C" company).

between Blackpool in the season and the Ganges. . . . The men think it a fine picnic, but we are going into the firing line tomorrow night. . . . There was a great din last night about 9.30. We could hear terrific rifle fire, and the French guns behind us started firing into the darkness with a boom and a whirr, and then a pause and a distant bang as the shell explodes. We have not heard what it was all about.

Here are the authentic first impressions of one whose letters, written home regularly throughout the campaign, correct time and again my own recollections, which I can back with no contemporary evidence except of purely military happenings.

The life in the rest camp was, indeed, pleasant enough as long as the general level of health was good, which was until the dust, the flies, and the midsummer heat became simultaneously acute. Till then our scattered days behind the lines were occupied with platoon inspections in the morning, bathing (subalterns with bathing parties, company officers and headquarters by themselves) in the evening, and working parties at night, the intervals being filled up by long and not unamusing meals which lacked the formality typical of the experienced campaigner, but which made up for this, for a time at least, in novelty.

The first of those constant changes in personnel which make up the ever-varied life of a battalion took place on landing, when C.P.O. Stewart, the battalion sergeant-major, was transferred to service afloat, and Sergeant-Major Lydiard succeeded him. His dapper figure jumping in and out of the company dugouts with a large note-book was one of the features of the landscape in those early days, only less vivid in recollection than the harassed spectacle of the adjutant searching for picks and shovels, or turning out his pockets in the vain hope that on one of the ninety-nine scraps of papers which were their normal contents some trace might be found of the battalion orders which he had written a few hours earlier, but which appeared always to have vanished in the stress of some recurrent emergency.

The serious work of the battalion was, however, hardly impeded by these eccentricities, as Colonel Wilson's order-book, circulated with such vivacity by the R.S.M., was the authentic fount of information, though when it came to details of time, place, and guides for a working party (and five out of. every six orders were concerned with these), nothing but a tape machine could have kept pace with the changes signalled every ten minutes from the staff captain's office.

When we remember now that the Gallipoli campaign was fought with at least a semblance of modern methods over rough scrub devoid of a single road which could be used (the Krithia road was too conspicuous a landmark to be used much even by night), the incessant fatigues, which were soon, in the unbearable midsummer conditions, to wear down the health of the men to breaking-point, are easily understood. It could even be plausibly urged that they were essential. Certainly, just at the time when the Hawke landed they were more urgent than ever they were later. The great assault on the Turkish prepared positions, before which our Army was at last entrenched, was to be made on June 4th.

The organisation of the divisional sectors and the reorganisation of individual units had only just been completed by the time the battalion arrived, and the intervening week had to be spent digging communication trenches for the extensive paraphernalia of a battle. This was the first task of the Hawke Battalion, and in its execution they made their first acquaintance with the Achibaba Nullah, the Brown House, the White House, Port Arthur, and all the other landmarks which lay between the rest camp and the three lines of trenches (Backhouse Road, Mercer Road, and Trotman Road), which marked the different stages of the Naval Division's advance since the May battles, and now formed a conventional front-line system.

The Achibaba *nullah* was, as its name suggests, a narrow gully carved out by a small stream flowing from Achibaba to the coast. The stream was, in summer at least, little more than a running brook, and the gully itself was the smallest of the three which ran down from Achibaba and divided the Peninsula into four roughly equal divisional sectors. It is, however, intimately bound up with the activities of the Hawke, as of all battalions of the Naval Division, in Gallipoli. The divisional sector was, for the first four months of the fighting, astride of this *nullah*. The divisional rest camp was among the trees which flourished in and on the edge of the valley into which the gully opened out as it neared the shore of Morto Bay, and the gully itself, from Backhouse Post onward, was, in the early days, the only covered approach to the trench system on this part of our front.

The way from the rest camps to the entrance to the *nullah* (the Hawke camp was some three-quarters of a mile from Backhouse Post) was marked by a line of ruined towers, ruinous before the war, more ruinous now, but which still challenged with mighty memories the assaults of time and the violence of man. For these towers were the ruins of a Roman aqueduct, now falling before the barbarous weapons of a younger civilization. Beyond them the valley narrows into a glen, remarkable for its monopoly of shade and the incessant croaking of frogs. This glen was not more than 50 yards in width, but extended for something between a quarter and half a mile, when the *nullah* opened out again and became unsafe for use except by night for small parties.

In this *nullah* the Hawke Battalion had its first experiences of war. Prosaic in retrospect, familiar in outline, they live in the individual memory. On the night of May 31st and June 1st the battalion was called on to supply 400 men for six hours' digging on the communication trenches alongside the *nullah* at its wooded end, and beyond the glen to the frontline system. The digging, though in the open, was well behind our front line, and in most campaigns would have been as safe as an Aldershot field-day. In Gallipoli, however, the Turks practised the art of rapid fire which the English regular army preached, and swept the hinterland of our trench system with method and skill. The task of digging and of supervising and organising digging under these conditions was one of overwhelming simplicity, which for a moment baffled the inexperienced officers and irritated the men. Surely, one remembers feeling, there is something which ought to be done, something which one has unpardonably forgotten.

After an hour or two common sense reasserts itself, and one is glad that the reality of war does not at the moment call for any personal interference with the schemes of staff officers and generals. The men take, in time, an equally prosaic view. But for a time they feel that "the officer" might move them to a safer place or interpose some effective barrier between themselves and bullets clearly not aimed at their unoffending selves. The hideous impersonality of war is not yet fully understood, but the work goes on, the officers and sapper N.C.O.'s walking up and down the long stretch of trench giving an order or two in the course of the six hours, but most of the time pretending that they enjoy the bitter cold and the bullets, and only wish that, they hadn't got to go away so soon.

Allied to these earliest recollections is that of the first visit of the Hawke Battalion to the trenches, which began on the evening of June 2nd and ended in the early dawn of June 4th, a day memorable, if not remembered, even in the vast panoramic history of the Great War. It cannot be claimed that the battalion avoided all, or indeed any, of the mistakes common in units on these occasions. Leaving the rest camp with a great show of efficiency and importance in the dusk of evening, all but two platoons and the Battalion Headquarters had lost their way in the space of half an hour, each platoon losing touch with each other with a facility surprising to no one except a civilian or a staff officer. The way was plain, as a matter of fact, and the need for haste was not apparent, but even the routine occupations of the infantry have their technique, and the battalion had to learn them.

The fatigue parties of the preceding evenings had been found from

"C" and "D" companies, and now the front and support lines were to be held by "A" and "B" companies. "C" company was in reserve and "D" company still farther back. After an evening of exasperation and feverish wanderings to and fro all the companies got eventually into position, and those in the front line proceeded to discover rows of Turks in no-man's-land threatening instant disaster.

Lieutenant (later Commander) Lockwood (then commanding No. 1 Platoon, "A" company), writes:

I shall always remember my first night in the trenches in Gallipoli. The trenches were not by any means scientifically constructed, though they were good enough for cover. Trench boards were non-existent in those days, and sandbags hard to procure. However, considering that there was an absolute lack of, or, at any rate, great shortage of, all timber, sandbags, etc., the trenches were not to be despised as such.

As soon as the outgoing troops had left us, we immediately started to look round and find good fire steps, etc., for every man. Whilst I was busy doing this a message was passed down to stand to, and that the Turks were advancing against us. This was somewhat thrilling, as we had had no time to find out who our neighbours were or, indeed, our way about the line at all. We got the men standing to on the fire steps and threw up a Verey light. I swore then, and still adhere to it, that some distance away I saw a line of men lying down facing us. Two or three of our officers and several of the men swore it also; but on another light being thrown up there was nothing to see.

Being in the line for the first time in an utterly unknown position, it was quite an exciting five minutes. One welcomes an attack when one knows exactly where everybody is, but I didn't even know where company headquarters was. To me it was, therefore, a distinct relief that it was a case of imagination.

Morning came and the usual stand to arms. We were then better able to take stock of our surroundings.

Water was the trouble. But we were able to send water parties twice a day to bring up sufficient water for the company, and though it was short and necessarily had to be economized, we had no real hardship from that source.

We were kept busy in the trenches day and night, digging and improving the line. Wiring kept us busy at nights, and it was an unpleasant business, for the Turks believed in a constant rapid fire by machine guns and rifles; though most of this was badly aimed and much of it fell behind our lines, it was not a savoury business to be out in front night after night.

But if the front-line companies had their moments of excitement (for the front-line trenches were still only earthworks hurriedly thrown up under fire, not nicely organised fortifications requiring a garrison of second-line troops), the reserve trenches had lost even the faintest savour of romance. One sat in them, and there was absolutely nothing else to do. The trouble was that "C" company had not yet reached that stage of lassitude when it is restful to do nothing, nor that stage of efficiency when one can do nothing in comfort. Neither had they suffered the necessary 60 *per cent*, of casualties which would have enabled them to fit into the allotted portion of trench.

These, however, were the minor excitements common to all young battalions launched into a campaign already in being, but not yet organised to absorb untrained troops by any gradual introduction to the practice of war. In the result the Hawke Battalion came through without mishap, and after a mere two days in the line came down to find itself in reserve for the historic engagement of June 4th.

This engagement, as it turned out, was to provide us with but the barest introduction to the real business of war, but, optimistic in our inexperience, we prepared busily in the small hours of June 4th to march up the slopes of Achibaba. The two and a half limbers which provided the battalion transport (the waggons and mules which had left England with the battalion had got no farther than Alexandria) were duly loaded up with ammunition, and even the officers and the company cooks resisted the desire to take off their boots. On the edge of a battlefield the war was a thing to be reckoned with, and the battalion, duly flecked with the dust of conflict after no less than two nights in the trenches, awaited the issue with a sense of legitimate importance. Were we not to see our first battle? And were we not at least a seventh of Sir Ian Hamilton's general reserve?

The attack, planned for the 4th June, was—I quote from the history of the Royal Naval Division, as I shall on future occasions where it is necessary for a moment to deal with the general rather than the particular—like those of May 6th and 8th, to be a direct frontal assault on the whole Turkish forward position. We started, moreover, with three advantages which we had not previously enjoyed: We were now right up against our objective, not vainly groping for it; we had limited the objectives of the first waves of the attack; and, finally, our troops, though not fresh, were infinitely more rested than they had been early in May. To this extent the modified optimism which prevailed was justified; but there was another side to the picture. The Turks had been

"A" Company lines, 1st Rest Camp. 1915

strongly reinforced and were deeply entrenched, and their left flank (against the French—that is, on the right of the Allied line) rested on the Kereves Dere Ridge. This position was unassailable except to an advance along the line of the ridge. Such an advance the French had attempted on May 6th and 8th, but had only pushed forward for a distance of two or three hundred yards along the crest. Seeing that the ridge ran diagonally to our front, it was clear that any failure to advance farther along the crest and the upper slopes in the forthcoming attack must prejudice our chances on the lower slopes, where were the Naval Division. Equally, failure there might imperil any gains in the centre, and must, in any event, reduce their tactical value. On this view the success of the operations as a whole must depend largely— far too largely, considering to what extent we were committing all our resources to the uncertain issue—on the success of the French

On the British front the attack was to be carried out by the 29th, 42nd, and Naval Divisions, each attacking the Turkish trenches opposite to their own. The Naval Division, which had the shortest sector (less than a thousand yards of front), had to supply two brigades, less one battalion, to the corps as a general reserve, and were left, for their share in the battle, only the 2nd Naval Brigade and the Drake Battalion. Holding the last-named in reserve, General Paris arranged with Commodore Backhouse for the Howe, Hood, and Anson to attack the first two front-line trenches and the redoubt on the right of the brigade boundary, and for the assault of the Turkish third line to be carried out by "A," "B," and "D" companies of Commander Spearman's Collingwood Battalion. The remainder of the Collingwood were held in brigade reserve under Lieutenant-Commander West, R.N.V.R.

Next to the Anson (on the right of the brigade) were French Colonial troops, and next to the Howe (on the left) the Manchester Brigade of the 42nd Division.

For the purpose of this record the battle of June 4th may be said to have begun (not, perhaps, uncharacteristically) with the departure of the Hawke Battalion for the rest camp shortly before dawn, when they and the Drake and the Nelson Battalions of the 1st Naval Brigade handed over to those three battalions of the 2nd Brigade who, a few hours later, were to go forward to the attack. The hour was a solemn one in the history of the Naval Division, and marked the brief interregnum between two epochs in its history. Ever since Antwerp the supremacy among the Naval battalions of the Howe, Hood, Anson, Nelson, and Drake Battalions had been tacitly admitted. Now on this 4th June the whole division was assembled for the first time since Antwerp, and for the first time, as well as the last, the division was in a position to go into action with twelve infantry battalions of its own. But the burden of the day was to be borne by the veteran naval battalions, the Marine Brigade was to be employed on detached duty, and the Hawke and Benbow Battalions were to witness the beginning of the battle from the rest camp. It was not really the reunited division which fought this battle, but the five Naval battalions which had escaped scathless from Antwerp, and had trained through the autumn at Bettysanger, while the Hawke Battalion was but an agglomeration of recruits being suitably nourished under glass at Sydenham.

The story of the ill-fated assault launched at noon, and brought to nothing by the failure of the French Colonial troops to hold the pivotal position on the right of the Allied line, has been often told. The Hawke Battalion in the rest camp heard only the news of our astonishing success (the Naval Brigade had taken three lines of trenches), followed in a bare half-hour's time by the no less authentic story of eventual repulse. The first news had seemed too good to be true, but the later news shattered a secret dream never to be dreamt again on that dedicated Peninsula. Historians and journalists are still talking in whispers of the day when the truth will be known, and no doubt some domestic scandals of the war period will be unearthed to gratify the salacious appetites of the next generations; but the main crises of the war were not only clearly marked at the time, but instinctively appreciated by the civilian soldier almost as quickly as by the staff officer "in the know."

Was it to be trench warfare over again (in which case the attempt to "break through" by getting round the vast trench system of the eastern and western fronts had failed), or was the campaign to develop on spectacular lines with the Turks in retreat from their Achibaba positions, and the whole force of the Allies on the move? June 4th gave the answer, and it came with singular directness to the Hawke Battalion. The waiting limbers were quietly unloaded, and the battalion (no longer in Army Corps reserve, but reattached to the division) was ordered to an intermediate position halfway up the Achibaba Nullah early in the afternoon. Here, by Backhouse Post, they waited for six hours, a prey to the wildest rumours, under systematic if intermittent fire from an unseen but exultant enemy; while a touch of the bizarre was provided by a strange smoke cloud, which looked for all the world like Turkish writing, stretched across the sky above the crest of Achibaba, and interpreted, at least by many of the miners, as a significant omen.

The new atmosphere in the already familiar *nullah* was something fresh in our experience. The first hint of it came when an excited staff officer rode past while we were yet on the way from the rest camp, and urged the phlegmatic Tyneside miners to keep cool. "Nothing out of the ordinary had happened, or, indeed, ever did happen," was the burden of his whispered colloquy to a group of junior officers. They were not convinced. The whole experience was, in fact, decidedly unconvincing, and the endless procession of wounded men and stretcher parties excused a modified pessimism. On one officer of the Hawke Battalion, at any rate, the 4th of June left an impression vastly different.

The battalion stayed at Backhouse Post all night, suffering a good many isolated casualties from spent bullets and occasional shells, and here Surgeon Bradbury was wounded—happily only very slightly.[6] Not even the slightest of wounds, however, could be treated on the Peninsula, and his gain was the battalion's loss, a loss universally felt, for "Brads's" ever-smiling sanity achieved a combination of light-heartedness and efficiency which most of us could envy more easily than achieve.

All through the night the stream of wounded coming down the gully was unceasing, but the tales of loss and disaster which still poured from the mouths of those men suffering every extreme of pain, thirst, and fatigue were no longer so alarming. It was by then definitely known that on the Naval Division front we were safely in our old front line, and that though the four battalions actively engaged so far (the Howe, Hood, Anson, and Collingwood) had suffered disastrous losses—not more than a dozen officers remained to the entire brigade—not a yard of ground had been lost. To the left of the Naval Division, moreover, we had achieved substantial gains, and to secure this flank the Nelson Battalion had been sent on the evening of the 4th June, and were believed to have been severely engaged.

In the early hours of the 5th June the long-expected orders reached the Hawke, and the battalion went up to the line to complete the relief of the 2nd Naval Brigade, which had been begun the day before by the Drake Battalion. Starting forward through the welcome shade of the glen, which begins just beyond Backhouse Post, the battalion soon arrived at the Brown House, the point of junction of all forward communications in the divisional sector. The sun beat down from a cloudless sky on the painted ruins, a dusty olive tree or two, and an expanse of sandy waste; trenches and excavations designed to shelter the innumerable dumps closed the view on all sides, and the ear was confused by the never-ending croaking of frogs, the chirruping of crickets, the whistling of stray bullets overhead, or their reverberating rattle as they struck the sandbags of the trenches in front. An occasional shell swelled the chorus, while the voices of officers and men, the noise of

---

6. Bradbury was back with the battalion early in July.

transport waggons loading or unloading, and the unmusical notes of picks and shovels provided a persistent undercurrent of sound.

Here, at this meeting of the ways, converging into inextricable confusion, were not only the fighting troops and their reliefs, but hewers of wood and drawers of water, stretcher parties from the Field Ambulances, engineers' and trench stores, ammunition carriers, signallers, dispatch riders from the base, runners from the front line, quartermasters, transport officers, chaplains, and dressing stations. The barren but crowded scene epitomized at once the ineffective complexity of modern war and the devastating simplicity of unchanging nature. Faced with both realities, the crush of fevered humanity merely cursed each other under their breath and carried on. Among them, struggling to find a way forward, uncertain of their direction like everyone else, still keen but already tired by their very inexperience, the companies of the Hawke Battalion were catching their first authentic glimpse of war.

As it turned out, one company was needed at once to relieve that Nelson Battalion company which had had the difficult task during the night of the 4th/5th June of effecting a junction between the Naval Division back in their old lines and the 42nd Division clinging to their gains on the immediate left.

Ker, ("C" company had been detached to this particular task), wrote:

> We found ourselves in a trench running obliquely to the general line of the front. It had only been begun the night before to connect up a new piece of the firing line; it was only half dug—less than half at one end. The Turkish trenches were 150 to 200 yards off, and we had been shoved in with no instructions as to what we were in for, and we had no picks or shovels. As we could not have existed there without them, we finally persuaded the company we were relieving to leave us theirs. Luckily, the Turks were fairly quiet at the beginning, and we were able to arrange ourselves. We were in the trench for about thirty hours.
>
> The worst of it was that the men were tired when they went into it, having been bucketed about for two days and nights without sleep; also our rations went astray, and they had very little to eat all the first day. They had been sent off from the base without their mess tins, and had nothing in which to brew a hot drink. Water was another difficulty, as it all had to be brought up from the reserve trenches in tins. Another thing was

that (as I said) the trench was only half dug, and passage up and down it was difficult. Also at my end we had no sooner started deepening it than we struck a spring, and in a short time, to get up or down, we had to pass through 20 yards of mud ankle deep. Efforts to drain this part failed. The engineers tried next day and could not manage it, so it was not our fault.

In the evening Stevenson, our company commander, was told that we were to be relieved, and had actually sent half a platoon out when the order was cancelled, so three and a half of our platoons remained.

My men undoubtedly were best off of our lot, in spite of the flooding. The Turks were 150 yards away, and the trench was fairly well dug when we got into it. At the other end, where the 10th Platoon was under Cotter, the surface had hardly been broken in places, and the nearest Turks were only about 30 yards away. However, they were partly covered by the trench with which Cotter's joined up. The Turks fire off a lot more ammunition than we do; they go in for rapid fire at a line of trench. This is all right when you are safely dug in, but when the trench is only half made it is disconcerting at times. There were a lot of snipers about, and being shot at when you are not replying (most of our men were digging) is always trying.

I dare say this makes rather lurid reading. As a matter of fact, it was uncomfortable enough, but it was not really bad, because the trench, except up at Cotter's end, gave perfectly adequate cover as long as one kept down.

One of the Turkish habits is to blaze away like anything during the night, especially if they are thinking to try and rush a trench, or think they are going to be attacked. They shoot very high though at night, and the most dangerous place to be is on the way up to the reserve trenches, half a mile behind. As the Turks were supposed to be lively along one part of the line, one man in two had to keep watch all night.

Our men were as keen as anything, and the difficulty was to prevent them from firing too much. As it was, they let the Turks have it pretty often, and there was no movement during the night. . . .

Unfortunately, early in the night Stevenson was hit just above the left eye, but it turns out not to be at all serious. He has remained, so to speak, at his post, though he was a good bit shaken for a day or two. I expect he will have to go away for a week's rest. The next morning we really had the worst time, because the Turks kept up a perfect fusillade at our parapet for a couple of hours, while we were still working away at it. We had a good many men hit then. I was lucky in my platoon, though I lost a petty officer.

To our ill-concealed delight we were relieved that afternoon. We were really pretty tired by then, but we had to spend the night in the reserve trenches, where there was very little room for us, and everything was extremely uncomfortable.

Meanwhile "A," "B," and "D" companies had been more fortunate, as their task had been to relieve the old, comparatively well-established Naval Division trenches. With a genius for pessimism which was to become even more accentuated six weeks later, the general staff issued the direst warnings of an impending attack, but the nights of the 5th, 6th, and 7th were, as always happened on these occasions, extremely quiet. On the night of the 7th to 8th the whole battalion was relieved, and returned to the rest camp to sleep soundly for eight hours. The battalion were for twenty-four hours in corps reserve, which meant sitting down doing nothing, instead of bathing by day and digging by night; but on the 9th routine began again.

On the whole, the succeeding days were pleasant, but one of the officers writing home on June 14th reflects the minor worries of the campaign.

We go back into the trenches this afternoon after a week here of so-called 'rest'; as a matter of fact, you couldn't get real rest, if you had had a bad time in the trenches, unless you went right off the Peninsula (hence the talk of a 'rest camp' on Imbros), because the whole of it is within artillery range of the Turks. Luckily, their shooting is not up to much, and also they seem to be short of ammunition, as they have made no serious attempt to shell us out of our position here, which appears sufficiently precarious.

There has been a strong wind from the north-east all the week, which hides the countryside from dawn to dusk in clouds of driving dust, and makes camp life rather a burden. They say that this wind goes on practically all summer; otherwise we have not much to complain of. The expected heat is not; it is no hotter than a hot summer in the south of England. There are no mosquitoes; I dare say it is too dry. There are a good many flies, but nothing very bad.

We have been rather worried during 'rest' with fatigues. There is nothing more wearying than to get orders constantly countermanded, or to be kept waiting for orders which never come or enterprises which never happen, but, on the whole, we have done quite well; good food.

I have had one or two good bathes. The view from the hill above Helles beach is worth seeing. Asia and Troy Plain, and the Rabbit Islands, and a busy dusty foreground with ruined forts, and horses and waggons, and Sikhs and Ghurkas, Scotch, Welsh, Irish, English, Australians, half-castes, Senegalese, and big buck Negroes, all doing any number of different things. Imbros, across the sea to the west, is perhaps the best view of all; almost like Skye, with a destroyer or two in the foreground.

Sawyer had been slightly wounded during the last spell in the trenches, and had left the battalion, as also had Lieutenant Lockwood (suffering from sunstroke), and Sub-Lieutenants Nicholson, Marvin, and Venn (all sick). A proportionate number of petty officers and men as well had fallen victims to a climate which was beginning already to be a handicap to successful campaigning, but the casualties were so far light. "C" company, in Nelson Avenue, on the 5th and 6th had suffered worst, a particular loss being P.O. Robinson, platoon sergeant of the 10th Platoon, actually the first member of the battalion to be killed in the line. A fine petty officer, with R.N.V.R. experience, he had been with the company from early days, and was the subject of a singular presentiment of death.

Months before (at the Crystal Palace) he had told the writer that he would only see a few days' active service, and he foretold his death to his platoon commander only a few hours before he was shot through the head by a sniper, whose bullet found a chance gap in the parapet at one of the few points in the uncompleted trench where there was a fair protection from rifle fire. The total casualties, however, to June 14th were no more than three officers wounded, eight petty officers and men killed, and thirty-five petty officers and men wounded. Yet the casualties on the 4th of June alone in the 2nd Naval Brigade exceeded 1,100, among them being sixty-four officers. The Hawke Battalion had had, in truth, a gentle introduction to war. Their next turn in the line, which began on the 14th, was to throw a darker shadow.

The battalion subsector was in the centre of the divisional sector, just to the right of the point where the Achibaba Nullah intersected the track system. On the right of the Hawke, next to the French lines, were the Drake, and on the left, across the *nullah* and holding Nelson Avenue (the scene of "C" company's trying experience on the 5th and 6th of June), was the Nelson Battalion. This was the entire strength of General Mercer's 1st Naval Brigade, for the losses on June 4th had been so severe that the Benbow and Collingwood had been disbanded to supply reinforcements to the Anson, Howe, and Hood, the Naval Brigades being reduced to three battalions apiece.

With the 2nd Naval Brigade thus consisting almost entirely of unassimilated drafts, the 1st Naval Brigade took pride of place as the stronger of the two R.N.V.R. formations, and, what is more relevant to this story, the Hawke Battalion found itself with a more secure status than it had enjoyed heretofore. The least experienced of the battalions of its own brigade, it was nevertheless signalled out as the only one of the three new battalions with a place in the new organisation. As a consequence, it was for the rest of the campaign to take a more equal share in the fighting. But the price of this distinction was now to be exacted.

The battle of June 4th had marked the definite abandonment of the hope of a decisive victory south of Cape Helles. Sir Ian Hamilton had realised—and it was still possible to say that he had realised in time—that a methodical trench by trench advance up the stubborn slopes of Achibaba yielded no such hope of victory as would justify the indefinite dispersion of our strength. If we were to win, it must be by some strategy which would enable our naval supremacy to play its part in turning the flank of an enemy now at no military disadvantage. From this clear and sane reasoning developed the plan for the Suvla landing, and it had its natural reaction on the front south of Achibaba. No further general offensive was to be attempted there, but at the same time there was judged to be a greater need than ever for the maintenance of a show of activity. The enemy must not for a moment suspect that our main effort now to be made elsewhere. With the merits or demerits of this policy of local and miniature offensives at Cape Helles, offensives leading to no immediate or calculable advantage in position or moral, this history need not concern itself much. It is sufficient to understand the policy, and to note the consequences.

The first condition of any further advance on the right or in the centre was the capture by the French of a further section of the commanding Turkish position on the heights of the Kereves Dere. Then the Naval Division line must be advanced to the higher ground immediately to their front which they had actually reached on the 4th June, but which they could not hold when their right flank was uncovered by the French retreat.

While the French commander was making his plans for his own attack on the ridge, General Paris was concerned to advance his firing line as far as he safely could by minor operations, so as to reduce the distance to be covered by any assaulting troops who might have to carry out on his part of the front the next attack on the main Turkish positions. It was clear that the line could be pushed forward without great hazard to a distance of nearly 100 yards, but opposite the centre section of the divisional front was an advanced Turkish trench, which it was felt ought to be at once easy to capture and useful to hold, and which, had it been either, would have assured an even more substantial advance. This trench it was decided to attack with the Hawke Battalion on June 19th. A daylight assault was out of the question, since every rifle and machine gun on the slopes of Achibaba and the Kereves Dere commanded the ground, and Colonel Wilson was left with no alternative to a night attack.

The first of the days before the attack were quiet, but the next two were of quite exceptional activity, though the Turks were not responsible. Generals of all descriptions with retinues of staff officers paraded every corner of the trenches, and several officers of the battalion, not yet hardened to their visitations, were guilty not only of expressing their own opinions on some things, but of admitting their ignorance of others. Only from General Mercer, who came round on the 15th, was advice and assistance invariably forthcoming, and in consultation with him the plans for the attack took final shape.

The trench was supposed to be held by the enemy lightly, if at all, and it was believed that no strong counter-attack could be directed against it, as the ground between the main Turkish positions and their advanced trench seemed enfiladed by our new position in Nelson Avenue. In the circumstances the main difficulty seemed to be to get into the trench rather than to hold it. A night attack without preliminary bombardment was the deduction, and Morgan's "A" company was to carry it out. The front line was held by "B" and "D" companies, and "C" company, in reserve, would provide reinforcements and reliefs if such were needed. From the left of the Hawke front line ("D" company's front) a sap ran out for some 30 yards in the direction of the objective, and from this sap, to be held in force by "D" company for this occasion, the assaulting platoons (the 1st, 2nd, and 3rd) were to move out to their assembly positions. The 4th Platoon (Sub-Lieutenant Milvain) was to dig a communication trench between the objective and the sap. The first move was to be made at 12.30 a.m. on the 19th.

Nothing marked the 17th and 18th—days of preparation undisturbed by Turks and generals—except the loss on the 17th of two excellent N.C.O.'s, P.O. Clements and L. S. Smith, killed by chance shots, from which no possible protection could be secured so long as the enemy held the high ground all round us. There were still many

60

rumours of enemy snipers behind our own lines, but these, in my firm belief, were unfounded. Certainly the most vigilant observation and patrolling between the trenches never found a sniper at this stage.

The night of the 18th was a dark, moonless night, and particularly quiet. The Turkish rapid fire was by now far less active, as our machine gunners learnt to keep the Turks below their parapets. Punctually at 12.30 a.m. Morgan led out his platoons from the sap-head, and giving the word himself led the attack.

From that moment the fortunes of this miniature battle alternated with bewildering speed. Advancing with more enthusiasm than method, and adopting the old-fashioned and probably mistaken habit of cheering as they advanced, the assaulting line was seen to reach the trench; then there was a burst of firing from the enemy and five minutes' pause, broken only by a confused shouting of orders by officers separated from their men; then a swift and inexplicable retreat. Morgan himself had reached the neighbourhood of the trench with some of his men, and had there been killed. That much was certain, but the rest was confusion. Each man had found himself alone, as indeed happens to men facing death at night in the open for the first time; someone had ordered a concentration on the right; another had directed his fellows to the left; a third had heard his officer call a halt; no one had countenanced a retirement, yet the chances of war had resulted in nothing less. The attack had failed, and Sub-Lieutenant Little and two men, who were the only party who had actually reached the trench unwounded, were obliged, seeing themselves isolated, to retreat themselves.

But the attack had not begun. Such, at any rate, was the view of Lieutenant Horsfield, Morgan's second in command, who had been left out of the first assault; and a new attack was immediately planned and immediately executed. This time there was no mistake, and the trench was taken at 2.30 a.m., Horsfield, Rush, Little, and Tremayne (M.G. officer), with the survivors of the first assault, reaching their objective with little loss. Now in the two hours of darkness that still remained the work of consolidation had to be completed. For a time there was peace. The Turkish garrison of the trench had fled, and silence reigned while their victorious successors filled sandbags and attempted to prepare a defensible position.

To quote from Lieutenant Rush's account:

> The trench, however, proved to be barely 4 feet deep, and was untraversed for almost its entire length, besides having scarcely any parapet or *parados*. It was apparent, moreover, that its position alone rendered it almost untenable. Attempts to consoli-

date were made by reversing the parapet, and by blocking the trench about 100 yards towards the left. Here the machine gun was mounted and got into action, though it soon jammed. Sub-Lieutenant Tremayne was here shot through the head whilst firing over the parapet. The garrison continued to maintain a steady fire until very heavy casualties, and the fact that there the enemy offered no very clearly defined target, made active defence difficult.

An hour before dawn the struggle entered on a new phase. Rifle and machine-gun fire was concentrated on the position from the Turkish trenches which dominated it, and the enemy advanced to the counter-attack. Partly by fire from the captured position, mainly owing to the vigilance of the Nelson Battalion in Nelson Avenue, this was beaten off, but our losses in the trench were becoming serious, and ammunition was running out. Moreover, as it grew lighter our communications had become insecure. In the half-light before dawn volunteers from "D" company (among whom A.B. Chalkley was conspicuous) took out ammunition and rifles to the now small and exhausted garrison, and came back, for the most part, safely,[7] but it was already clear that the position would be held with difficulty. The garrison was dangerously reduced. Lieutenant Horsfield, wounded in the first assault, had been wounded again, this time mortally. Sub-Lieutenant Tremayne, the battalion machine-gun officer, had been killed. Of the original assaulting party, not more than twenty were unwounded.

Sub-Lieutenant Rush made his way back to Colonel Wilson, watching the situation anxiously from the sap-head, and gave him a detailed account. Whatever the issue might be, it was clear to Colonel Wilson that "A" company must be relieved, and Lieutenant Cotter's 10th Platoon ("C" company) was ordered up.

Before this platoon had reached the front line, however, the adjutant, who was in charge at the sap-head of the digging parties and other arrangements, got a message from the garrison that another officer was wanted.

He writes:

Being on the spot I went over and found the trench, which was only about 3 feet deep, an absolute shambles. Soon after, Cotter arrived with his platoon, and as dawn was breaking, and there was about 20 yards of open ground to get over, I ordered the

---

7. Though six men of this fine company—L. W. Young, S. G. Brown, J. S. Menhinnick, L. H. Salaman, E. W. Langland, and H. W. Stoessiger were killed.

'A' company men to crawl back one by one; the Turks spotted this and turned a machine gun on to them, and it was then that Little was killed. In the trench there was no field of fire, but we kept the Turks back with bombs. When these were exhausted, the Turks crawled up and bombed us; this was at about 8 a.m., and as we were badly enfiladed it could only have been a question of time before we would have been all wiped out. I then gave orders to withdraw one by one. Poor Horsfield was lying badly wounded in the trench, but managed, the Lord knows how, to crawl as far as the commencement of the communication trench, where Cotter and I found him and got him back to the front line; he died the next day. Of Cotter's platoon, which had held the trench for not more than half an hour, more than half had become casualties.

And so by 8.30 a.m., after alternations of fortune as confusing at the time as they are now in recollection, this minor but disastrous operation came to what must probably be regarded as its inevitable ending (though it was not so regarded in all quarters until a few days later, when a party of marines under Major Grover had attempted the same task, and succeeded no better).

The loss of so many officers and men, including the gifted commander of "A" company, was a severe blow to the battalion, but it was only an event in a campaign where such incidents had to be accepted. General Mercer's signal to Colonel Wilson, received at 1.25 p.m. on the same day, showed, as always in his case, a just measure of sympathy and appreciation.

> I congratulate the Hawke Battalion on their gallant second attempt on the enemy's trench, and regret it was impossible to hold on to what had been won. The enemy's losses were, however, far greater than ours, the cross-fire from the Nelson accounting for about 150 dead. I regret exceedingly your loss of so many gallant officers and men. Please accept my most heartfelt sympathy.

The exact losses in the operation were four officers and twenty-five Petty Officers and men killed, and one officer and seventy-four Petty Officers and men wounded. Unfortunately Sub-Lieutenant Milvaine, wounded while in charge of the working party early in the operations, died on the way to Alexandria.

Sub-Lieutenant Rush was promoted to Lieutenant to command "A" company, Lieutenant Bennett (originally of the Nelson Battalion, who had returned after being wounded at Anzac) became machine-gun officer, and Sub-Lieutenant Southon was transferred from "C" to "A" company. A number of men were transferred at the same time to "A" company to take the place of their casualties, and the first reorganisation of the Hawke Battalion was quickly completed.

With this operation we may close a chapter in the history of the battalion. Just as the optimism and novelty of the period of training can never be quite recaptured, so the strangeness an excitement of the first weeks of active service have a flavour of their own. Impressions of these days are apt to be unreliable and probably those written here are no exception. But they appear more crowded with incident than the later days of experience, merely because a battalion takes longer to learn the art of living a natural and easy life under war conditions than it takes to master the prescribed tasks of war itself. Officers and men alike come to judge their later periods of service by conditions behind the line; a canteen, an estaminet, a billet, or a camp focus their memories; but in early days the fighting is the thing. It even throws a shadow forward, and only the experience of loss brings the faculty of endurance—almost resembling indifference—which makes the strain of prolonged active service tolerable, and more than tolerable in times and places where fortune smiles.

And so, though the months that were to come brought extremes of heat and cold, acute physical discomfort, considerable danger, and constant ill-health, they brought more than a measure of compensation in a growth of confidence, and the recapture of a sense of humour temporarily in the balance. And in these months the battalion was to organise itself in the haphazard fashion of all things British along lines which could still be traced at the distant ending of the campaign nearly four years ahead. On the long view these, and not those spent at the Crystal Palace and Blandford, were the days of preparation.

CHAPTER 4

# Not Without Dust and Heat

Throughout the rest of June, and until July 7th, the Hawke Battalion were in or about the trenches. The 2nd Naval Brigade had been sent to Imbros to reorganise after the disaster of June 5th, and the result was that the three battalions of General Mercer's Brigade had to do eight days in the line to every four days out, while even these brief intervals were occupied with nightly fatigues. The practice common to corps staffs of requisitioning infantrymen from the trenches to build dugouts and offices for those more fortunately situated was, moreover, developing just at this time in an acute form; many military landing officers, supply officers, ordnance officers, and such-like must have owed the small comforts which they enjoyed through the autumn of 1915 to the activities of the Naval Battalions in their hours of leisure.

The feud between "the beach" and "the line" was, of course, more theoretic than practical. The former had all the luck, and stuck to it, but personal relations, stimulated by the occasional gift of a bottle of whisky, a ham, or a cup of tea and rum for the infantry officer in charge of the working party on a particularly cold night, and by similar, though necessarily rarer, acts of "fraternisation" between the N.C.O.'s and men, remained reasonably cordial. Moreover, the infantry were learning all the time, and could by the autumn more than hold their own with the beach-combers as pickers-up of unconsidered trifles of other people's goods.

On the beach, in the gullies, in the line, it was always the same task: to dig, to go on digging, and then to dig a little more. The experience, novel then, became later familiar, but the conditions were unparalleled, and remained so, because of the universal ill-health of the rank and file of all infantry units. It is safe to say that after the end of June no one was really fit for sustained physical exertion, yet this was precisely what was required of everyone except the officers, and sometimes even of them. Among the statistics bearing on the results of inoculation against enteric, I have seen none which pointed out that the percentage of cases of sickness of a kind singularly similar to enteric among the troops on the Gallipoli Peninsula in the summer of 1915 were nearer 100 *per cent*, than 90 *per cent*. The cases were described—and no doubt correctly—as gastroenteritis and enteritis, more or less according to taste, and by all lay accounts the sickness, though equally disabling, was a good deal less severe than that classified as "enteric fever" in the South African War. But the facts remain, and any glib assumption that inoculation is a serious safeguard for the continued efficiency of troops operating in infected areas under insanitary conditions would be too dangerous to pass unchallenged. The history of the Gallipoli campaign would have been different had the special medical problems created by the conditions then prevailing been even partially solved.

This is a digression, but hardly an irrelevant one. In the months of July and August more than half of the Hawke Battalion and of the surviving members of the other naval and marine battalions, as well as of the 29th and 42nd Divisions, left the Peninsula sick. The other half remained—almost equally sick—and left in September and October.[1] The number of officers and men on the fighting strength of battalions who survived both wounds and sickness was nearer 5 than 10 *per cent*, in the Naval Division, and possibly even less elsewhere.

In the circumstances the battalion over this period was in a state of constant change. From headquarters the quartermaster, quartermaster-sergeant, and battalion sergeant-major disappeared during July and August—all sick, and all, happily, to recover, but not to rejoin the battalion. "A" company, so sadly depleted by the tragic events of June 19th, retained only the indomitable Rush (whose ten hours in the Turkish trench had cost him nothing more than a hat, which, however, nothing would induce him to replace), now in command,[2] and formally promoted. "B" company lost Price, Peckitt, and La Fon-

---

1. Many of the September and October "casualties" were due to jaundice, which became in the latter month almost as universal a complaint as enteritis had been in July. Among the victims in the Hawke were Lieutenant Lockwood and Surgeon Bradbury, R.N., though the latter, as before, was soon back.
2. Though Lieutenant Lockwood returned for a few weeks in July before again falling sick.

taine (the last wounded by a chance bullet on July 13th), leaving only Harmsworth of the original officers. "C" were hardly more fortunate, Stevenson, A. P. Herbert, and Southon (the latter after being lent to "A" company for some weeks) going away sick by the middle of August. In "D" company George Peckham and Farrow alone remained at the beginning of August,[3] and Farrow was killed by a chance bullet when commanding a digging party behind the front line on August 25th—a great loss to his company and battalion.

The adjutant, never at a loss for novel methods of organisation, preferred to function without a regimental sergeant-major; he acquired instead a strange bodyguard of personal servants, whose place in the scheme of things was one of the mysteries of the lesser lights who had merely to command companies or platoons. C.P.O. Bailey, however, assumed the part of R.Q.M.S., and played it with a suavity which was as welcome as it was unusual, until he, too, fell sick (on September 5th), and was succeeded by C.P.O. Price, a great character of piratical appearance and language, but by no means intractable to those who could withstand a preliminary bombardment of unmitigated scurrility stimulated from time to time by rum.

C.P.O. Wapshott—C.S.M. of "A" company—went sick at about the same time, and was succeeded by C.P.O. Davey (a riveter from the Clyde, I think). "C" company lost C.P.O. Wilson (reported to be a detective in private life, but enjoying a less ungenerous reputation as the custodian of the company stores), and were compensated by discovering one of the real "characters" of the battalion in C.P.O. Malpress, who can be found now, as before the war, in charge of a flourishing newspaper stall at Wimbledon Station. As became a Cockney, he had unfailing resource and a keen sense of humour, and would work in his own way and at his own time without regard for orders or regulations. He had an unerring eye for what he and others would, in a perfect world, have been entitled to, and he preferred to trust to it rather than to indulge in superfluous calculations. The result was that he was equally at home under all conditions and a few shells at the dump, a battle, or a battalion move never disturbed him to the point of inducing him to cease his efforts to get for the company more than their fair share.

He was, in the circumstances, marked out for early promotion.

To follow the changes in "D" company is no task for a short history.

---

3. Marvin being invalided on May 27th, Venn on June 13th Nicholson July 15th and Wolfe Barry on July 27th.

Lieut. the Hon. Vere Harmsworth after bathing near
"V" Beach, Gallipoli, July, 1915

Here was talent without end, and the army, the corps, the division, the brigade, and the battalion drew on it without mercy. Blackmore, the original company sergeant-major, was commissioned on October 3rd, and remained with the company till the end of the campaign. Davidson, Tomson, and Aron were commissioned in turn to be machine-gun officers; Poole to command a "D" company platoon; Bessell to a platoon in "A" company; Codner and his beard[4] to take charge of lumbers and catapultists.

While the battalion was selecting—almost at random—men of the world to carry on the urgent work of active fighting, the corps artillery begged for the choice of some of the younger blood in the company to mould to the approved pattern of officer. The authorities at home were equally zealous in commissioning those in whom a public school education had induced an especial acquaintance with the elementary classics, and constant driblets of petty officers and able seamen drifted home to new responsibilities *via* Alexandria, Cairo, Malta, and all the other bases that the zeal of the War Office had contrived to bring into being.

Meanwhile reinforcements began at last to dribble in, though in quite inadequate numbers and rather short of training. The first arrivals, towards the end of July, were the least satisfactory; the departure of the division from Blandford in March, April, and May had taken away the bulk of the trained officers and men, and most of those who had remained behind had done so for some good reason. This was a temporary difficulty which never recurred. By the summer of 1915 arrangements had been made which ensured a continuous flow of recruits, and later drafts in August, October, January, and February were thoroughly efficient.

This is not to say that there had not been even in May, 1915, a surplus of highly efficient officers for whom vacancies could not be found in the battalions which were going overseas, and a number of the best petty officers and men as well had been kept behind on the depot staff as instructors.

Even these, however, created their own problems, and the arrival of a regimental sergeant-major[5] of four months' total service and no experience and two officers senior to every company commander in the battalion created problems which all Colonel Wilson's diplomatic

---

4. These two were inseparable. But see Chapter 7.
5. C.P.O. Todd, a most energetic N.C.O., who did excellent work in many capacities, till finally appointed Quartermaster-Sergeant of "A" company in 1916.

skill was needed to resolve. [6]

Resolved, however, they had to be. For the Hawke Battalion was beginning, especially in the hard and anxious weeks of July, to take some definite shape. The process of trial and error may be an expensive one, but it is the only one by which a raw battalion can become a fighting unit. And so we find Rush, Harmsworth, and George Peckham in permanent command of companies, which they led until the historic but fateful 13th November, 1916. The same applied elsewhere, subject to further changes, which took place in October, 1915, when the adjutant fell sick and returned *via* Egypt to England. He was succeeded by the writer of this record, "C" company coming under the charge of Lieutenant A. V. W. Cotter, with Lieutenant Ker (promoted for much distinguished service in the autumn of 1915) as second in command, carrying perhaps more than half the burden of responsibility till his death at the head of his company in 1916.

C.P.O. Gillard, of "B" company, became regimental sergeant-major, and when Lieutenant Gilbert was invalided, C.P.O. Day from the same company became quartermaster, a post he held without a break until 1919, and with unfailing success. C.P.O. Nadin—a resolute Irishman from "A" company, who had distinguished himself on June 19th—became company sergeant-major of "B" company. C.P.O. Ross was put in charge of the transport,[7] an invaluable ally to a succession of transport officers and quartermasters who found the management of horses, and even of mules, easier than the management of brigadiers and staff captains.

Another whom one recalls as figuring characteristically in many changing scenes was P.O. Macdonald, in charge of the battalion signallers, a veteran who had learnt his soldiering, and a good deal else besides, on the South African *veldt*, and was now reliving his youth under conditions which sent men of half his age to hospital every day. His one weakness was a taste for killing Turks, a paradoxical relaxation, but perhaps his wanderings round the trenches with a periscopic rifle, when by all the rules he should have been taking in messages in a dugout in the reserve line, brought back some savour of more adventurous

6. These officers were Lieutenant-Commander Robson and Lieutenant Gilbert. Robson was temporarily lent to the Nelson, and Gilbert became Quartermaster, till he was invalided in November.

7. Up to October the scanty battalion transport had been in charge of Sub-Lieutenant Brereton, an eccentric firebrand, whose fighting tastes were, it must be presumed, gratified when the shortage of officers made it necessary to transfer him to the command of a platoon in "D" company.

and piratical wars which he had fought, I fancy, unhampered by the responsibilities of a sergeant's stripes.

In strange contrast to this veteran war-horse, frankly contemptuous of the ways of peace and the war of position, was Petty Officer Grieve, who in no other war since (but perhaps excepting) the siege of Troy could have found fruitful employment in the fighting line. In 1915, however, a melancholy temperament which expected nothing but the worst, a taste for carpentry, and a hatred of anything in the shape of a uniform marked him out for the command of the pioneers, a body of men whose distinguishing characteristic is, as is well known, that they would be the very men to do the job which so badly wanted doing, were it not for the fact that they happened at the moment to be doing something else. The problem of the proper employment of pioneers is, of course, not a new one.

H.R.H. the Duke of Cambridge, inspecting a battalion on one occasion, touched on the subject when he innocently asked the commanding officer what the pioneers were at that moment doing. He was informed that they were on parade. This was too much for His Royal Highness. "Bring them to the front," he said, determined to solve once and for all the problem of their proper employment, "and tell them to dig a very large hole; then they can bury your bloody battalion." The Hawke Battalion pioneers did not achieve quite this measure of superiority to the terrestrial fate of their colleagues, but their occupation remained a mystery to which the inscrutable melancholy of Petty Officer Grieve afforded no clue. Commander Fairfax was believed to be in the secret, but the Silent Service tells no tales.

Surgeon Bradbury deserves a chapter to himself, but he must content with an inadequate paragraph. He was, of course, the busiest man in the battalion, and the only man who never lost his temper. Not even the order, which preceded the evacuation by an unjustifiable interval, to destroy all stocks of alcohol provoked more than momentary solemnity. Yet a perpetual melancholy would have been almost justified. At no time or place can the work of a battalion medical officer have been more difficult or more responsible than June, July, August, and September, 1915, at Gallipoli. The prevailing sickness could be staved off for a bit, but could not be cured. The battalion doctor's task in the circumstances was to judge how long individuals could stand the strain of constant work under bad conditions, and keep them there so long and no longer. This required a deeper knowledge of men than of medicine, and no merely academic training. Absolute confidence on the part of all ranks in their doctor was the only thing which could keep a battalion together under these conditions. "If the doctor says I'm all right, I am." This was the belief which had to be implicit beneath the mere formal acceptance of discipline. In the Hawke Battalion at this time I don't think there was ever any doubt on the matter.[8]

These few notes have no ordered sequence. Some of the changes recorded took place in July, others in August, September, and October. The beginning of the last month marked the most important change of all (though only a temporary one), for Colonel Wilson was invalided to Egypt, and the command of the battalion passed to Commander Fairfax; Lieutenant-Commander Robson then rejoined the battalion, and acted for the time as second in command.

But before the placid days of October and November, when officers and men kept their letter-writing to occupy them in the trenches, the battalion had to endure the dust and heat of July and August. In plain fact they were not endurable, and most of the significant changes recorded above took place in these months; but the work went on. I cannot give a better account of the battalion activities at this time than is to be found in William Ker's letters, from which I have quoted earlier. They have only one defect as history, that they reflect a temperament singularly equable and courageous, and fortunate also in keeping in good health. A. P. Herbert, in the earlier chapters of his novel, *The Secret Battle,* reflects the more acrid impressions left on one who lacked nothing in courage or cheerfulness, but a good deal in digestion.

July 7th, 1915, 9 a.m.

Here we are back in the rest camp again. We were relieved last night by the 7th H.L.I., who have never been in the trenches before. We had another eight days in there this time. That is, out of the last twenty-one or twenty-two days, we have spent sixteen in the trenches. 'C' company had the first three days in the firing line, and then went back to supports (only about 200 yards behind), where they were shifted about a good deal and not given much peace. My platoon alone remained fairly stationary. The men had a good many digging fatigues, but the

---

8. A word should be added here of Surgeon Schuler and Surgeon Cox, who successively filled Bradbury's position when he was away in the autumn. Schuler was unfortunately severely wounded after a few days with the battalion. Cox survived to dine with us many times in France.

On the road to "V" beach, June 1915

officers had little to do. It is a ludicrous existence. For three days in the supports I did absolutely nothing except take a two-hours' watch at night, and occasionally inspect a rifle or two. I spent the time in a vain endeavour after a comfortable position and some shade in a trench that was apparently designed by the architect of 'Little-Ease,' and that lay open to the sun at every point. . . . We saw a lot of Turks as large as life this time. The French attacked on our right, preceded by a lot of high-explosive shelling. We saw the Turks rushing about on the sky line—*perturbabantur Constantino-politani.*"

July 12th.
We have been pretty busy; not much rest for the men at any rate—exactly one day, to be accurate. A lot of big digging parties. . . .
The R.N.D. left the trenches altogether when we were relieved last time, and we were said to be going to have a rest from them for some time, but today we seem to be going to be pushed in again somewhere. There is an attack on in one part, and we are even now (7.30 a.m.) waiting to move off. We are in reserve, and, of course, may well not come into action at all (this was what happened to us on June 4th). There is an incessant din going on just now—the so-called intensive bombardment. I must stop."

July 19th, 1915.
Life is only tolerable here between the hours of 7 p.m. and 7 a.m., though between those hours it is very pleasant indeed. Still cloudless nights we have, full of stars, the Milky Way with an un-English brilliance, and (just now) a yellow-horned moon. Twilight is short, and the sun goes down behind Imbros with an almost audible plop. It is too hot to be comfortable during the day now, and the lack of shade is a serious problem. Dug-outs fairly contain the heat, and a waterproof sheet over the top does not do much to keep one cool.
Our company mess is at the foot of a double olive tree, which is worth a good deal to us, although the foliage of olive trees is hardly luxuriant. The tree is inhabited off and on—weekend visits—by a creature which makes a noise like a starling in its worst mood, only much more monotonous. In a moment of unexampled energy the other day I tracked the creature up the

tree (which is about 18 feet high), and finally came face to face with an insect about an inch long with a large flat face and long wings. It stopped its raucous cries on my close approach, and regarded me with an owl-like, but unconvincing, gravity of expression that quite put me out of countenance. I re-descended the tree in haste, and left Ismail (that is his name) to his own devices and his strident song. I have not seen or heard him this time. . . .

Last Wednesday (July 14th, wasn't it?) we were roused out at 3 a.m., and got under way for the trenches at once, being told, just to prevent any undue elation at that hour of the day, that an attack on some Turkish trenches by certain Scotch battalions had failed,[9] and that we had to go and take them (on a cup of cocoa and a biscuit, and jolly lucky to get that). We arrived at the reserve trenches, and mucked about there all day and the next night (the attack business was off, of course), and finally strayed into the firing line by degrees, where we remained till we were relieved the day before yesterday by some marines.

Though it was the shortest spell we have had in the trenches (four days), I think it was the most unpleasant.

There was a big attack in our sector at the beginning of last week (July 12th), and we had the uncongenial task of relieving the trenches immediately afterwards. They had taken a trench or two, and we were pushed into a scene of indescribable chaos and mess to hold and improve and clear up the new line, and possibly to make a further advance. This was not a pleasant task . . . there can be few things more trying than being landed in an ill-dug and unsanitary trench in the height of the Turkish summer to wrestle for two days and nights with the combined duties of scavenger, navvy, grave-digger, sanitary inspector (officers only), and—last, but not least—soldier. I do not care for the personality of the Turk, if his trenches can be taken as any indication of it.

In the Mohammedan religion cleanliness apparently does not compete with Godliness. I should have been sorry to be a non-smoker. The men were very good about it, and 'C' company did some useful work. We found the trench in a hopeless mess, and rather ghastly, and left it comparatively safe and clean. We

---

9. This, as a matter of fact, was very far from being the case, as the rest of the letter shows.

also materially improved some sapping in the direction of the Turks.

We were glad to get down here again. I hope we shall not be spirited away for some days ... (two shrapnel shells came over at this point and burst just above our olive tree. I had to get under the wall of the dugout; no damage done to anyone. There are a good many shells going about this morning). . . .

July 20th, Tuesday.

I hear that we are due to go up to the trenches tomorrow, for a short time only, they say, but then, when they get you there, you never know when you will emerge. It is unfortunate that the colonel has gone away—to Lemnos, I think—for a few days with gastritis. Also that Stevenson is down with a similar complaint, and will not be able to come to the trenches. Most of us have got something of this sort in a greater or less degree. Lieutenant-Commander Fairfax (R.N.) will be in command of the battalion meanwhile, and Jerrold in command of 'C' company. . . .

A lot of reinforcements from Blandford arrived the other day[10]—also Boot, now a lieutenant. He has returned to this battalion, I am glad to say. It is impossible to reorganise here. It takes time. Hope we shall get away after this go in the trenches. We thought we were going the time before last when the R.N.D. was relieved altogether by H.L.I. and K.O.S.B. (T.F.), which were newly out. But we had to go back within a week when this attack came off. . . .

We get coffee and rice from the French in exchange for jam (which they never get otherwise). Alleged remark of a French Artillery man, summing up his gallant Allies: '*Les Anglais—oui—beaucoup de confitures, mais pas de munitions.*' It is apparently quite true."

July 25th, 1915.

We were relieved from trenches according to previous contract (actually carried out) after forty-eight hours—that is, on the

10. This draft included Lieutenant-Commander Robson and Lieutenant Gilbert, already mentioned, and Sub-Lieutenants Ellis ("D" company), Matthews and Goll-man ("C" company), Paton and Bowerman ("B" company), and Collins, Potts and Cookson ("A "company). Gollman und Potts were, however, invalided almost immediately.

day before yesterday, July 23rd. The battalion, however, was kept in some old reserve trenches until the following day— yesterday—when we came back to the rest camp, which had been occupied in our absence by some new troops; consequently, we found the camp gutted. Luckily we had not left much to gut, but they got all our wood (not much), including the essential part of our company mess table, which is (was, rather) biscuit tins full of earth, with a few pieces of packing case on top, and an ammunition box or two which we used as cupboards. The Sherwood Foresters relieved us in the trenches. . . .

One could stand a lot of this if one could keep well inside. The climate, if you could meet it half-way, would be good, but when the conditions of life actually accentuate its bad points it becomes rather trying. Nearly everyone is rather upset inside. This is due to nothing in particular, but to the rations and the dust and the life in general. The great thing about being dyspeptic here is that it gives you something to talk about. We all discourse at length about our internal economies, and none of us believe that there is anything the matter with anyone else. As a matter of fact, you must not think we are in a bad way. I think it is rather astonishing that the men keep as fit as they do. I know I could not go alternately trenching and digging on bacon and Maconochie 'Meat-and-Vegetable' ration, and biscuits and tea as staple diet. They grouse, but survive. . . .

I must go and bathe this evening. . . . I spend most of my time here pursuing the shade round our olive tree, and smoking more cigarettes than are good for me. This is not a good climate for a pipe, even with Smyrna Mixture. Wonderful moonlight nights just now—getting near the full. I understand that for Mohammedans this is *the* month, the sacred month of *Ramadan*, and that this full moon is the great feast of the year. The staff thought the Turks might consider it an opportune moment to drive the infidel into the sea, and we have been much (too much for comfort) on the *qui vive* lately. Personally, I imagine the foe are probably thinking that they celebrated the occasion considerably more pleasantly last year. I do not think the recent operations have done much to convince the faithful of the holiness of the war, which the authorities have been at so much pains to impress upon them. The papers do not tell you much. We rather smile when the dispatches finally reach us. All

I will say is that the view from our trenches is very much the same as before, and, as far as I can see, is likely to remain so for some time.

July 30th, 1915.

. . . Herbert unfortunately developed a temperature of 103.5° that morning (he is not strong, and has been unwell all along), and was taken off to hospital, out of my ken, off this seething Peninsula. Stevenson (company commander) emerged from the field ambulance looking pretty bad, and went off for a week's sick leave, leaving Cotter, Jerrold, and me. Jerrold was, and is now, pretty seedy, so Cotter and I sat down before the accumulated stores, and for that evening gravely made hogs of ourselves.

August 17th, 1915.

All the so-called non-combatants in England seem to be working a good deal harder than we are. Strange times when I, exiled for an indefinite period in the less accessible parts of the Turkish Empire, look westwards to a world where one of my female cousins (care of the Young Men's Christian Association) scours France in her car; where my most homely (old English meaning) uncle runs a temperance canteen beneath the statue of Jeanne d'Arc, while my most adventurous one forms platoon in a London park, and handles stores throughout a fourteen-hour day in a suburban goods station; where my sister and her likes wrestle with uncongenial accounts, wash dishes in unfamiliar pantries, or cope day and night in hospitals with refractory sick and wounded and truculent matrons; where, lastly, my mother, in the name of charity, fills her drawing-room with the undesired presence of the neighbourhood. What a life. . . .

You will have read about the new operations here—the new troops landed higher up the Peninsula. A. de Selincourt and some other people I know are up there. I fear we shall have no news of them except by casualty lists from home for some time, but may we meet soon—at Chanak, though frankly I do not think this is at all likely. Things are naturally in a state of uncertainty—from our point of view, I mean. Unless something decisive happens very soon, we shall have to prepare for the rains, however that is to be done. We are rumoured to be going back for a spell in the trenches soon. Personally I have had a good rest during the past three weeks, and am as fit as when we landed, but others are not, and a lot of men have been going to hospital. . . .

August 23rd, 1915.
. . .We go back to the trenches tomorrow with the new lot and all. I do not look forward to it. We go to a new part of the line, west of Krithia this time. As most of the men are either quite raw or rather seedy, I doubt if our week (or whatever it is) in the trenches will go with the usual roar.

September 1st, 1915.
We were relieved from the trenches on Monday (this is Wednesday) by the Marines, after a week up there. It was a quiet time; 'C' company had two days in supports, three in firing line, and two in supports again. I spent most of my time in contemplation of the Turks through a periscope and my glasses over a barricade which we held, where we and the Turks are in the same trench, with barricades about 40 yards apart, and no-man's trench in between.

'C' company was in the southern barricade. A lot of bombs were thrown about, but no damage done by theirs, and not very much, I should say, by ours, though we had a catapult. We had a lot of periscopes broken by a persevering sniper, but never one that I was looking through. My glasses (that is, father's) are much admired, especially as they are perfectly suited for trench work. They are so small that you can get both eyes on to the mirror of a periscope with ease. You can see a good deal through glasses at 50 or 100 yards. I saw a number of Turks as large as life at different times. There was one place where we had an extra good view into their trench, only they had it very well marked by their snipers, and on the strength of this used to show themselves, when going about their lawful occasions, with boldness, not to say presumption. . . .

To the left of our part of the line there was a deep gully,[11] and from one part of the trenches we could look right across it and see the ground on the other side, which is lower, and the opposing trenches laid out before us like a map. There were a good many Turks to be seen there, too, through a glass, and we did a good deal of sniping at anything up to 1,000 yards, with

---

11. Gully Ravine.

a man observing through a telescope. It is an odd sight, the two firing lines curving about more or less in conformity with each other, with some strange contortions—as in our own bit—the maze of communication trenches, etc., behind either line, the uninhabited space between, and the line of wire in front of the Turks all spread out before one over a moor of thyme and wild flowers in the sun, and sloping away down to the bluest of seas. It always struck me as queer and subtly comic (when from some safe position in the supports I was admiring a view—whichever way I turned—that was, I suppose, in its way, worth coming miles to see) that no one could get out and stroll upon that sunny sweet-smelling heath without getting a bullet at him before he had gone 2 yards.

Exercise is what I lack; on some of the golden evenings I would have liked to walk up Achibaba and watch the sun set over Samothrace from the top. There must be a grand view from up there. But I never succeeded in doing so. Coming back here from the trenches was a tedious business. We marched right down the gully, which is picturesque, and will, I feel sure, in after years be visited by streams of tourists as the scene of some of the heaviest fighting of the war, where they will examine the remains of the Turkish entanglements (they are at present almost intact), and will joyfully pay exorbitant prices for bogus war relics manufactured in Birmingham, and sold on the spot by the erstwhile indigent Greeks, who made a modest fortune by a little honest spying for the Turks when employed in a labour party on West Beach.

However, we could almost have done without the gully on this occasion. As it was, we must have walked about three times as far as the direct distance between the trenches and camp. Also, as we had not had much to eat (that was eatable) in the trenches, I was conscious of a void somewhere inside me, which I was enabled on return to effectually banish through the agency of an orderly who foreran us and had got hold of some real food. We were so long in arriving down that there was no time to bathe when we got back. Hence, we went to bed dirty, and not the first morning. Yesterday morning I went to bathe off Cape Helles at 6 a.m. Our old bathing-place, called by us 'The Goats,' has been spoilt by some work that they (the French) are doing down there. It now crawls with black men—real niggers, not

Indians, Senegalese—who are picturesque at the proper distance, but essentially offensive at close quarters, especially in the mass. They look rather striking in mustard-coloured uniforms and crimson or vivid blue *fezes*, and faces black as coal. They stand about in large parties with shovels and things, and talk a great deal, but under the French they seem to get through some work all the same.

I like going among the French soldiers here, and seeing and listening to them. A remarkable people. Pleasing contrast to us out here in the matter of organisation and administration. I believe it is the same everywhere.

September 5th, 1915.

This is Sunday, and I am apparently to celebrate it by hiking 100 seedy men with picks and shovels to delve for the A.S.C. on West Beach for six hours, when I might be singing ' All people that on earth do dwell' with the Rev. F. Cairns[12] by the cook-house, there being a Presbyterian service this evening for once in a way.

We go back to the trenches on Tuesday. Another part this time. We were on the left of the R.N.D. sector last time; this time we are to be on the right, goodness knows why. So many men are going sick that soon we shall be quite unable to hold our part unassisted. Our company strength today is 117 and four officers—Cotter and I, and two new ones. We came out with 212 men, and had a draught of sixty-eight men a fortnight ago, so you can judge. I think I forgot to tell you in my last letter that Jerrold had retired to Mudros (Lemnos) in an advanced stage of physical decay and internal disturbance. Stevenson is at present attached to Divisional H.Q., and has a job in connection with trench supplies at a fairly comfortable spot about half-way between here and the firing line, so Cotter is O.C. company. . . .

*Later.*—Since the above I have spent an intensely aggravating five hours in the neighbourhood of the beach, the men professing to dig drainage trenches for the A.S.C. It does not seem to occur to the authorities that the Naval Division may need some

---

12. Padre Cairns was a great character. When asked on his first Arrival in June what he thought of it all, he replied: "Aye, mon, it's hell of a place. If anyone had suggested that I should ever live to share it hole in the ground with a worshipper of the Scarlet Woman, I should have called him a damned liar!"

drains of its own when it begins to rain. It will now, however, be forced upon their attention, as I gave a lurid (but strictly accurate) report to the colonel, who dashed off at once to send in a protest. He spends a large part of his time in sending in much-needed protests. . . .

How I dislike the genus of beach officer. The men who dwell in cliff dugouts of a million sandbags (much needed in the trenches) live upon the fat of the land (or rather the sea; there is not fodder for one consumptive goat on this arid but fair plateau). The A.S.C. officer, as a matter of fact, proved himself not beyond redemption by giving me three cups of tea (out of a china cup—*china*, mind you) and a strawberry jam sandwich (strawberry jam, which we never see). Most of them, as a matter of fact, turn out all right on acquaintance; it is only in theory (and when we have to take out working parties for them in the middle of the night) that we condemn them. . . .

I am writing now by candlelight in our dugout beneath the olive tree, with the usual brilliant arch of stars above. It is as warm and as cool as you could wish, and so still that you can hear the olives getting ripe—except when Asia (or that gun or guns known rather vaguely to some as 'Christians, Awake') drops a shell into the French lines; or the French battery near us looses off at large into Asia (a more noisy affair, and not to be encouraged, especially at night).

There must certainly be worse places to be stranded on than an outlying promontory in the Ægean, though it has its drawbacks. Even coming from or going to the trenches we hardly ever fail to get some glimpse of sea, land, sky, and islands, which rivals Ben Lomond at its best. With an effort I can nearly always raise the energy to appreciate it. The climate is fine now that the heat is over. But I expect most of us are weary of this blue and gold world; I am not sick of the country, but of the general mucking about here. I should like to be back in your soft grey land again. . . .

September 11th, 1915.

Saturday, 11th September, was a day of beauty—sun and clouds, and a wind that was too cold to be pleasant at night Like a tip-top English (Scotch) day in end of August. Wonderful views from Munster Terrace (our trench) of Achibaba Krithia, and our lines and theirs to the right; then farther over hills of Asia in varying blues, greys, and mauves, and regular Ben Lomond clouds over them. Then a little farther round to Morto Bay and the plain of Troy, and so on to Helles and a hospital ship or two at Tenedos. I have no camera, so I make a prosaic note of what was to be seen, because it was worth photographing or painting.

Biliousness not improved by the coldness of the night watches,[13] or the attentions of the as yet undaunted flies during the day, prevented my taking much interest in the landscape, or the Turks occasionally visible in the trenches which we overlook from here, or the sniping thereof—or in meals. . . .

September 12th.

Saturday night was beastly cold again to us poor creatures long unused to anything in the nature of a low temperature. I had got hold of two overcoats (one good, the other rather played out). I also wrapped the summer number of *Land and Water* round my back under my tunic (as far as it would go), and a page or two of *The Times's* 'England for the Germans' campaign round my front—this eked out by a Shetland jumper and Margaret's invaluable and ever-present woollen scarf. Thus fortified, I lay down in due course on a ledge covered with a few empty sandbags and a waterproof sheet, and was (excuse me) cold. The fact that my indisposition (above hinted at) did not during this period develop into acute gastritis, or enteritis, or gastric catarrh shows either that there is more in *Land and Water* than meets the eye, or else that there is something still to be said for Britain's hardy sons.

If yesterday was a Scotch summer day, today was autumn, and no mistake. Grey sky, clouds high but quite thick—chilly wind, no sun. The weather is certainly changing; we have never had anything like this before.

Eight days in the trenches is a beastly long time, especially when the prevailing motif in your spirits is a feeling that you have every right to be elsewhere. There is nothing to look forward to except *(a)* when in the trenches, being relieved; *(b)* when in camp, the next meal. . . .

Sunday, anyhow, was a gloomy day, and chilly withal. We spent it as usual, doing nothing in this particularly uninteresting sector.

13. Particularly unfortunate was the lot of those who, following the Australian example, had converted their trousers into "shorts" earlier in the campaign.

The supports there are more interesting than the firing line, as they are higher up, and you can see much more from them. We were in the firing line from Tuesday till Friday, then supports till Monday, then firing line again till relieved on Wednesday, I sent my orderly down to camp to get some Bovril, a blanket, and some biscuits, not being able to eat anything but that (not the blanket). As a matter of fact, it was a good deal warmer on Sunday night, and we were fairly comfortable, until it began to rain at about 5.30 a.m.; a good thing it was not sooner.

I wish our men were a bit more like the Puritan soldiers, and would sing psalms in the trenches on Sunday or something like that. It would keep things going and might annoy the Turk, whether a devout Moslem or not. There is none of the mutual amusement league business which is boomed so by the ha'penny Press as happening in France, and I believe does actually occur sometimes. Any efforts on our part to get in touch with or pull the leg of the Turk are regarded with disfavour by the authorities. Even noise is discouraged. A. P. Herbert sent up a Verey light (star shell) once in broad daylight[14] to try and make the Turk think some unique sinister scheme was on foot. We stood by to note the effect, which was nil—whether due to lack of imagination on the part of the enemy, or to the fact that they were not looking.

What may have been a laudable attempt to establish a social understanding (as far as this is compatible with a certain temporary political antagonism) took place last night, when a strange man approached a 'D' company look-out from the direction of Achibaba. It is rumoured that he brought a dog with him (one barks in the Turkish trenches regularly; I don't know whether it is a pet, or their method of solving the fresh-meat-in-the-trenches problem). The 'D' company man, who is new out here, showed a self-control and consideration worthy of the public school which was largely responsible for him, and, after challenging him three times in best Blandford manner, apparently allowed him to walk off unmolested. . . .[15]

---

14. This, of course, was in July. Herbert had been invalided long before the date of this letter.
15. An eyewitness casts doubts on this episode, alleging that the dog was unaccompanied. If so, it must have been out without a licence—surely another breach of the Hague Conventions.

September 13th, 1915.
We were relieved on Wednesday, September 15th, by Marines at
3.0 p.m., or 15.00 as they call it here, to please the French, and
proceeded through the mud to the rest camp. I say the mud. It
began to thunder and to lighten at 4.15 a.m., and then to rain
in a crescendo and diminuendo for about an hour and a half;
very unpleasant. . . .

At this point this vivid story is interrupted, as the writer was sent
off on duty to Alexandria, a pleasant interlude which, as it happened,
came as the worst period of strain was drawing to its close. The last
phase of the campaign was indeed approaching. The offensive at Suvla
had failed, the battalions at Cape Helles were thinned by sickness and
severe losses (the Hawke Battalion was, indeed, the only battalion in
the division whose actual battle casualties were not, in a comparative sense, severe), and the uncertainty and disappointment inseparable
from unsuccessful adventure were infecting the optimism of the staffs
and the authorities at home. The result was an inevitable reversion to
a more or less strict defensive, which, though it was varied by occasional minor "stunts," permitted at least of a regular trench routine and
regular reliefs. For a time, however, the sickness continued unchecked.
Perhaps it is for this reason that the records of the campaign for October, November, and December contain such frequent references to
the loss of "moral" among the fighting troops.

These references reflect, however, a very inaccurate diagnosis not
uncharacteristic of the times. If the resolution at home had been maintained, adequate preparations for winter on the Peninsula could have
been made, and the line which "had every conceivable military disadvantage could have been made as strong as countless sectors on the
western front, which resisted more resolute attacks than were likely
to be made by the Turks. Granted, however, that there were to be no
enforcements, no fresh guns (except "L" battery of the R.H A., sent to
the East for a rest from the infinitely more placid conditions in France,
with guns no longer dependable for accurate firing), no timber to
enable the trenches to be secured against the winter rains, and shell-
proof dugouts to be built for the garrison, it was not loss of "moral,"
but common sense which told even the infantry subalterns that the
campaign might, in the event of an offensive relentlessly pressed, come
to an untimely end.

After all, it is the job of the infantry subaltern to know under what conditions front-line trenches can be successfully defended, and to express his opinions when the essential requisites of security are continuously withheld. That opinion, freely expressed, could have been heard in the Hawke Battalion lines any day during the autumn of 1915, and certainly did not indicate a loss of "moral," nor any slackening in those preparations which, without engineering material and with the battalion reduced to the strength of a company, and under-officered at that, were still pressed forward.

The new front line, which the battalion had taken over in August, was a part of the old Turkish trench system, and was joined to the present Turkish line by numerous communication trenches, watched from barricades generally within hand-bombing distance of the enemy. These barricades marked almost invariably the scene of the most bitter hand-to-hand fighting. The bodies of English and Turks alike were built into the walls of these rough-and-ready fortifications, and others were buried only a few inches below the ground. In the rest of the front-line trenches the conditions were only a little less unhealthy. These conditions accentuated during August and September the prevailing sickness. The numbers available for duty in the trenches fell constantly, while the length of the divisional sector could not be correspondingly reduced. In the result, the hours of duty were lengthened, the reliefs were less frequent, the fatigues were more arduous.

If active fighting was at an end, the strain of the defensive war carried on under these difficulties was considerable. Moreover, in face of the possibility of a winter campaign communications had to be improved, a trench drainage system had to be prepared, and a new front-line trench had to be dug and wired. Our trenches were so sited as to be extremely open to effective bombardment, and the work of reconstructing the sector was dangerous, as well as irksome, to the depleted garrisons.[16] Throughout this period a semblance of an offensive war also had to be maintained, if only to forestall any possible Turkish attack. To this end saps were pushed out, barricades pushed forward, and intensive trench-mortar bombardments added to the horrors of war. Few of these constant activities are referred to in the letters we have quoted.

The period of maximum activity did not, indeed, begin till mid-October, when the health of the officers and men began definitely to improve, but there is another reason which must account also for

---

16. And to the Engineers, whose energies were unfailing. It is certain that no division was ever better served by its field companies than was the Naval Division.

many seeming omissions from this record. The construction of saps and trenches, wiring at night, pushing out barricades, digging in the open, patrolling in no-man's-land are the common employment of infantrymen which occupy a working day which varies from sixteen hours to twenty-four. The life of the Hawke Battalion was lived in the scanty intervals between these hours of tedious, if rarely dangerous, employment. Only on infrequent occasions do the normal activities of the front-line soldier touch the dramatic level. The experiences of July 14th, 15th, and 16th alone, of the events covered by this chapter, stand out in recollection, and even here the sequence of events in which the Hawke Battalion played a part had no conceivable military significance. The memory of these three days remains, however, and one or two incidents not mentioned in the letters quoted above may be worth a short record.

As on June 4th, the opening of the attack of July 12th had found the Naval Division in the rest camp. The attack, moreover, had, as far as the Naval Division's sector was concerned, been directed against the same objective as the earlier attack, except that the capture of Achibaba and the opening of the road to Constantinople played a smaller part in the calculations of the staff, and, so far as is known, no transport was loaded up for the pursuit of the enemy. The other difference was that the heights on the right of the Naval Division sector, which the French had failed to reach on June 4th, had been taken by them on June 21st. The attack on the Naval Division front could thus be made without risk of disaster from causes beyond the control of the attacking troops. For the purpose of the attack, the 52nd Division had relieved the Naval Division, but as it happened the Hawke Battalion had played the same part as on June 4th in corps reserve.

The issue of the attack was, on the whole, successful. The first and second lines of the Turkish position were reported captured, and portions of the third line were also held. But the inevitable order to the reserve troops to move forward into the gully, which reached the Hawke late on the 13th July, following on news of an attack by the Nelson, Chatham, and Portsmouth Battalions on the afternoon of that day, had an unpleasantly familiar echo. The promptitude with which the battalion was ordered forward from the gully to the line was another "disquieting symptom." No doubt we should in those early hours before the dawn have been thirsting for military laurels, but it was the fashion in 1915 to take the chances of war as they came—we were then able-bodied and of military age—and the prospect of plunging into a battle under unknown commanders without reconnaissance and on an empty (and rebellious) stomach was in no figurative sense nauseating.

However, it was all quite simple. It was only a small matter of a redoubt at the point P, a few bombs, a rush forward to the objective, and we should have done all that was required of us. The point P! Hardly, perhaps, an objective to kindle the imagination, but still a nice, well-defined position, with no depth or breadth. It was clearly devoid of any embarrassing features.

It would be easier to give a concise and ordered account of the ensuing operatings if the point P had ever been located. A. P. Herbert, in his capacity of Intelligence Officer, made a searching investigation with Geoffrey Price, whose company, in conjunction with the Chatham Marines, who held the front line on the morning of the 14th, was detailed for the attack. But the plain fact was that, beyond the enemy second line, which the 52nd Division had reached and held, the enemy's positions were not where, according to all the rules of the proper conduct of war, they ought to have been. On the left, by the Achibaba Nullah, round about the northern end of Nelson Avenue which "C" company of the Hawke had helped to dig after the disastrous 4th of June, the Turks had played the game, and their rear lines of defence corresponded accurately to the indications on our maps. On the right, however, of the 52nd Division line the preparation of the third line, the correct position of which was quite clearly marked on our own carefully drawn maps, had been unaccountably overlooked by the Turkish staff; in no place was it more than 18 inches in depth, and over a large stretch of front it was non-existent. At no place was it less existent than at the point P.

The first intention of the staff had been to make a direct assault on the missing portion of the enemy third line, the point P being on their map the left boundary of the objective. This plan had, however, been abandoned early on the morning of July 14th, and it was in these circumstances that the point P assumed importance in the minds of its ever-ingenious inventors as being, in the language of the *communiqués*, a *point d'appui* of great importance. The idea was that, with this miniature fortress in our hands, the enemy positions on the right and left would yield easily to bombing attacks directed to either flank.

The Chatham Battalion faded from the picture at this stage, and it was to be left to Lieutenant Price and his company, assisted by no fewer than seven bombers (an arrangement which gives a hint of the colossal scale on which the operations were planned), to rush the point P from the head of a sap (LP. on the maps) after a preliminary bombardment of bombs. The attack was to be made at 1.30 p.m. on the 14th.

The whole company was assembled when the usual order arrived to postpone the attack till 3.30. Once again the company assembled, when an eleventh-hour message arrived to the effect that if the Turkish resistance seemed likely to be serious no attack was to be made ! This placed a certain strain on the anticipatory powers of the leaders of the attack, but the party advanced, headed by Price in shirt-sleeves and pink braces, a distinctive emblem which might, no doubt, had events turned out otherwise, have assumed a no less historic importance than the white plume of Henry of Navarre immortalized by Lord Macaulay. But the advance up the sap was unopposed, and the leading bombers found themselves in an uninhabited waste of derelict trenches commanded by the distant Turkish positions on the right. Why not seize them after a short bombardment directed against the *point d'appui?* The idea occurred to Lieutenant Price, and a fusillade of bombs and trench mortars was directed against an unoffending mound of earth, which had, it must be assumed, a "point P-ish" appearance. Stung to fury, the Turks responded, but their fire, oddly enough, was directed on precisely the same spot.

Had they captured one of our maps? Perhaps! But clearly the destruction of so formidable a position was better achieved by enemy ammunition, of which there was plenty and to spare, than by our own. And so the point P passed out of history to the accompaniment of a low but unmistakable titter from the retreating ranks of "B" company of the Hawke Battalion. The whole line was taken over shortly afterwards by "C" company, and it fell to A. P. Herbert to establish barricades and place guards on the saps leading to this historic position. "Stay where you are," he was overheard to remark to the rather dour miners whom he selected to man this particular outpost of Empire, "and regard all Turks with the gravest suspicion." After their unpardonable omission to defend the point P, the inscrutable enemy could certainly not be taken on trust.

# CHAPTER 5

# The Triumph of Routine

The last chapter closed, perhaps irrelevantly, with some random recollections of the days when soldiers had to earn their shilling a day at Gallipoli. The aftermath of those days of muddled anguish, and sorrow, and humour we have also described, and the slow dawning of routine in the new sector on the left of the Peninsula. Routine reached its apotheosis with the evacuation of the Gallipoli Peninsula. If there be any wish to cite a classic example of what good staff work can achieve, this operation, perhaps one of the world's irreparable disasters, can safely be quoted. Mr. Winston Churchill has written General Monro's epitaph in the book of history in a pregnant sentence. He omitted to add, however, that superb staff work was necessary to enable the General to win his exotic laurels. Routine and discipline had, indeed, here their unmistakable triumph.

The superimposition of order and method against the romantic background of the Dardanelles was a gradual process. For the Hawke Battalion the first sign was the digging of a new, symmetrical, rectangular rest camp on the left coast of the Peninsula, directly behind the new sector taken over in August. The move took place in October, and its complications were a remarkable tribute to the acquisitiveness of the British soldier. Here, in small round holes cut spasmodically in a sandy desert, we had lived four months of intensive activity. Nowhere in the vicinity was even an outpost of civilization. Yet when we moved, Barkers or Shoolbreds would have hesitated before the vastness of our accumulations. Furniture made out of packing cases, food and clothing from England, dead men's waterproof sheets, loot from the trenches and the beaches, ration issues hoarded by capable quartermaster-sergeants, battalion stores accumulated at the risk of countless courtsmartial—the whole amazing collection of odds and ends was characteristic of the infinite adaptability of the English civilian to the most incalculable conditions. They had found a solitude and made a home.

Genuinely, we were sorry to leave, and sorrier still when we found that before the same luxurious standards could be regained many hours of intensive digging—which, as it added to no one's comfort but our own, would not be accounted to us for righteousness—would be necessary.

It was at this point in the fortunes of the Hawke Battalion that Colonel Wilson was invalided to Egypt, rather seriously ill with dysentery and enteritis, and he was followed a day later by Shelton, the Adjutant. The change came when the battalion was at its weakest, and marked the lowest point in its numerical strength; but in Commander Ramsay Fairfax it found a leader more than equal to the demands of a very difficult situation, and with reinforcements in October and November the battalion never lost its shape as a fighting unit. The outline of the organisation which had been growing up has been traced. It remains only to pick up the threads of its day-today occupations.

These consisted in the main of digging the new rest camp when out of the line, and draining the trenches when in the line. The Turks made not the slightest attempt during October and November to hinder us in either task, though the staff made fevered attempts to scare the life out of the infantry by circulating day-to-day news of the approach of 15-inch guns from Austria, against which, as they hastened to add, we had no adequate protection. The guns, however, never arrived, and the work went on with greater vigour as the weather grew colder and reinforcements arrived. Early October was, indeed, the lowest point in the trench strength of most of the battalions at Cape Helles, and the recovery from that point was fairly rapid. Ker's letters, from which I have quoted before, give a true day-to-day picture of the closing months.

*October 18th (Ker has just returned from Alexandria).*—I returned to find an even more emaciated battalion pottering forlornly about a camp of half-made dug-outs with an inadequate supply of sandbags and waterproof sheets on the high (or rather higher) ground about due north of our old warren—that is, as you will see if you consult any map, on the Imbros side of the Peninsula, and about a mile nearer the trenches than we were before. We have come from a land of intermittent olive trees and white dust next the French camps to heather and red soil, treeless and hillockless (no slopes to dig into when making dug-outs), stretching north-west to the cliffs over the beach. The point being that we are a lot nearer our part of the firing line, which is on the left, and also that there is some chance of a certain proportion of the water that is about to fall draining away from our new camp to the lower ground.

We are, in fact, in our winter quarters, which we are in the act of hewing out of the middle of the moor. The disadvantages of the position, apparent at the first glance to the eye of the least intelligent observer, are that every wind that blows will (does) sweep the place with the keen searching force of a well-plied hose, and that there are no natural means of getting water when it does not rain, or keeping it out when it does. Consequently, the site, excellent as it would be for a hydropathic (with golf course attached), or a hospital for the open-air cure of consumption, makes, in the present circumstances, but little appeal to us. . . .

At this point the camp-stool, bought in Alexandria for a quite exorbitant sum, on which I was seated, gave way, and I sat upon the ground. As the damage (to the stool, not to me) seems beyond repair tonight—as it is late (9 p.m.; one goes to bed ridiculously early now that it gets dark at 6), and I have only three sandbags to sit on, and there is no roof to this so-called mess dugout, and the breeze blows chill enough about me, and the half-moon floats vaguely in a sky of filmy clouds, and the candle in the camp lantern gutters, I shall go to bed and my dug-out forthwith. I bought a bed in Alexandria, and my dugout, though only half-finished (they have given us a pattern in which they must be made, and about half the material necessary for making them), has several waterproof sheets over the place where I sleep, and would keep me fairly dry at a pinch, which is just as well, as it has been raining gently off and on for the last few days. But not like Scotch rain—no, no. None of that all-pervading dampness. We do it differently in these parts. . ..

However, to return to hard facts before I retire to rest, or lose the thread for ever, I got back to find that Cotter had gone off with dysentery the day before I landed; Jerrold had got back, but was doing adjutant; hence I am in command of the company, which has now diminished to seventy men. The colonel and the adjutant have both gone sick. Also Lockwood (O.C. 'A' company). And D.H.Q. were asking O.C. battalions to state what steps have been taken to secure a supply of Christmas puddings from England. . . .

*October 19th.*—A gorgeous Scotch morning with a northerly wind and a ruffled blue sea, white flecked over to Imbros, which reminds me more of Arran than ever, with the cloud shadows chasing across the hill-sides. I am busy with the thousand and one trivial things which in the present life make up an O.C. company's day. And I must go down to the beach and look for a kit-bag of mine, which contains many purchases made in Alexandria for other people, not to mention a large quantity of gear of my own. . . .

We go to the trenches tomorrow for seven days. There is nothing doing there. Some London Territorials have come out to reinforce our division. Even so, it is much below strength. Everyone in the battalion is pretty seedy and fed up, though, in most cases, ten days even in Alexandria, would probably set them up again. It has made a good deal of difference to me, quite apart from physical ailments. My health is much the same as when I left—that is, quite good—but I can't deny that I am at the moment remarkably fit. Fitness, like happiness, is a thing you don't realize you have until you have it no longer, but on mature consideration I am compelled to acknowledge that I am very well just now. . . .

I missed a pleasant diversion here the night the news of the advance in France came. We organised a demonstration—all the troops ('C' company was in the firing line); at a given signal (a volley of various coloured star shells) everyone cheered and yelled, and the Scotchmen's pipers' band played and the French brass bands and bugles, and we let loose with artillery and bombs of all descriptions from the trench mortars, etc. Consequently, the Turks thought the devil's own attack was coming, and opened a tremendous fire on our trenches for half an hour, which we (our men) enjoyed, smoking at ease in their lairs. We also sent a lot of bully-beef tins (full) over, with the good news written in Turkish on tracts wrapped round them. It was very picturesque, I am told; wish I had been there. It is so seldom that we are allowed to give vent to our ever-bubbling *joie de vivre. . . .*

*November 2nd,* 1915.—It certainly gives one a new interest in
things to get charge of a company, even though that only happens by the elimination of senior officers (largely by sickness),
and though the company itself only numbers sixty men, as it
did last time in the trenches—proper strength being about 220.
Since the new draft we have four officers and about ninety-five
men all told. The last lot all came from Paisley, a fact which becomes apparent the moment they open their mouths. . . .
Trenches again tomorrow. Very few men get hit nowadays; considered very bad luck if one does. As long as they don't suddenly decide to make us take a trench or two under the influence
of those threadbare catch phrases, 'straightening out the line' or
'keeping up the offensive spirit,' we shall be all right . . . . .

*November 16th,* 1915.—We go back to the trenches tomorrow
as usual (Wednesday). A week down here goes all too fast, as
this camp in normal weather is really pleasant. There is nothing
to do, of course, in the way of amusement, but I have a roof
above my head, a bed to sleep on, a chair to sit on, and a table
to sit at. The last two articles belong to other people: the table
to Lockwood, who is sick at Alexandria, and not, it seems, likely
to come back here; the chair to the Marine, one Morford, O.C.
'C' company, who shares this dugout. Box and Cox, you know.
Have you grasped the situation? In normal weather, I say. Last
night the weather was less normal than anything I have ever
experienced.
There was, in fact, a thunder-storm which came up from the
south and took us in the rear about 8.30 p.m. The rain was
amazing while it lasted. The men were flooded out in rows,
because most of their dugouts were not finished or properly
drained, and none of the roofing of waterproof sheets was adequate; the water came through the joins. Half of my dug-ut
was perfectly dry. This was entirely due to a tarpaulin which
Morford stole off West Beach one dark night. But that is another story. The drains outside, however, had not been cut; consequently, the greater part of the water that streamed off the
sloping roof collected in the lowest place handy, and with an
unnatural observance of the conventions entered by the door.
Luckily the half of the dugout with the bed in it happened to

94

be higher than the other, so it stayed in the hall, so to speak, and was gently but firmly removed by my orderly in the morning. I used the sea-boots with pride for the first time here. The rain was not tropical at all, but by the nature of the state of the camp there was bound to be some flooding. . . .

We are going to be in the firing line again; this time I shall probably take some more photos. Last time we were in reserve, endless fatigues for the men and nothing to do for the officers. It rained a bit in the trenches, too.

Last week we did what in these days passes as 'a stunt.' That is, we pushed out one of our barricades 25 yards nearer the Turks one night. A barricade in this business means (as you probably know) an erection across a trench. I think I once drew you a map of this part of the front before. We and the Turks were in the same trench, and barricaded it opposite each other, with about 40 yards of deserted trench between; now there is 15 yards between. The work was done by men from this company under Hancock, the new officer, who worked very well; so did the men. It was a dark night, and the Turks did not spot anything; even when daylight came, they took very little notice. We expected to be bombed considerably.

They don't seem to be holding their front line much at all; but they are waiting for us with redoubts and machine guns in the second line, I expect. Why we should push out the barricade, God and D.H.Q. alone know. From where we were before we could bomb their trench well by means of a catapult, but they could not touch us with hand bombs. Now they can bomb us if they take the trouble. As the thing was well organised (by the battalion), however, and went absolutely without a hitch, there was not the vestige of a casualty. . . . .

Firing Line, Gallipoli, 23rd November, 1915.

After six months I still write the above address with something of a thrill, and a lurking feeling, suspiciously akin to complacency, that it looks well at the top of a letter. There is no getting over the fact that a certain zest is added to any pleasures one may have here, and the edge taken off most of the unpleasantnesses, by the idea at the back of one's mind that one acquires merit by being at the front, however stagnant things may be there. . . . .

However, this sententious vein can hardly be too strongly deprecated. The bald fact remains that this is Tuesday, and tomorrow we wend our unreluctant way back to camp. Much as we should like to remain permanently in the firing line, all-consuming as is our ardour to outwit the Turk, and whether by sub- or superterranean means to reach Krithia before the winter of 1920, there is a general feeling that it would be hardly fair to the Marines to monopolise the trenches, and to leave them for ever to the inglorious life of the rest camp. So tomorrow we go down, not, you may suppose, without a sigh.

The thought uppermost in my mind just now, 'The recuperative powers of the common fly,' would make a not unsuitable subject for a monograph by anyone who happens to be interested in entomology. Here we are having weather in which the ordinary human manages at nights to keep body and soul together by dint of wrapping himself in as many great-coats, blankets, waterproof sheets, and empty sandbags as he can lay hands on, and, behold, a glimpse of November sunshine about midday, and out crawl, hop, stalk, creep, leap, and hobble a myriad of these odious insects, and proceed slowly but inevitably to thaw into the flying and aggressive state.

True, they are not in their best summer form, but it remains to be proved that a fly is the less offensive. because, instead of sporting light-heartedly about one, it lands with a complacent buzz upon one's collar, and thence proceeds to crawl without undue haste down one's neck; or because, while retaining an ungovernable partiality for any food one happens to be eating, it is no longer capable of emerging from the dish when threatened with a fork. . . .

'C' company has been in the firing line all this week—at least, I have. Part of the company was moved back into reserve after three days, and spent the rest of the time in ration fatigues in the direction of the beach and working parties in the barricades. Such is the doubtful pleasure of being in reserve. We ('C' company) are holding that merry little salient where we pushed out the barricade last time up. It is called the Southern Barricade. We did our stunt there the night before we were relieved, and abandoned the place without regret on the following day to the Marines. They—dear fellows—acting no doubt from a praiseworthy, if misplaced, desire not to queer our pitch, left the new piece of trench annexed severely alone— that is, they sat in it, and regarded our handiwork (which was naturally but roughly finished in one night) with an admiration which was purely detached. There is no petty spirit of emulation about them. Hence we found any amount of work to do when we arrived this time. We have polished off a good deal of it. Some of it is grisly enough. . . .

I told the Doctor-Surgeon Bradbury, R.N., an Irishman—who has been with us since the start—the other day that I was shortly leaving the Peninsula. ' What's the matter?' says he, 'Home sickness,' says I. 'Agreed,' says he, thinking of Ireland. And there we left it. . . .

We had a bad start this time in the trenches, which took us several days to get over. We got up there just before dark, and a violent rainstorm arrived a couple of hours later. The trenches flooded in no time, and I found myself splashing about near our infernal barricade with the water in places well over the boot-tops. I had no kind of a dugout at the time; it was our first night up, and I did not know what the Turks might have in store for us at the barricade. Added to which a new order had come out that day saying, ' No cooking in the firing line,' so we had been launched at one swoop into all the intricacies of company cooking in the trenches. The men have always cooked their own rations in their own dixies before. The cooks, who had been sent on ahead to get a place in a convenient communication trench and start on the men's tea, did not turn up for hours. When they did, fuel (an eternal difficulty) was short, consequently the men got nothing hot that night at all. By Jove, it was miserable! To the morbid mind our misfortunes assumed nightmare proportions . . .

For some weeks past rumour, which ranges wide, has given up insinuating that the R.N.D. is to be relieved and go home the day after tomorrow. Speculation, however, dallies with the question of a complete withdrawal from this ill-chosen spot. But we hear no rumours at present. Personally, I am sure, D.H.Q. don't yet know themselves what is going to be done. Anzac and Suvla are in just the same state as we are, only possibly they (the troops) are less comfortable there. Interest has shifted away from Gallipoli altogether, and centres round the Salonika business, and as far as I can see is likely to remain there. . . .

LIEUTENANT WILLIAM KER, R.N.V.R.

*25th November.*—We had an uneventful journey down—trenches all the way from camp to firing line—down hill most of the way into the eye of the westering sun, with Imbros giving its celebrated imitation of Arran on a September evening, and the parapets of the mule track (5 feet wide by 4 feet deep) glowing red-gold in the sunset light. We passed the ruins of a cottage on the way down with a few acres that were obviously fields a year ago in the middle of the moor, and an old stone well with a path leading to it from the house; The whole place looks as though it might have been there since the days when this was the Thracian Chersonese. It struck me, as I sauntered past in the trench at the unexhilarating pace which you must keep to when you have a hundred laden men in single file behind, that the picturesque, if dirty, farmer who pottered round that patch twelve months ago—or his wife shuffling along the stony path to the well—probably did not, in the wildest flights of their vivid imaginations, guess that a year afterwards 100,000 men would be fighting around their front door.

Cotter is here from Malta, not in the best of health, and with the usual tales to tell of the almost insuperable obstacles placed in the way of men trying to get back to the Peninsula when discharged from hospital. . . .

A particularly dull man said the other day in a letter I censored that he didn't think he would be home for his Christmas dinner, as, in his opinion, the first seven years of this war were going to be the worst. . . .

Herbert, A. P., and I decided long ago in July that it would be highly desirable in this climate to activate (our word), if you take my meaning, but it is becoming increasingly obvious nowadays that it is quite as necessary to hibernate here—in fact, that the only two times of the year when one is inclined to be alive are April and October. I am beginning to look on my B.W. (for which I always had a weakness) as my best friend. . . .

*9th December,* 1915.—Two nights ago we were told that our relief from the trenches by the Marines, which should have happened yesterday, was postponed for two days, and later that a brigade of another (old) division would relieve us to-morrow (Friday). We spent an evening in happy speculation. Castles in the air. The division was to be relieved (we had no definite news). The betting was 10 to 1 against England, and 2 to 1 was taken against Alexandria, Anzac, Malta, or Salonika. But the popular view was a period at Alexandria, and then Servia. Then yesterday we were told that we were merely shifting our sector here. No further news; we do not know the why and wherefore. But any shifting is a nuisance. . . .

*13th December,* 1915.—Hancock had to take a working party to unload lighters on the beach last night. Among the cargo were a lot of stores for some General. It was a dark night. This morning we are the proud possessors of a roll of waterproof (tarred) felt, a hurricane lamp, and a pair of live chickens. . . .

*21st December,* 1915.—We are installed, if not settled, in the new camp, which was till lately, all too lately, occupied by the Cannibals. We are back in the region of white sandstone and olive trees. We are pretty high up, and have a fine view of Achibaba, our old camp, Morto Bay, the Straits, and the Asiatic side. There is a good deal of tin roofing about, and we should be able to keep fairly dry. Our company is particularly lucky in this way. We are very cramped at present. The men are like sardines, but, like sardines, they are under tin, so they prefer this to the roofless roominess of the other camp. There are not enough officers' dugouts, and they are very small for two to share. Two feet below the surface of the ground you come on sandstone, which makes the digging very hard.

The stone has to be howked out in chunks, and is used to make walls for the dugouts, with mud for mortar. There are no sandbags. There are wooden doors on the officers' dug-outs, and windows in some—not in mine, which would be all right if it did not remind one so strongly in appearance and in smell of the tomb. We shall have to get some more places dug, especially as we are threatened with another draft (we always are) in the near future. It is fine weather (several magnificent days and nights lately), but there is a very heavy dew at night, and it is as well to sleep under cover of some kind. . . .

We go up to the trenches tomorrow (Wednesday), so we shall have had twelve days out for our nine in. We have spent all our time preparing to move, moving and recovering from the move; shifting camp is a great nuisance. . . .

To me the salient feature in the attitude of the men here is that it never occurred to them that we may be beaten by Turks or Germans, or anyone else. The psychology of the ordinary Tyneside or Paisley man in the ranks is sufficiently impenetrable. The journalist who has to get copy from the front gets over a little difficulty like this by inventing a complete set of thoughts and views for him.

The men know that blunders have been made, are being made, and will be made, and they seem to regard their superiors in proportion increasing, according to rank, with a tolerant scepticism. It never enters their heads that they will not ultimately beat the Turks or Germans, staff or no staff. . . ."

*26th December,* 1915.—The mails are becoming eccentric. There is a rumour that the last mail from here has been held up for a week or two to prevent our telling what you will know by the time this reaches you, that Suvla and Anzac have been abandoned, very successfully, no casualties—about the best organised piece of work that has been done on the Peninsula. . . .

"On Wednesday night we waded up here. Trenches almost knee-deep in water in many places. A foot or two of mud in others. The battalion on our right has 5 feet of water in its trenches in places. Almost 15 *per cent,* of the battalion had rubber thigh-boots. This was all right for the lucky ones (of whom I was one), but not much consolation to the remainder. 'C' company in the firing line again. It was fairly dry, and now completely so. We go into support today, where you get plenty of working parties and shells. There are a lot of the latter about (for here), and the disadvantage of being more than 50 yards from the Turks is that they can shell our firing line. They celebrated Christmas Eve by giving our sector a very hot time for a couple of hours. There is nothing more unpleasant than sitting in a trench being shelled.

There are plenty of good dugouts in this part of the line— tin roofs. The French had the sense to get lots of the stuff, which incidentally all came from England.

Harmsworth went off yesterday to England, nominally to take up a job in the Colonial Office, but he will go to sea or into the Army, I should think, when he gets there. He was sorry to go, in a way, when the time came, but he needs a rest and deserves it, having not missed a day in the trenches for seven months. . . .

Colonel Wilson is back, looking very well...

There is a big draft imminent. We shall, for the first time for ages, be almost at full strength in affairs. Pray that we may be lucky in the new ones. Where we are going to put all the men in the new camp I don't know.

Christmas Day was gorgeous as far as weather and views were concerned, though I have spent it in more congenial surroundings. No genial exchanges between us and the enemy. The Turks were jumping last night—thought we were going to attack. We all had some plum pudding for dinner, which was a good effort for someone. (Was it the *Daily News* ?) . . .

Rather dramatic things seem to happen to me when I am writing letters with nothing to say. A Battalion H.Q. orderly came to me with a note (Cotter being asleep at the moment), which said: 'To be communicated to all ranks. The 8th Army Corps will be relieved here by the 9th Army Corps in the near future,' or words to that effect—news which makes most of us smile long and fatuously.

How soon we shall go, or where or how, I do not know. We may go Arab twitting in Egypt or Bulgar baiting at Salonika, or the R.N.D. may cut itself adrift and go to England. . . .

This was the last letter of the series to be written from the (Gallipoli Peninsula. The warning of the impending relief of the 8th Corps, universally understood as an intimation of the impending evacuation, turned out to have been so intended; three days later the orders were definitely issued, and the remaining period till January 7th was occupied with incessant preparation in very scanty intervals of leisure, for the Naval Division was in the line till the end.

The new sector mentioned in the letters was on the extreme right, held till December by the French, and taken over from them to avoid the dangers of a bilingual withdrawal! The billets taken over were also of French construction, and the whole stretch of country was new to the Hawke Battalion. Its chief characteristic was that it was more rocky and infinitely better wooded than the left of the Peninsula, and that the provision for the comfort and safety of the troops was, on the whole, greatly superior to that in other sectors.

The battalions left the Gallipoli Peninsula almost at full strength, draft after draft arriving throughout October, November, and December. The last draft actually reached us less than ten days before the evacuation. With these later drafts had come some valuable officer reinforcements, notably Lieutenant-Commander Robson, Sub-Lieutenant Hancock, and Sub-Lieutenant Rackham. Commander Robson served with the Hawke only for the last three months of 1915, and at Mudros and Imbros for the following January and February, acting in Colonel Wilson's absence as second in command, and later in command of "B" company. But he was one of the most eccentric of many personalities associated with the battalion, and if he had forgotten more about soldiering than most of us ever knew, he had remembered at least as much. And for one service, at least, he deserves more than a passing mention.

The battalion arrived at Mudros on January 9th in a state of acute thirst, and for two or three days remained in this condition. Robson, however, was about and doing, and one memorable morning saw the officers' mess installed with two large barrels of beer. Where they came from was never known, but their arrival did not pass unnoticed among other units in the neighbourhood, and Robson's invitation to "partake of a glass of nut-brown ale" became so unvarying a formula as in the end to be taken for granted by every Naval Division officer passing within a mile of the Hawke Battalion mess. Many decorations have been awarded for less tangible services than this.

This may seem a digression, for we have carried the story of the Hawke Battalion on as far as Christmas Day, 1915. But, in truth, there is little more left to tell. The evacuation, when it came, was only a final and uninspiring incident of a campaign rich in its earlier days in dramatic excitement, memorable later for its call on the endurance and morale of the troops engaged in it, but in its closing days degenerating into a dull and hardly dangerous routine. Christmas Eve, indeed, and the two days following provided a break, which, however, we hardly welcomed when it came, since a very heavy bombardment on the Hawke sector caused the most serious losses we had had for nearly five months. The battalion, indeed, in killed and wounded, lost between sixty and seventy men in three days, and among them many who had served scathless through the whole campaign. One of those killed was the Rev. Davis, who had served in the ranks of "D" company as a combatant since their expectant and enthusiastic arrival on the shores of the Peninsula, which not all were now to leave.

Yet must one confess that at this interval the perspective changes. Now the losses of one campaign or another are alike, sacrifices to a grudging fate which asks much and gives but a memory in return.

Then we lived for the hour, and the losses of one day were bitter, at a time when the next day might bring, if not peace, at least rest and relaxation. The news of the impending evacuation was, in the circumstances, to us not so much a sentence as a reprieve. Sacrifices had been vain, hopes had proved to be illusions, but the future remained.

And so we passed from the period of an anxious, stubborn, and even costly defence to days of bustle; light-hearted days for those blessed with irresponsibility. Only another week! Should we be lucky enough to see it to its destined, safe, and unexpected ending?

The days of stress were the last days of the old year, when we did our last tour of duty in the trenches, and Rackham, the latest-joined officer, complained to his company commander in the thick of a severe bombardment of a deluge of "spare parts" unearthed and scattered among his platoon by the assiduous 8-inch howitzer, which was the nearest the enemy could do in matching the apocryphal 15-inch with which our intelligent staff had endowed him.

The spare parts were indeed a legitimate subject of complaint, for Turkish legs and arms are not at their best under such conditions. The spirit underlying the solemn complaint was more than legitimate. It was characteristic of the battalion and its future Adjutant, who was to serve with it continuously on the fighting front for a longer period than anyone else.

On December 29th the Hawke Battalion left the front-line trenches for the last time, and returned to the new rest camp for three days' badly needed rest. The plans for the evacuation now took more detailed shape, and the closing days of 1915 were devoted to packing surplus gear and assembling it ready for embarkation. The rôle of the Hawke Battalion was to provide the garrison of the Eski line for the entire divisional front. The general scheme was for the four battalions who, in the normal course of things, were in the line at that time (the Drake, Hood, Anson, and 1st R.M.) to remain there, and for the Nelson and Howe and the two London Territorial Battalions to embark before the final operations began, while the Hawke Battalion supplied the divisional reserve, and the 2nd Marines garrisoned the beach defences. Under these arrangements neither the Hawke nor the 2nd Marines left the Peninsula till the last night, but on the last night but one the Hawke withdrew to the rest camp, while parties from the four front-line battalions took over the Eski line. Thus, on the last day and night the Anson, 1st R.M., Drake, and Hood held the whole of the trench system on the right of the Peninsula in depth, while the function of the Hawke was limited to standing by in the rest camp till the time came for the embarkation to begin, which it did at 7.30 p.m.

The dates of "Y" and "Z" day were left uncertain when the orders were issued on January 1st, but the general expectation when the battalion moved to the Eski line on that night was that their stay would be for two or three nights at most. The expectation was, however, falsified, if local gossip was correct, not only by the wind which delayed the embarkation of stores, but by New Year's celebrations among the working parties on the beach, who found themselves engaged at this particularly inappropriate season with the task of loading up on lighters the reserve supplies of the rum ration. Other factors contributed, however, to the congestion and confusion which, for the first time, almost overwhelmed the beaches and their staffs.

The rough outline which we have given of the Naval Division's dispositions conveys no idea of the inevitable complexity of the arrangements. The garrison of every post and every trench had to work out to an exact number, so that the lighters for the final embarkation should, as each party reached the beach in ordered sequence, receive their exact complement of 400 men. This meant that in the rest camps and attached to the corps troops on the beaches were numberless detachments of surplus men from innumerable battalions, and these provided the only source from which the beach working parties could be drawn. These men were not always the most experienced or the best disciplined. That the work of loading up the stores, not only of battalions and divisions, but of an entire field army, of embarking guns, horses, transport, and ammunition from open beaches with no proper piers and no skilled labour available was yet carried out was one of the miracles of the campaign. The delay in completing the work was simply inevitable.

To this task of embarking guns, mules, and stores the Hawke Battalion, like every other of the fighting units, made its contribution, a party of some sixty N.C.O.'s and men under Sub-Lieutenant Paton being detailed for beach duties on the 1st January. This party remained on the beaches under corps orders 8th January (the ultimate "Y" night), when they embarked for Mudros.

The chief feature of the last days of the battalion in the Eski line was the arrival hour by hour of new rumours of delay. All through these anxious days we watched the weather, which grew threatening, with high winds at night, which held the menace of actual disaster. The situation seemed to us most serious of all when an order came to destroy all stores of alcoholic liquor, coupled with a request for a telegraphic report to the effect that the order had been carried out. Within the appointed time the Hawke Battalion orderly room reported that "All *surplus* stores of alcoholic liquor has been destroyed," but it appeared that this qualitative interpretation of the intentions of the staff was incorrect, and thirty-six hours later the mistake which had been made (by the writer, it must be here confessed) was pointed out in terms which were commendably explicit. Happily, by that time the withdrawal was at hand.

On the 5th January the final decision, meaning nothing but a relief from anxiety to officers and men in the line, but throwing an incalculable responsibility on the staffs responsible, was taken. On the night of the 8th and 9th January the Army was to enter on the final, the only gamble of the campaign.

On the 7th January, the last day to be spent by the battalion in the trenches for many months, the Turks directed an attack against the left flank of the British position, involving the sector formerly held by the Naval Division. The day before, an aeroplane reconnaissance in the morning, accompanied by a good deal of shelling, had seemed to indicate that the attack might be on the right, and it seemed impossible that the Turkish or German observer in one particular aeroplane, which came right over the Eski line flying very low, could have failed to observe the absence of guns. On the left, this was not a serious matter, as the fleet could and did give splendid assistance. Where the Hawke were, however, there was no serious help to be expected, and had any serious attack developed, it must have been necessary to disembark men and guns in support. Happily, the necessity did not arise. Sub-Lieutenant Tomson and his machine guns were responsible for the last shots fired in anger by the Hawke on the Peninsula, and the Turkish aeroplane went back apparently no wiser than it came.

On the night of the 7th to 8th the battalion went down to the camp, leaving the adjutant, two signallers (P.O. Macdonald and L. S. Davidson), C.P.O. Gillard (R.S.M.), and L. S. Steele to hand over the dispositions of the buried stocks of ammunition and other stores to the detachments of the front-line battalions who formed the final garrison of this position. Of this small rear-guard of the battalion only the ever-faithful L. S. Steele remained with the battalion on November 11th, 1918.

The last day spent by the battalion on the Peninsula was uneventful, and at 6.30 p.m. we turned our backs on the enemy and marched

106

down to the beaches. In the energy of preparation the main road to the beaches had been cleverly blocked with barbed wire entanglements of a peculiarly intricate kind, and the wire-cutters issued to the battalion on landing were used for the first time to clear the way for our orderly but yet furtive retreat; yet the grey dawn of January 9th found us, none the less, in Mudros Harbour.

# CHAPTER 6

# Organised Warfare

The Hawke Battalion made only a short stay at Mudros—a brief interlude of endless rain and bitter cold, brightened, as far as the officers were concerned, by our two barrels of beer, and for the men by the presence of an authentic canteen not staffed by Greeks. At the end of January we moved to Imbros to garrison the island.

The chief task of a garrison is to maintain itself in a decent obscurity, and in complete isolation from the inhabitants, the Civil Government, and the Naval and Military Headquarters. These conditions can never be wholly fulfilled, but at Imbros it was possible to achieve a great deal. The Naval Division Headquarters were at Mudros, and so was Admiral de Robeck's flagship, which was obscurely understood to be ultimate authority. Moreover, even the status of the Naval Division in the Imperial forces was less obscure than the status of the Imperial forces in Imbros. The result was that we were inspected on different occasions by a Marine General, an Admiral, and a foreigner (perhaps a Greek) in a top hat, but were otherwise left severely alone, residuary legatees of the grandeur of Army Headquarters, the typewriters and office equipment of the R.N.A.S., the mess fittings of the 11th Division, a grand piano, fifty turkeys, and a flourishing trade in contraband between the island capital at Panageia and the military camp. It was not magnificent, but it was war.

With the aid of new drafts of officers and men the battalion was reorganised on the basis of the effective organisation built up in the trenches at Gallipoli in the autumn of 1915. For a short time Brigadier-General Mercer was in command at Imbros, but when he left for England to take up in a few months' time the important appointment of Adjutant-General of the Royal Marines, Colonel Wilson was promoted to command the 1st Naval Brigade, and Commander Ramsay

Fairfax once more assumed command of the Hawke. In other particulars, the reorganisation was as follows:—

O.C.: Commander W. G. Ramsay Fairfax, R.N.
Second in command: Lieutenant-Commander H. R. Robson,
R.N.V.R.
M.O.: Surgeon W. Bradbury, R.N.
Adjutant: Lieutenant D. F. Jerrold, R.N.V.R.
Assistant Adjutant: Sub-Lieutenant Hancock, R.N.V.R.
Transport Officer: Sub-Lieutenant C. S. Codner, R.N.V.R.
Quartermaster: Hon. Lieutenant H. A. Day, R.M.
Machine-Gun Officers: Sub-Lieutenant G. Tomson, R.N.V.R.,
and Sub-Lieutenant E. M. Aron, R.N.V.R.

| *Regimental Sergeant-Majors.* | *Regimental Q.M.S.* |
|---|---|
| C.P.O. Gillard.[1] | C.P.O. Bailey.[2] |
| C.P.O. Foster.[2] | C.P.O. Malpress. |
| C.P.O. Finlay. | |

| *"C" Company.* | *"A" Company.* |
|---|---|
| Lieutenant H. H. Rush | Lieutenant A. V. W. Cotter |
| Lieutenant W. H. S. Wallis | Lieutenant W. Ker. |
| Sub-Lieut. J. H. Bessel. | Sub-Lieut. F. J. Matthews, |
| Sub-Lieut. A. C. Black. | Sub-Lieut. B. B. Rackham. |
| Sub-Lieut. C. B. Tompkins. | Sub-Lieut. M. C. Henderson |
| C.S.M.: C.P.O. Davey. | C.S.M.: C.P.O. Miller |
| C.Q.M.S.: C.P.O. Roger. | C.Q.M.S.: C.P.O. McCombie. |

| *"B" Company.* | *"D" Company.* |
|---|---|
| Lieutenant O. J. Wainright. | Lieut.-Commander G. Peckham |
| Sub-Lieut. T. S. Paton. | Sub-Lieut. E. Ellis |
| Sub-Lieut. R. Bowerman | Sub-Lieut. R. Blackmore |
| Sub-Lieut. J. A. Cooke. | Sub-Lieut. S. G. Poole. |
| Sub-Lieut. A. Cooke. | Sub-Lieut. H. A. Burr. |
| C.S.M.: C.P.O. Nadin. | C.S.M.: C.P.O. Relton. |
| C.Q.M.S.: C.P.O. Todd | C.Q.M.S.: C.P.O. Wright |

This battalion, reclothed, well fed and housed, and now for the first time drilled as a battalion (for 70 *per cent*, of the officers and men had never done any battalion training with any formally constituted unit),

---

1. Transferred to sea service in March, 1916.
2. These N.C.O.'s were gazetted to commissions (not in the Hawke Battalion) in the spring of 1916.

was the product in all other particulars of eight months' of active service, which had demanded its sacrifices and brought its compensations in experience and the opportunity it had given for the selection and training of N.C.O.'s.

This was fortunate indeed. No worse place for training or disciplining a battalion could have been found than Imbros in 1916. The troops were kept within a cordon, and more than half of them were always employed on picket duty of an informal and inexacting kind, which had all the disadvantages of relaxed discipline with none of the incentives of active service. The chief incidents from week to week were provided by the deaths of sheep or goats on the hills surrounding the camp, processes of nature which the passage of years might have led the Greeks to regard as normal, but which were invariably followed by a claim for compensation from the owners on the ground that the animal in question, if not actually done to death by a naval bayonet, had at any rate received a fatal shock which could not be disassociated from the worries of a military occupation.

Otherwise, however, the relations between Greek and English were friendly to a degree, and nothing but the poisonous quality of the alien brandy could have availed the sentries against the blandishments of the picturesque bandits who carried the trade of the country over its rugged hills and scented valleys with a smiling patience in the face of the law's delays, a patience acquired through centuries of petty larceny in a golden climate all too productive of a comprehensive charity.

In camp things were almost ideal from every point of view, except that of military efficiency. The men were perfectly comfortable, well fed, and not overworked, while the officers and N.C.O.'s were more comfortable than at Blandford. The one fly in the ointment was the price of whisky—seven shillings a bottle! When shall we look upon its like again?

Eight officers and some of the N.C.O.'s and men went on leave to England early in 1916. The first to go—Commander Ramsay Fairfax, Peckham, Rush, and Cotter—returned on the *Olympic* early in March; The rest were taken back by the *Olympic* on her return voyage, and heard when the time came for their return that the division was coming to France. The scene of action had indeed moved westward, but farther west than France, and the sharpest engagement in which the division had been engaged was waged in March, 1916, in Whitehall.

For those of us who were on leave at this time, the time chosen for this pitched battle was opportune, as it prolonged our leave. But the atmosphere of ill-will which the dispute engendered did little good to the division, even when reason conquered prejudice and it was finally decided neither to disband the division as a fighting force nor leave the battalions at Mudros, Imbros, and Tenedos to fade away from inanition.

The facts were that the executive authorities in France had formed the meanest opinion of the quality of the troops engaged at Gallipoli, and of the Naval Division in particular, while the administrative services dreaded the complications of a heterodox formation trying to fit itself in, without modification, into the more rigid organisation of the armies of the West. However, the right decision was eventually taken, and the scene changes to Abbeville, which marked, as for so many divisions, the first plunge into the highly developed warfare of the western front.

As the troop trains rolled up from Marseilles with the different battalions of the divisions, the hearts even of their protagonists must have sunk. Never had a stranger spectacle burst upon the orthodox military eye. The battalions, the engineers, the divisional train, all alike had come without stores of any kind, with rifles that would only take ammunition obsolete long before the war, with all the "old soldier's "tricks and none of his experience of the (very different) conditions. The material was there, no doubt, but the appearance had somehow worn off. The reports from the base-camp commandant at Marseilles were hostile to a degree; the faces of the hordes of Generals and staff officers in the area of concentration were a study. But the Tyneside miners remained unmoved. Not, perhaps, till the Germans attacked in March, 1918, was this particular capacity of theirs for remaining unmoved appreciated at its proper valuation.

Before that, indeed, these dogged North Countrymen, who could be as smart as paint on parade, but who refused to imitate the bearing of soldiers when standing outside the estaminet, gazing with undisguised curiosity at passing motorcars with curious-looking flags on their bonnets and elderly gentlemen in khaki inside, were to show that they could fight tolerably well. Immediately, however, we had to study appearances, and for the officers there was the constant preoccupation of the first weeks in France. Appearances and the endeavour to comply with the demands of the thousand and one schools, courses,administrative and grandmotherly services which battened like leeches on any battalion so foolish as to linger behind the fighting line.

The Hawke Battalion was heartened on its arrival in France by the return of Colonel Wilson to command it, and by the return of Vere Harmsworth to command and to look after his beloved "B" company. Unlike some others, Harmsworth had decided to refuse the staff appointment which was waiting for him, and to stay in the fighting line.

Behind the lines the standard of efficiency in France was far higher than anything we had experienced even in England. For the first time, while at Doudelainville, a few kilometres from Abbeville, the battalion was properly fitted out with up-to-date rifles, Lewis guns, Stokes mortars, transport, field kitchens, etc., and other mobilisation stores. Then, as soon as the mounted officers had got used to the unwanted encumbrance of a horse, as soon as the battalion transport had been organised and the necessary quotas had been provided for the brigade machine-gun companies and trench-mortar batteries, and when, finally, the Lewis-gun sections, bombing sections, rifle-grenade sections, scouts, and other passing fancies of an over-enthusiastic staff had been attended to, the battalion marched off to La Compté on June 3rd for a definite period of training.

Only one sad mischance had marred the initial stages of preparation. This was a disastrous bombing accident, on June 2nd, involving the death of Sub-Lieutenant Hancock and two men. The cause was, without doubt, a defective bomb, which robbed the battalion of a very keen, capable, and popular officer.

At La Compté we were left to ourselves to a good extent for the first week, and were able to do a small amount of company training. To do bayonet exercises, however, without a sack of straw suspended on a gallows in front of each participant was painfully old-fashioned. Had not the authorities discovered and enunciated in unquestionable terms that *all* soldiers preferred to have the sack of straw to play with, and that *no good purpose* whatever was served by bayonet exercises of any other kind? It was the same with tactical exercises. The attack, as practised in pre-war days, moved forward in *lines*. Now the word had gone forth that movement must be in *waves*. Those who were ignorant of this development were indeed barbarians, though the difference between a line and a wave was to the crude civilian mind which predominated still in the Hawke Battalion none too great.

Moreover, we had retained a pathetic faith in the value of platoon and company drill, and in the rifle as a weapon. We now learnt that physical training was the only thing conducive to really sound up-to-date discipline, and that the bomb was the only infantry weapon of serious military account, at least behind the lines! We did not take these sweeping judgments too seriously, especially as it was by no means certain that those few officers and N.C.O.'s, whose proficiency in the mysteries of bayonet fighting (new style), P.T., and bombs was the only redeeming feature of the battalion in the eyes of inspecting Generals, were, in actual fact and without exception, the dare-devil fellows which their *élan* in front of a sack of hay appeared to suggest to our visitors.

None the less, these barrack-square revolutions were a source of constant worry, since those unfortunate people who had to run the battalion—such people, for instance, as colonels and company commanders, warrant officers, Adjutants, and the like—knew literally nothing at first of the technique of the new aids to efficiency. We were saved (the officers, at least) from absolute disaster only by a capacity for bluff born of long practice at poker. The N.C.O.'s, too, responded gamely, though perhaps with less success, and I fancy that few people were ultimately deceived. Happily, the Naval Division in France was seldom behind the lines for long.

The present was no exception, for the loss of a portion of Vimy Ridge hastened the arrangements for the taking over of a portion of the 47th Division sector on the left of that key position. Before the orders came to the Hawke to go forward the staff had, however, made a serious onset on us, and by June 14th no fewer than fourteen officers and 216 men had been detached for one Course of instruction or another. What remained of the battalion went forward to Barlin on June 15th, and thence by easy stages into the trenches.

It was not till July 17th that the Naval Division formally took over a sector of the line, for these things were done on a systematic and by no means unsound plan, whereby platoons, companies, and individual battalions were attached for preliminary tours of duty to a division already in the line and accustomed to the local conditions. Like most things, however, in France at this time the system was less excellent in practice than in theory. The reason was not far to seek, and of some intrinsic interest. The ruling passion of G.H.Q. at this time was standardization. Starting from the assumption (which was, to be perfectly just, more a working hypothesis than a serious belief) that all formations of the new armies were wholly ignorant and unreliable, and that all regular officers were cast in the Napoleonic mould, it followed that the new armies could only be usefully employed if their activities were restricted to more or less routine tasks, the whole organisation, both of attack and defence, being in charge of specialists specially trained by and working under the direct control of Corps, Army, or General Headquarters, as the case might be. The triumph of this system was the assault on the Messines Ridge in 1917. Its failures have left a more decided imprint on the world's history.

The fact, of course, was that the antithesis between the war of movement and the war of position was almost wholly false, that once a battle was launched its success depended on the rapid exploitation of any local success by local commanders, who must be skilled, not in the successful organisation of a routine, but in the personal control and direction of men in the field. To those familiar, even to the extent that we were, with the more elementary but more elemental campaign of Gallipoli, the mechanical routine of the trench defence system in France, which we had to learn by gradual and carefully graduated stages, seemed less impressive than it ought to have done. It was not that the Hawke Battalion, at any rate, had not got much to learn. But we did not learn much of it in the Souchez sector.

Yet these were pleasant days. The work was arduous, but not anxious. The demands of the staffs for working parties and for officers and men for detached duty or courses of instruction, the routine work of draining and rebuilding trenches, laying buried cables, digging deep dugouts, bringing up trench-mortar ammunition, clearing mining saps of filled sandbags (a task comparable only to the cleansing of the Augean stables) took on the shape of so many obstacles to be overcome by those conscientious enough to wish to defend at the same time the trenches nominally entrusted to them. The game could be played good-humouredly if the staff took it all in the right spirit, or as a serious and sometimes bitter wrangle if either side lost its temper.

Happily, A. P. Herbert rejoined us in July and became assistant adjutant, in which capacity he became the Correspondent-in-Chief with Brigade on all controversial matters. This brilliant writer can seldom have been seen to better advantage than in some of the never-ending correspondence which he conducted from this vantage-point of mingled authority and irresponsibility. Captain Bare and Major Sandilands, front their entrenchments at B.H.Q., responded with almost unfailing geniality, though the Staff Captain had doubts, I feel sure, as to whether this wordy badinage was wholly consistent with "playing the game" in the true public school sense of the term. But the times were not very serious at Souchez.

Another old friend who rejoined was E. M. Lockwood, now a lieutenant-commander, who became Brigade Intelligence Officer, and upheld the cause of the Hawke Battalion, and of A. P. Herbert in particular, at Brigade Headquarters on every occasion when a crisis seemed to be in the air. These crises were brought about, as a rule, by telegraphic refusals to supply working parties in excess of the numbers available. Other battalions, we were told, had "ante-d up." Why was the Hawke invariably the defaulter ? I have often wondered whether the same point was put, *mutatis mutandis,* to other battalions, or whether we really put up a harder fight for battalion autonomy. Anyway, we were never courts-martialled.

Other officers who joined us for the first time in July (when we had a pleasant and sunny fortnight at Dieval after our preliminary tours in the line) were G. H. Inman and R, S. Stewart (who went to "C" company), Lieutenant Melland (second in command "B" company), O'Hagan and "Bill" Knight ("D" company), Rowden and Gibb ("A" company), Lyall ("B" company), Elphick ("A" company), Edwards (signalling officer), and Pizzey ("C" company). The battalion with this reinforcement[3] was greatly over strength in officers, and the demands for officers for detached duty could at last be met with equanimity.

From July 17th onwards the life of the Hawke Battalion centred officially round the Souchez II. sector. Without a doubt this was the quietest sector ever seen, though by no means easily defensible had it been attacked. The Souchez Valley runs roughly east and west, immediately to the north of Vimy Ridge. Our line, as elsewhere, ran north and south. Immediately behind us was the famous Lorette Spur, and this was the real tactical position. Our front trenches were, however, in the low ground well in front, pushed forward across the Arras-Bethune road, and ran from the Souchez River itself (the right divisional boundary) through Angres and Liévin to the outskirts of Lens. The 189th Brigade (the new name for the old 1st Naval Brigade) held the right of the line (Souchez I. and Souchez II.), the 188th Brigade (the old Marine Brigade) held the Angres sectors, and the new 190th Brigade (an Army Brigade attached to the Naval Division to complete its establishment) held the two battalion sectors farther on the left.

Souchez I. was held throughout our stay in this part of the line by

---

3. Another change of importance was the arrival of R.S.M. Sands, of the Royal Marines, to act as Regimental Sergeant-Major in place of C.P.O. Findlay, who was demobilised to work in the Clyde shipyards, at that time dangerously short of skilled labour.

the Hood or Drake Battalions, while we did turn and turn about with the Nelson, a pleasant, easy-going battalion who forbore to indulge in those weekly recriminations and reports to Brigade Headquarters on the state of the trenches which so many units regard as the only conclusive proof of their own efficiency. Our one quarrel, indeed, with the Nelson was on the subject of their taste in pictures, which tended to an inharmonic blend of Kirchner and Bairnsfather. In this respect, if in no other, the Hawke Battalion was rather in the Spartan tradition.

The only peculiar feature of Souchez II. as a sector was that it had clearly been for months the scene of a furtive but systematic retirement. Whole stretches of trench, and sometimes those nearest to the enemy, had been tactically abandoned or allowed to fall into decay on the curious ground that they were "dangerous." As far as could be observed no one had put this hypothesis to an exhaustive test, but the fact remained that a whole group of trenches were derelict and so situated as to provide a possible avenue of approach for enemy patrols. An obvious solution was to reoccupy them. This, however, was easier said than done, as the work of rebuilding them would be laborious, and most certainly observed day by day by the enemy.

Now in trench warfare the enemy can, of course, render any particular stretch of trench untenable at any time. He is, however, human, and gets used after a time to the established front line. Nevertheless, digging operations and similar outward and visible signs of activity disgust him. So much we knew, and had almost determined to do nothing in the face of such undeniable difficulties, when we discovered "Archie." Archie was a wholly perfect *papier-mâché* soldier, life-size, and far too smart and well equipped to have passed at close quarters for one of our battalion. But the enemy could not know this, the only weakness of an admirable plan. The plan, in brief, was that night by night different conspicuous positions in the derelict trenches should be occupied by this gallant soldier, and that day by day our front line should enjoy a perfect immunity from enemy action, while his efforts were concentrated on the demolition of Archie and his invisible but surely-to-be-presumed-on comrades.

A. P. Herbert, I think, was responsible for the scheme, and certainly, in his capacity as scout officer, for carrying it out, in conjunction with the invaluable P.O. Kent, formerly of "C" company, but now in charge of the scout platoon (an organisation insisted on at this time, though soon abandoned on the not altogether convincing ground that every officer and man ought to be a scout—a *dictum* which carries one in actual practice little farther than Clough's unsupported assertion that every woman is or ought to be a cathedral).

The first expedition saw the intrepid Archie safely installed in an exposed position in what up to that memorable hour had been no-man's-land. Now it was ours, and for two days German barbarism, excited to fury by our intrepidity, rained rifle grenades on this outpost of Anglo-Saxon culture Like all good things, the enemy's anger came to an end in time, or so we thought, and it was decided to move our brave comrade to another point of vantage. Unfortunately we had built better than we knew, and Herbert and Kent, setting out on their errand of mercy, were fired at by an enemy machine gun trained on the line of approach. Clearly they were supposed to be a ration party, but circumstances did not enable them to clear up the mistake in identity. The shameful sequel was that our too-realistic comrade was left to fight his own battle while we thought out other methods of irritating the enemy.

This was perhaps rather superfluous, as the enemy did little except when roused by our own activities. Our own Stokes mortar battery (just behind Kellett trench, which was the Hawke Battalion support line) was indeed the only real source of danger. In retaliation for its depredations Kellett trench itself was blown in two or three times a week, happily without serious loss, but still at the constant risk of casualties. Whether we inflicted on balance greater loss and discomfort on the enemy is necessarily uncertain. The infantry as a rule doubted it, and the Stokes mortar batteries did not. The staff were in a stronger position, since they experienced few of the dangers either of our own troops or of the enemy, and consequently had no hesitation in assessing the losses of the latter as double our own.

But danger, though it existed from time to time, was only a negligible factor in the daily life of the Hawke Battalion at this time. Every other week we were out of the line, and when in the line our real occupation was to dig ourselves and everything else deeper and deeper down. The surface activities of the infantry were only a small thing, employing a bare quarter of our strength.

What was even pleasanter was that half our time was spent out of line in conditions very gratifying to a battalion which had been cut off from even the cruder comforts of civilization for a long time. A quarter of an hour's ride or half an hour's walk took one back still at this period into conditions of absolute peace. On the Somme, in Belgium, at Arras in 1917 there was a wide belt of devastated country—

so devastated, indeed, that it remains so to this day. But Coupigny, Hersin, Barlin, and Bruay were all within easy distance of our huts in Noulette Wood, or of the other reserve position on Lorette Spur. Indeed, Day, Codner, and the transport lived all these weeks at Coupigny, and had as their mess a sitting-room with a plush table-cloth and two real horsehair sofas, which represented peace and comfort past understanding, perhaps, to a later generation, but not to us on hot summer mornings when our thoughts were of war and we were correspondingly thirsty. Nor were these delights for officers only. The estaminets remained open even under fire on the Bethune road, actually nearer the trenches than our hutments, and farther back they were plentiful (and perhaps a little cheaper). Nor was there no suggestion of profiteering anywhere nearer to the front than Bruay, where a permanent garrison of A.S.C. Subalterns in field-boots and spurs had undoubtedly exercised an unfavourable influence on the price of the sweeter varieties of champagne.

Noulette Wood itself was by no means uncomfortable. It had the merit of being perfectly safe, and Generals dined in our mess with alarming frequency. There was also an indisputable parade ground and a Lewis-gun range, so that in the intervals of digging we could play at soldiers to our heart's content. Ablain St. Nazaire and the Lorette trenches were more romantic, and here we went for two weeks out of the lines in August. Here the company officers and men lived in real trenches amid all the debris of the great battles which had been fought for this hill by the French in 1915, and won by some miracle of gallantry and devotion. The hill was the gateway to the west at this point, and while we held it the front-line trenches were secure, for we had command from here of the whole panorama of the German positions.

The idea of losing so important a *point d'appui* had occurred to no one, and its defences were of the most casual order. The trenches were tumble-down, very exposed to fire from the heights of Vimy Ridge, and without any secure communications with reserves on the reverse slope of the hill. These reserves were, however, usually away on a working party, so the point was perhaps of no importance. Behind the hill was nothing. Not a battalion, I fancy, within fifteen miles. But from that day till November, 1918, our hold on the position was never challenged, principally because we held a portion also of Vimy Ridge, and, later, the whole of it. Now no doubt the scattered bones along its battered slopes are buried, and the church has perhaps been rebuilt, and in any case its fame has passed it by, eclipsed by more decisive victories. Then it was a formidable position wrested from the enemy, as formidable, though, alas! less vital, than Achibaba itself, and we lived in the desolate and extremely insanitary trenches with a feeling of vicarious importance as we looked down on the silent lines of the opposing infantry beneath us, our meditations broken only by the formidable sounds of battle carried on the wind from the south. How soon should we exchange our desolate but peaceful post of vantage for the tumult of the Somme?

Meanwhile we worked hard, and constructed a model swimming bath out of a small stream which flowed through the ruins of Ablain St. Nazaire. This fine piece of marine engineering was regarded by the staff as a sign of grace, and certainly improved the amenities of the dirtiest trenches I have ever seen.

Apart from the dirt, the difficulty of communication between the different companies was the chief hazard. It may be more blessed to travel joyfully than to arrive, but men waiting for rations, or for relief by another company, take a less philosophic view. When it came to the exchange of hospitality between the different company and headquarters messes, the situation was delicate in the extreme. It was difficult to arrive; having dined, it was virtually impossible to return. Those of junior rank were in the circumstances well advised to stay at home, or at least to choose their hosts with discrimination. An invitation to "D" company's mess, pitched on the very edge of a steep bank leading down into a slimy marsh, was a particularly incalculable hazard, and "C" company's mess on the forward slope of the hill was out of bounds, except for teetotallers or members of the Alpine Club. Unfortunately there were none of either in the Hawke Battalion.

Inevitably, things were too good to last. Yet they lasted for nearly three months, and no news came, except orders for a raid to be carried out by "C" company on a small German salient opposite our front line in Souchez II., and rumours of a more extended but still local operation against the trenches recently lost on Vimy Ridge. Somehow neither the orders nor the rumours impressed us much, though "C" company profited greatly by them, being taken back behind the lines (to *Fosse* 7 —a group of slag-heaps and some very clean miners' cottages near Barlin) to rehearse the intended operation in the thorough fashion of those early days when war seemed so simple.

The rehearsals of the raid proceeded according to plan, but the scheme was brought to nothing at 10 p.m. on the night of September

16th by orders for the relief of the battalion (then resting in Noulette Wood) by the 18th Battalion of the Yorkshire and Lancashire Regiment at 11 a.m. the next day.

The task of moving a battalion at such short notice was not an easy one, but the orders read like the beginning of a divisional relief (which, indeed, they were), and the excitement compensated even for the necessity of returning in the middle of the night a piano hired at the utmost expenditure of time and diplomacy for a battalion concert the following night. Why in the world no adequate notice of the move should have been given remained, and remains, a mystery. But as this was the only occasion during our stay of four months in this area on which authoritative advance information had not been obtainable from the local estaminet, we felt that the staff, for once, had scored. And for once we forbore to grudge them their unexpected success.

The next four weeks, spent at Fresnicourt, Monchy Breton, and Villers Brulin (in the IVth Corps training area), and at Forceville (a training centre for the reserve army on the Somme, to which we were to be attached) marked a kind of climax in the history of the Hawke Battalion. For almost two years we, alone of the battalions of the division, had escaped drastic reorganisation or severe losses. Obviously, an end was coming to our immunity, but the remaining interval must be a memorable one. And brigade could do their worst!

We had to work hard in the intervals of changing billets, and the trials of brigade and divisional field-days rained on us as a matter of almost daily routine. But the weather was fine, and the day's work ended in time for good dinners and much excellent poker—for the officers—varied with company and battalion concerts. Not that the men were any more in need of organised amusement here than we were ourselves. They had the hospitality of the villages to themselves, and enjoyed it. The only limitation on their freedom was the placing a sentry on one estaminet out of many. This was for the sole use of officers—an unusual but clearly sensible arrangement which left everyone well pleased.

Three evenings of this period I remember well. The first a farewell dinner to Commander Fairfax, appointed to the command of the Howe Battalion;[18] the second a twenty-first birthday party given by Vere Harmsworth at Villers Brulin; the third a battalion concert at Monchy Breton. The first a gathering of senior officers, the second of

18. He was succeeded as second in command by Major H. du Cane Norris, R.M., formerly second in command to Colonel Ramsden at Blandford.

junior officers, the third of the whole battalion, but each one a meeting of friends, whom, if we cannot meet, we cannot ever forget.

We were, moreover, a good deal more efficient in the conventional sense when we finally entrained for the Somme than we had ever been before. In Gallipoli days there had been so many things that we could not do if only because we had never had to; We had no transport (had never had any except for a day); half the mounted officers couldn't ride; our rifles were out of date; we had never seen a Lewis gun. Now we had filled all these gaps in our knowledge, and had even acquired a long-service Marine N.C.O. with at least two medals as Regimental Sergeant-Major, of the most approved type on parade, though off parade the mildest and most diffident of men. These things were, perhaps, less important than they seemed to generals who had grown up in the pre-war routine, but their possession gave us a certain freedom from care, a feeling of *abandon* in the face even of an exacting inspection or a divisional field-day which we had sometimes lacked, and were soon, owing to an incalculable mischance, to lack again.

CHAPTER 7

# The End of a Chapter

The Hawke Battalion left the training area on October 7th, and arrived the same evening at Forceville, a small town some four miles east of the Thiepval Ridge, and one of the recognized concentration centres for units arriving to take part in the Somme battles.

The *hinterland* of the Somme was not impressive. The roads churned up into seas of mud, the congestion of traffic, the daily cancellation of orders, the insanitary billets, the continual working parties under impossible conditions—all this spoke of an immense concentration of certainly uncoordinated and perhaps unimaginative energy.

To those of us, indeed, whose experience had been gained on the barren shores of Gallipoli, where shells were counted in units and bombs by boxes, where sandbags had to be extracted in half-dozens from despairing ordnance officers, there was a bright side even to the chaos of Forceville; material at least was available. But the noise, the confusion, the almost universal irritation, the criticisms of the infantry on the staff, of the staff on the regimental shortcomings, of brigade on brigade and division on division were more significant signs.

We must look for a moment at the general situation on the front which the Hawke Battalion was now to take over (a situation which gave rise to the battles of the Ancre in November, 1916, and February, 1917).

The campaign on the Somme had opened on a wide front north and south of the Ancre, but all attacks north of the Ancre and against the Thiepval Ridge immediately south of the river had failed in the early stages of the battle. Much the same had occurred on the extreme south of the battle front. In other words, the enemy had stood fast on both flanks, and our own advance had continued perforce on an ever narrower front, so that our gains at the end of September were represented by a sharp and actually rather dangerous salient. On September 30th we had captured Thiepval, but the enemy still held the whole of their original front north of the Ancre, and till we could dislodge them we could not advance safely any farther on the front south of that river.

The main pivots of the enemy's defences north of the Ancre were, from north to south, Serre, Beaumont Hamel, and Beaucourt. The last was some distance behind the enemy's front-line, but was the key position commanding the actual valley of the Ancre. A little way behind Beaucourt were two farther ridges, which, if we could capture them, would command the gun positions defending the German positions behind Serre, and even farther north.

The capture of these positions along the Ancre Valley was a matter of the highest consequence, for on this depended the possibility or otherwise of enforcing the long-awaited German retreat. The task of capturing them was allotted to the Naval Division. To the 51st Division fell the hardly less difficult (perhaps, indeed, equally difficult) task of capturing Beaumont Hamel.

The line taken over in October, 1916, by the Naval Division was just in front of the small village of Hamel on the reverse slope, the crest and the forward slope of a ridge which faced up the Ancre Valley. The Ancre itself was the right divisional boundary, and the valley defences were part of the left of the two divisional sectors. This was the sector taken over by the 189th Brigade, and on October 19th by the Hawke Battalion.

Straight to our front, two miles away, and exactly parallel to our own line, was the Beaucourt Ridge. Intervening between this and our front line was, first, at a distance varying between 150 and 250 yards, the German front-line system, consisting as usual of three lines of trenches. The last of these trenches was to form the "first" objective in the forthcoming attack, and came to be known later, for that purpose, as the *Dotted Green Line*. Behind the German front-line system, and separated from it by a valley, through which ran the road known as *Station Road,* was a second ridge running from Beaumont Hamel to Beaucourt Station. On this ridge was a strongly fortified position, later called the *Green Line*. This was the second defined objective. Except on the right front of the divisional sector, the country immediately behind this line was featureless.

On our right, however, immediately in front of Beaucourt, the ground rose sharply, and the crest of this small hill commanded the enemy's communications with his forward systems. On the western face of this hill was a trench, which continued parallel to our front across the more level ground on the left. This trench was known later as the *Yellow Line,* when it formed the division's third objective. The final objective, known as the *Red Line,* was a roughly defined position to be taken up beyond Beaucourt, the capture of which would be, for the Naval Division, the real proof of success.

It may be convenient to summarize here the final arrangements for this attack, though these were not, of course, definitely settled till the middle of November. The first and third of these objectives were to be attacked by the 1st Royal Marines, the Howe, the Hawke, and the Hood Battalions, each advancing in four waves. The second and fourth objectives were to be attacked by the 2nd Royal Marines, the Anson, the Nelson, and the Drake Battalions. The plan, in detail, was that the first four battalions would rest on the first objective (that is, in the enemy's front-line trenches) and reorganise, while the other four battalions passed through and captured the Station Road Valley and the Green Line. They, in their turn, would rest and reorganise, while the first four battalions passed through to the Yellow Line. The final assault on Beaucourt was then, after another pause, to be carried out by the battalions who had reorganised on the Green Line. With each battalion was to go a subsection of the brigade machine-gun company, and trench mortars were to follow as soon as possible.

So much for the ground to our front and the objectives of the forthcoming battle. These, however, occupied but a small portion of our thoughts. The triple *rôle* of the infantry, sappers, beasts of burden, and fighting troops never pressed more heavily than it did at this place and at this time. The villages behind the line, which we of the Hawke must always associate with the rather weary period of waiting before the attack of November 13th, were Mesnil and Engelbelmer. Both were entirely deserted by the civilian inhabitants, and Mesnil was only a heap of ruins covering insecurely a handful of cellars, where, when in support, we sat and shivered underground by day and night alike. Engelbelmer provided at least a little comfort, though very little safety. Here by day men could walk about or sit down above ground with at least a roof over their heads.

When at Engelbelmer, however, we were required to supply working and digging parties to our total available strength, and a good deal beyond it, every night. These parties began with a march of three miles or more to the trenches at Hamel. From there would be an

Scene of the Hawke Battalion advance in the Ancre Valley,
November 13, 1916

impossible progress through slime and mud, either to dig assembly trenches in the open or, worse still, carrying up trench-mortar ammunition. This routine was punctually carried out, but the only possible result was a high wastage from sickness directly due to over-exertion and exposure. From this cause alone the Hawke Battalion lost nearly 150 men before the time came for it to go into action.

The real difficulty was the condition of the trenches as taken over by the division. These were indescribably dirty, with no deep dugouts, no traverses, in some places barely knee-deep, and planned without the slightest regard for any military consideration. Possible lines of communication on the lower slopes leading down into the Ancre Valley had either never been opened up, or had been allowed to fall into disrepair for lack of proper drainage. Now a wet autumn had come, and at a time when material had to be brought forward in vast quantities for the impending attack there was only one shallow trench leading over the exposed crest of the ridge above Hamel, without drainage or duckboards, and cut out of chalk which gave inadequate foothold even to officers lightly equipped.

For working parties the conditions were insupportable, and they were worse for the garrison in the line, many of whom could not even sit down, but could only stand forlornly in the mud for hours on end. Did they curse the enemy or those nearer to them ? They must have cursed someone, for the Hawke Battalion, thank Heaven, were human, but I have often wondered precisely what they thought. There was only one consolation, that they never cursed us. We were fellow-victims; that, at least, was accounted to us for righteousness.

The tendency to curse had been accentuated by the misfortune sustained by the division within a few days of their arrival at Forceville, when General Paris was severely wounded in the course of a reconnaissance of the trenches. He had been succeeded in command by Major-General C. D. (now Sir Cameron) Shute, in later times a friend, and even an admirer, of the division. At this critical period, however, he expressed himself much dissatisfied, and it was rumoured, I believe with complete accuracy, that he had asked G.H.Q. to replace a very large number of the senior officers of the naval battalions (by no means excluding the Hawke) with army officers.

The news was hardly welcome, but it was less immediately troublesome than the general's fondness for inspecting guards, billets, and trenches. Guards were not our strong point, and the efforts made by the Hawke Battalion guard to turn out before the general's car had actually passed did not offer any attraction as a subject for a wager, for the car invariably won by several lengths. Our only triumph was when a formal complaint was lodged on one occasion by the general himself that the guard had not turned out at all. It was explained, at first gently and then firmly, that there was no guard there, but only one sentry, who, as far as could be ascertained, had done everything that the drill-book prescribed for these difficult occasions.

Yet our triumph was short-lived, for General Shute, equal to any emergency, visited us in the line the next day. This time we had no answer, for it had been raining at least a fortnight, and the General's statement that the trenches were in a disgracefully muddy condition could not be denied. Another trouble was the habit of our predecessors in the line of using boxes of S.A.A. to pave the trenches. They were not wholly ineffective, but their presence, however deep down below the surface, was bound to be discovered, as until one's foot touched one of these one continued to sink. The result, as will be realized, was that whenever General Shute was standing anywhere sufficiently firmly to be able to criticize with his accustomed vehemence, he was standing on a box of S.A.A., which, according to orders reiterated every day, had no business to be there. The crisis came when George Peckham, rising to the occasion with every appearance of indignation, ordered the offending box to be instantly removed. It was removed, and disclosed a box of bombs of the most precious and costly variety, which might, moreover, be expected to explode on far less provocation than that afforded by a general's boot.

Between Mesnil, Engelbelmer, the trenches, and General Shute, the Hawke Battalion spent a troubled and laborious five weeks, varied only by an excursion to Hédauville and Puishvillers, where the sun came out for the first time for weeks, and we went hurriedly back to the line after a brigade inspection by the divisional general, and a pleasantly informal visit from the commander-in-chief, who inspected the companies one by one on their company parade grounds, and searched vainly for members of the senior service among the officers and N.C.O.'s till at last, despite a strong measure of encouragement from George Peckham, who persuaded himself that on this particular occasion he was a Marine, Sir Douglas Haig gave it up in despair just before shaking hands with our own only authentic sailor.[1]

Our stay at Puishvillers was, however, marked by one incident of great moment—the first encounter between General Shute and Cod-

1. Lieutenant Wallis, R.N.V.R.

ner's beard. The epic significance of this and subsequent incidents was set out in A. P. Herbert's *"Ballad of Codson's Beard,"* which appeared in *Punch* shortly after the incident on which it was founded, and there was, indeed, much that was typical of the Hawke Battalion and of the whole Naval Division, both in the beard and the poem. A quality of unconventional exuberance, perhaps justifiable, but certainly in need of justification. Yet we could not have selected a better issue on which to challenge the military hierarchy. Our guards might be slovenly, our transport muddy, our trenches paved with bombs, but our beards were an unassailable prerogative. If we had lost Codner's beard, for it became soon far more ours than his, we lost everything.

By November 9th, however, even Codner was forgotten, for we were back in the line, and the attack on the Serre-Beaumont-Hamel-Beaucourt positions, so many times postponed, was finally ordered for 5 a.m. on November 13th. The remaining days were occupied with the reissue and distribution of stores—in rather unmanageable quantities—and with the completion of the arrangements for the assembly of some thousands of troops on to the frontage normally allotted to a single battalion. We ourselves, being in occupation of the right sector up to the time of the attack, were intimately concerned. The main difficulty was that the two battalions to lead the attack on the brigade front, the Hawke (on the left) and the Hood (on the right), had to be lined up on the forward slope of our position, since the reverse slope of the very steep crest of the ridge was needed to conceal the two supporting battalions. Farther back still, in what were, normally, the reserve and support companies' trenches, had to be packed two battalions of the 190th Brigade.

In addition, there were attached to each line of the attack details of the machine-gun companies, trench-mortar batteries, etc., for whom special assembly positions had to be found. To move these numbers of heavily encumbered men within two to five hundred yards of a watchful enemy would have been none too easy at any time. As it was, the operation was attended with every element of risk, since the condition of the trenches, and still more the absence of adequate communications, made movement very slow, made it impossible to retrace any false step, and made retirement impossible in the event of the enemy detecting movement and opening a bombardment.

Unfortunately for us the battalions whose ultimate position was in front had to be first in position, and we, being already in the line, and having to make room for others, were actually first to move, as early as

6 p.m., on the 12th November.

Before that, on the morning of the 12th, all "surplus" personnel had gone back to the transport lines in Hedarville. These included the second in command and the assistant adjutant, one company commander (Lieutenant Cotter), and three seconds-in-command of companies (Lieutenant Wallis, Lieutenant Melland, and Lieutenant Matthews). As we left our comfortable Battalion Headquarters a fierce, though happily brief, bombardment broke out along the only communication trench, a bombardment which tragically killed Colonel Saunders of the Drake Battalion. We, however, were luckier, everyone getting into position without a casualty. The imperturbable Peckham led up his company in his individual style, and was distinctly heard behind our lines halting his company on the forward slope of our position within a couple of hundred yards of the enemy as though he were back on the Blandford parade ground. Had the enemy overheard, it must surely have convinced them finally that no serious attack was impending, but whether they heard or not must remain uncertain. The important thing was that "D" company heard and appreciated once more their commander's imperturbable quality.

Of the four Hawke companies, "B" was on the left, next to Commander Fairfax's Howe Battalion. On the left was "C" company, strengthened by the two headquarters Lewis guns, and in touch with the left of the Hood Battalion; behind them were "A" and "D" companies; each company was in two waves of two platoons each, platoons being in single lines. The battalion was very much below strength to begin with, the average being about twenty-five N.C.O.'s and men in each platoon, and it had been further depleted by a heavy trench-mortar shell from one of our own batteries, which fell on one of "B" company's dugouts late on the afternoon of the 12th.

The damage was happily slight, but a large number of men were buried for some hours, and ten or more were too shaken to go forward. Incidentally, more than fifty men had to be hurriedly re-equipped, a contingency not foreseen, of course, by anyone, and thus causing an eleventh-hour renewal of hostilities between ourselves and the brigade staff. Ultimately the difficulty had been solved by the discovery of a salvage dump in Hamel, which provided stores good enough for a battle, though hardly up to the standard exacted on more serious occasions.

The night of the 12th to 13th November, memorable for individuals, is bare of detail for the historian. We waited in darkness, silence, and the most complete discomfort I shall ever experience for an event unknown in our own collective experience, stereotyped in the accidental circumstances of its routine, of importance to most now only in its recorded result, but to us a night of significance, marking the indisputable end of a period crowded with lively recollections which, for the last time, we could look back on without the company of ghosts.

Waiting for zero hour is a sufficiently common experience. On this occasion it was literally a case of waiting and nothing else. No movement of any kind was possible for platoon commanders or their men, lying out on the exposed slope of our position in trenches so narrow that one man could barely pass another. Battalion Headquarters, shared with the Nelson Battalion, who were to advance immediately behind us, was a minute affair where six people could neither sit down nor stand up, and every square yard of ground outside seemed to be taken up with men. For a time we occupied ourselves in wondering whether the intermittent shells passing over our heads were the beginning of a destructive bombardment which must bring irretrievable disaster. But even this topic languished after a time.

The plain fact was that everything had gone off with peace and quiet, and for five whole hours we were even spared a signal from Brigade Headquarters. At 4 a.m. there was a sudden change. The time of waiting was almost over; the last orders had been given hours since; but officers and N.C.O.'s could be seen, or rather felt, on all sides creeping about, bringing sleeping men to life with impalpable gestures, repeating in whispers for the thousandth time the vital points in the orders, synchronizing watches, satisfying themselves, if no one else, that they were not only eager, but ready, for the fateful hour of attack.

A little later Battalion Headquarters, reduced to a skeleton—Colonel Wilson and his adjutant, Bowerman (now bombing officer), two or three runners, P.O. Macdonald, and some signallers—moved forward to the front line to watch the battalion go forward, and to go forward themselves at the earliest opportunity to the enemy second line. Battalion Headquarters was to "move forward in bounds," according to divisional orders, and were not to misdemean themselves by that halting and painful stumbling across shell-holes swept by machine-guns, littered with barbed wire, and populated with dead and dying men, which is the only mode of progress open to less exalted personages across a battlefield. Still, it was going to be an interesting experience, and we prepared to "bound" with the best possible grace, if with the least possible anticipation of success.

Suddenly, standing talking in the front-line, one was overcome by the silence—a rare thing when 10,000 men are concentrated in as many square yards. We looked at our watches. One minute to five. Another moment—we, too, were silent now—and then a deafening explosion, and the smoke and fumes of war were added to the thick November mist. Without a word, without half a second's hesitation, we saw the first wave of the battalion move from their trenches and pass into the mist and out of sight while they were still not more than 70 yards away. At intervals of less than half a minute the other waves followed. Soon the fourth wave, 50 yards behind the others, was itself out of sight. Through the November mists, deafened by the explosion of guns, almost choked with fumes of lyddite, blinded by smoke, we saw the last of the Hawke Battalion as we had known it.

Less than twenty of those men, and none of those officers, came back unhurt. We went into action with twenty officers and 415 men. Our official casualties were twenty-three officers and 396 men.

This may read like an anticipation of the results of a two-days' battle, crowded with incident, uniquely successful in its results. In actual fact, during the ten minutes that Colonel Wilson and his headquarters watched the battle from the front line almost the whole of these casualties had been incurred.

Looking out on the front nothing could be seen, and not a man came back. Our barrage could be heard moving forward, and there was every reason to imagine a sweeping and immediate success. Either the battalion had reached and entered the front line, or it was held up and was fighting in no-man's-land (which it certainly was not). So we reasoned, little guessing the truth.

At 5.20 a.m. we went forward, feeling our way through the smoke and debris of battle till we got a sight of the enemy front line, only to be fired on by the enemy machine guns, undamaged by the barrage, dominating what should have been a captured position.

As we lay out, such of us as had survived, we could take some stock of the position, which remained, however, inexplicable to us, since, owing to the lie of the ground, we could see but little to our right and left. There were, indeed, very many wounded and dead lying like ourselves in shell-holes, or where they had fallen in front of the German wire. But not the whole even of the Hawke Battalion. Yet the whole stretch of front line which we could see was, as a matter of visible fact, in possession of the enemy. It was, of course, the now famous redoubt which faced us, the whole strength of which had been directed against the Hawke Battalion, who attacked directly opposite to it.

On the left of the redoubt, in touch with the right of the Howe Battalion, Vere Harmsworth, wounded for the first time in no-man's-land, led the relics of his company to the second line. Here the last of them were hit, and Harmsworth himself mortally wounded. Sub-Lieutenant J. A. Cooke of this company was also killed, and Sub-Lieutenant Paton seriously wounded. Here, too, fell C.P.O. Nadin, a fighting Irishman with all the characteristic qualities and defects of a rare but genuine type, who had first attracted notice in the engagement of June 19th at Gallipoli. "A" company, following behind "B," had the same disastrous experience. Nine-tenths of them fell in front of the redoubt. Only a few on the left got through, but in such numbers as to be too weak to overcome the enemy garrison in the second line. Three officers of this company (Rush himself and two platoon commanders, R. C. Gibb and Rowden) were wounded in front of the first German line, and Sub-Lieutenant A. C. Black was killed a moment or two later. "C" company, on the right of the battalion front, and "D" company supporting them, had almost the same experience, except that on the extreme right, where the ground sloped away to the Ancre and was "dead" to the garrison of the redoubt, some twenty men and two officers (Sub-Lieutenant Stewart and Sub-Lieutenant Henderson) got through on the flank of the Hood Battalion.

Seven or eight of them, and about as many from "D" company, actually joined up with the Hood Battalion, and fought through to the Yellow Line in front of Beaucourt. Both officers, however, were wounded in the neighbourhood of Station Road, though Stewart, before being hit, was able to do some damage with a Lewis gun, which he brought through and trained against the enemy garrison in the Green Line till it was reached and carried by the Hood and Drake Battalions on his right. Sly, the remaining platoon commander of this company, was wounded in no-man's-land, and Ker, the acting company commander, was killed in front of the redoubt. In front of the same position fell Poole, Turnbull, and Knight, of "D" company, and at the same time and place Lieutenant-Commander George Peckham was seriously wounded. Battalion Headquarters, going over a little later, as has been told, suffered in the same way; Colonel Wilson and his Adjutant were wounded within two minutes of going over, and the same burst of fire killed the signalling officer, Lieutenant Edwards, and the brave and tireless P.O. Macdonald, who died trying characteristically to go forward after being once severely hit.

Surgeon Ward went forward a little later with Surgeon Cox of the Nelson, and reached the front line to the right of the redoubt, where he was killed by a bomb thrown in the course of the fighting here being carried on by the Drake arid Nelson Battalions in the endeavour, ultimately successful, to localise the activities of the unconquered redoubt. Incidentally it may be explained that the same essential but very difficult task was undertaken on the left of the redoubt by the Howe Battalion, led by Commander Ramsay Fairfax in person.

This is not the place for an account of the long, hard-fought, and complex battle of the Ancre. The full story has been written elsewhere. The share of the Hawke Battalion, which, as a battalion, ceased after the first five minutes to exist, has been told. Like all battalions, we had our cynics and our pessimists, but the reality of this, our first full-dress battle, surpassed all imagined possibilities. And yet the battalion had played its part. While the German machine gunners, untouched by the barrage, took toll of the eight lines of the Hawke and Nelson, directed frontally against a position which (granted its extraordinary immunity from our severe bombardment) was absolutely proof against infantry assault, the attack swept by on either side, and the lodgements effected by the Howe on the left and the Drake on the right (with a few of the Hawke officers and men living for perhaps half an hour on the flanks of either battalion) were consolidated. The redoubt and its garrison were isolated, and their efforts to bomb outwards and to clear their flanks were delayed till it was too late for success.

The point of controversy is the immunity of the garrison of the redoubt from the effects of the barrage. One explanation was that the Hawke must have fallen behind the barrage; another that in the dense mist the first waves had passed the redoubt, and thus enabled the garrison, lying concealed while the barrage rested on the first and second lines, to come up behind them. Neither explanation is accurate. So well did the men follow the barrage that they had, according to Sub-Lieutenant Sly, who led one of the platoons in the first wave, to be halted while crossing no-man's-land. As for missing the redoubt, no one got past the redoubt, except at a considerable distance on either flank.

The only possible explanation, and the true one, is that the exact position of the redoubt was unknown to us, that for this reason no special artillery bombardment was arranged for, and that a strongly fortified group of machine guns, skilfully and bravely handled, was proof against the strategy of the creeping barrage. The point need not be elaborated here. The new strategy of infiltration is, in fact, the expert answer to what is now an admitted fact. Specially strong positions can only be dealt with by special measures. As far as the infantry are concerned, they must be passed by and isolated. The doctrine, like most maxims of war, is as old as the fortress warfare of centuries ago, but it had been forgotten, and to this plain fact is due the annihilation of the Hawke and Nelson Battalions, as well as of a large part of the Howe and Anson. As it was, these battalions had their orders, and they carried them out.

Hardly to be wondered at, in the circumstances, that there are no recorded instances of personal achievement on the part of officers or men of the Hawke in the engagement. Some were wounded mortally, others recovered, and there is little else that can be said. The only officers unwounded were Sub-Lieutenant Bowerman (not detailed for the attack, but charged only with the organisation of the supply of bombs, but who found occasion, nevertheless, to go forward and get valuable information) and A. P. Herbert, who went up with Major Norris late on the evening of the 13th to join Colonel Freyberg's force in front of Beaucourt. These two officers were present at the actual assault on Beaucourt, a strange, almost ridiculous climax to a desperate engagement, when two thin lines of tired men charged up the shell-swept hill into the German stronghold in a desperate adventure against heavy odds, only to be met by an instantaneous capitulation from a far superior force, who bore down in unarmed scores upon their 200 assailants.

On November 14th the Naval Division was relieved, and the remnants of the different battalions assembled and reorganised in the captured front-line system—the redoubt having surrendered to a tank attack in the early morning of the same day, actually an hour or so before the fall of Beaucourt. Lieutenant-Commander Lockwood, till then acting as brigade intelligence officer, took over command of the Hawke, the only other officers with him being A. P. Herbert, Bowerman, and Rackham. Major Norris, who had, as we have said, taken part in the capture of Beaucourt, was wounded in the severe bombardment which had followed on our success. Sub-Lieutenant Gold, who had gone up at the same time, had been killed during the assault.

The number of N.C.O.'s and men of the Hawke collected on the ground after the battle was under twenty, and the total remaining with the battalion was not much more than a hundred, including transport men, cooks, N.C.O.'s kept in reserve in accordance with orders, men on leave, quartermaster-sergeants, and men on detached duties. These all joined up with Commander Lockwood at Engelbelmer, from where the battalion was taken in motor-buses to Arquéves, well behind the fighting zone. Here, on the 16th November, a memorial service was held for those of the battalion who had been killed in the engagement. "A very pathetic little battalion" is the simple description in the unemotional battalion diary of the attendance at this service.

And then, rightly, the future takes hold again, and the diarist records only the details of the march back from Arquéves to St. Firmin, with halts each night at Gezaincourt, Berneuil, Garennes, and le Plessiel, when not a man fell out in the five days of marching, and generals halted the battalion at intervals to express their "satisfaction."

Soon, indeed, the sun came out again, but not at once in its spring-time brilliance. The Hawke Battalion as it had gone into action, could look back on two years of varied experiences shared in common. The old atmosphere could never quite be recaptured. What new commanding officer would fight the battalion's battles with Colonel Wilson's determination and almost unfailing success? What was "B" company without Vere Harmsworth, always fighting friend and enemy alike on behalf of his company, and usually carrying the day by sheer force of personality; or "C" company without Ker, so gifted that his most strenuous efforts seemed effortless, yet moved to vehemence by patent folly or injustice—a personality of rare promise and still rarer charm.

Nor could "D" company be quite the same without George Peck-ham, happily recovering from innumerable wounds, but not likely again to be late on parade, or to break through a hedge in the middle of a commander-in-chief's inspection, called from the neighbouring estaminet by a sense of duty not diluted with too much soda. In-evitably we write of those whom we knew best; others, would write differently, and with equal truth. The loss of friends is a stern reality which calls for no pose of reticence, least of all in the record of bat-talions which, if they be not cemented by good fellowship, will never be hammered into fighting trim by discipline.

"Discipline," however, was precisely what, at this point, the army authorities deemed to be necessary. And St. Firmin threatened to rain down an unending supply of "competent army officers" to step into the shoes of those men of a different stamp whose achievements, paid for to the uttermost farthing, had given so much "satisfaction."

The situation, as far as the Hawke was concerned, was limited to the arrival of a Commanding Officer (Lieutenant-Colonel Whiteman of the Middlesex Regiment) and a second in command (Major Freeland of the Indian Army). But the threat of further incursions was a real one, and the relations between the fighting troops and their commanders grew decidedly strained. Minor causes of war were Codner's beard and Herbert's idealisation of the late William Whiteley as the ideal brigade commander (a thesis advanced for the personal edification of General Phillips,[2] with memorable results), but the solid grievance was the scheme, ultimately defeated by the zeal of friends at home, for formally militarizing the division by re-enlisting the men and recommissioning the officers.

This must have meant, definitely and finally, the end of the Hawke, as of the other naval battalions, for the proposal was to give the officers commissions on the "general list." They would thus have been available for service with any formation, and the division would, there is no doubt, have been used, on the first convenient occasion, as drafts for other regiments. The scheme sounded purely destructive—and, indeed, in ultimate effect it would have been so. But the immediate object was to reduce the seniority of the R.N.V.R. officers by transforming the R.N.V.R. lieutenants into the army lieutenants, and so opening the way for the infiltration of captains from other divisions to command companies in the Naval Battalions.

There was a schoolboyish simplicity about this plan which makes it difficult even to guess at its origin. The bait, clearly, was supposed to be transformation of our uncouth semi-civilian, semi-naval selves into "*pukka*" soldiers, for which no price seemed higher than we should be ready to pay. Commander Lockwood, as became an obedient commanding officer, represented the merits of the scheme to the Hawke officers and men during their first week at St. Firmin, but the response was not encouraging.

Colonel Whiteman was no more successful, and after a few weeks nothing more was heard of the proposal. Instead, the work of reorganising the battalion was put in hand. A. P. Herbert naturally became Adjutant, with B. B. Rackham as Assistant Adjutant. "A" company was commanded by Lieutenant Wolfe Barry (the original "D" company commander), "B" by Lieutenant Matthews (lately second in command "B" company), "C" by Lieutenant-Commander Shelton (the original Adjutant), and "D" by Lieutenant Ellis (promoted). Two other officers who rejoined the battalion were Sub-Lieutenants Blackmore and

---

2. Commanding the 189th Brigade.

Wilkes, both of whom were attached to "D" company. With these and the officers left out of the November attack—Sub-Lieutenants Collins, Lyell, Bowerman, Elphick, and O'Hagan—and with the Transport Officer and Quartermaster remaining, the battalion was a good bit more experienced than had seemed likely on November 14th. Among the N.C.O.'s, Sergeant-Major Sands and C.P.O. Malpress were still available, and under their supervision a new generation of company sergeant-majors and platoon sergeants, many of them newly arrived N.C.O.'s from Blandford, soon found their feet.

With the progress of reorganisation, helped by Christmas festivities, the poker parties began again, with alternating evenings of song and dance to more topical tunes than those on which we had to rely in those dim backwater days before General Shute made the most historic of his inspections. For officers of junior rank, the only problem presented by these evenings of lyrical exuberance was the tendency of voices to carry in the quiet of the early morning as far even as the Colonel's billet.

On the Somme this risk was minimized by a series of sound tests timed to synchronise with dinner at Battalion Headquarters. I forget the first test; it was mild, and usually quite inaudible. But the crucial test was the singing of "Michigan"; and on more than one occasion an echo of the chorus reached the headquarters mess. "What was that?" the colonel would ask, scenting possibly a visitation from enemy aeroplanes, or an untimely encounter between General Shute and a sentry improperly dressed. But no one could solve the mystery. The evening's concert, however, would be moved to a more outlying billet, where our anxiety "to go back" could be voiced with completer freedom. The alternative of a quieter rendering had seemed somehow inappropriate to the mood of those exciting days.

Now at St. Firmin they had changed the words and the voices, but the tune was surely the same. In the same spirit the battalion was going back to the old battlefield. "Do you remember? . . ." Yes, they remembered well enough, as they marched past Hamel on January 19th along the Ancre Valley, where Freyberg had shown the way only two months ago up to the Yellow Line, now the support position to our front-line trenches beyond Beaucourt.

CHAPTER 8

# A Fruitless Victory

The Hawke Battalion in 1917, on the Ancre, at Gavrelle, at Passchendaele, and at Welsh Ridge, were taking part in active fighting almost continuously and almost as a matter of routine.

To give a detailed and critical account of the military operations in which the battalion took part in this troubled and disastrous year would require a separate volume. The passage of historic events in Europe, in Asia, in America, and on the high seas, one and all directly influencing the character and conditions of the infantry battle, could not be ignored. Still less could the ill-concerted but unfortunately interdependent actions of the different Armies, French and English, on the western front. Why was it that the Hawke Battalion, victorious in November and reaping, in two small engagements in February, 1917, fruits almost unexpected, sharing in May in the successful attack on Gavrelle, and in November in the slow, cruel, costly, but still victorious advance to the Passchendaele Ridge, should in December of the same year have been fighting for its life, and incidentally for the safety of our line, on Welsh Ridge? Victory followed victory, advance followed advance, in all weathers and at all points, yet the enemy by the end of the year had placed us on the defensive.

Was it merely that we were outmanoeuvred? Should the pursuit to the Hindenburg line, to which the laborious and costly efforts of the Naval Division on the Ancre were so definite a contribution, have been an action of a different character, pressed to a more decisive conclusion ? Should the success at Gavrelle have been exploited ? Should the Naval Division, instead of dissipating its strength at Passchendaele, have been thrown in two months earlier into the gamble of Cambrai? Or was it only that the pressure of outside events dictated our tactics and our strategy, and led us as irresistibly to the *débâcle* of March as to

138

the subsequent victory of November, 1918?

Grave questions these for the historian, but not to be discussed here. They were in the background of men's thoughts, and overcast the different scenes with lengthening shadows, but not as questions calling for an answer. Front-line troops in the grip of events assume easily the *role* of Pilate. They may doubt, but they cannot wait for an answer, and the intervals of reflection are devoted to jesting.

In the circumstances this record of the 1917 fighting will be predominantly personal in character, based as far as possible on contemporary letters and notes, and ignoring to a large extent the why and wherefore of the engagements which followed each other in quick succession.

On January 18th, 1917, the Hawke Battalion had, on their way forward, reached La Vicogne, and on the 19th they moved up in buses to the old Yellow Line just behind Beaucourt. For three days the battalion supplied working parties to the Nelson lying in shell-holes in front of Beaucourt; the Hawke Headquarters were near the village, with a reserve company in old German dugouts. On January 23rd the battalion went "into the line." There was no line; only a number of shell-holes half-joined to each other, which were no sooner joined than abandoned. We were slowly creeping forward up the slope behind Beaucourt towards the enemy trench system (Puisieux and River trenches) on the ridge which commanded Grandcourt across the Ancre. Beyond this ridge lay another, covering Miraumont, Pys, and the gun positions behind Serre. When these two ridges (with the corresponding positions across the Ancre) were in our hands, the enemy would, it was anticipated, be forced to retreat; as things were, our position was as bad as it could be.

Beaucourt itself lay in a hollow, honeycombed indeed with excellent dugouts and trenches, but thoroughly familiar to the enemy, who watched us from Puisieux trench. As we pushed our posts forward (the Hawke made some 300 yards of ground on the 24th January) we merely got closer to the enemy, more directly under his observation, farther from our own reserves. The garrisoning of our outpost line was not a task for novices. It could not be visited by day, and had to be rationed by night at great risk, not only from the enemy's fire, but of losing the way and wandering into the enemy lines. In the different posts themselves movement was virtually impossible, and without movement it was bitterly, dangerously, cold.

Lieut. A. P. Herbert inspecting the Guard at St. Firmin, December, 1916

The battalion had, it was soon learnt, been sent into the line in preparation for an attack against the trenches immediately in front of them, and as soon as they had had time to learn the lie of the ground they were relieved and sent back to Forceville for the final preparations.

This was on the 26th January, and the next day they marched even farther back to Lealvillers, where the usual preliminaries of battle, conferences, inspections, speeches, rehearsals of the attack, night operations, and the interminable issue and reissue of stores, occupied nearly a week. The only sign of improved organisation was that, when the last order had been cancelled for the last time, and the time came to move off, motor-buses were provided as far as Mesnil, where, as once before, the battalion had to bid a provisional goodbye to the comparative comfort which even a ruin affords in the middle of a desert.

As before, the battalion's stay in Mesnil was short, and they moved forward at dusk to the old German front-line position, the accepted station of the support battalion. On February 3rd they moved forward to their assembly positions in no-man's-land, in front of the line of outposts.

The formation for the attack repeated that of November 13th, the Hood coming in on the right of the Hawke to attack along the Ancre Valley, while the Hawke moved to the left of the battalion sector and attacked with the Hood on their right. Here, however, the resemblance ended. This was battle in miniature: a fight by two battalions for the crest of a hill immediately to their front, with the river as a natural protection on the right, and a disused communication trench (Artillery Alley) running at right angles from the left of the objective into our own support lines, as an artificial boundary on the left.

The left of the objective, and the responsibility for forming a defensive flank, was assigned to Lieutenant-Commander Shelton's "D" company. On the right of that came "B" company (Lieutenant Matthews), and between "B" and the Hood was "D" company (Lieutenant Ellis). "A" company was in support.

The novel feature of the attack was that it was to be made at night. It was timed for 11 p.m. on February 3rd, and was to be made in two waves, the first of which had to push on to the enemy's second line (River Trench), while the second "mopped up" the first objective (Puisieux Trench). The only exception was in the case of the left. ("C") company, when there were three waves, the third of which had to assist the Nelson Battalion to form the defensive flank.

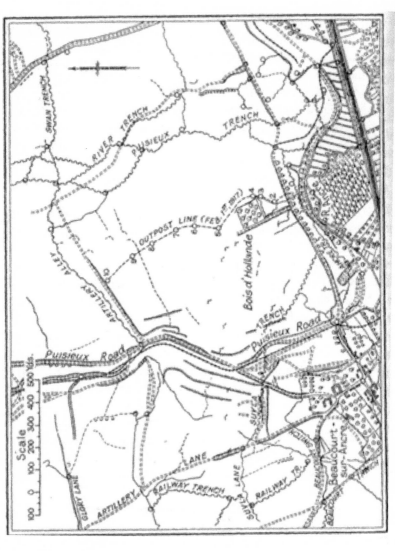

MAP ILLUSTRATING OPERATIONS OF THE HAWKE BATTALION EAST OF BEAUCOURT, JANUARY–FEBRUARY, 1917

Except on the "D" company front, everything at the start went according to plan, the barrage was perfect, and "D" and "B" companies both reached their objectives. The 6th Platoon (of "B" company), under Sub-Lieutenant Stephenson, distinguished itself by capturing a strong point and its garrison of sixteen men with little loss, while P.O. Rosewarne and L. S. Ker of "C" company showed the greatest gallantry in capturing a hostile machine gun between Puisieux and River Trenches, which threatened for a few minutes to hold up the advance of the left flank.

On "D" company's front the position was less satisfactory. Here history had repeated itself, and the Hawke Battalion had found itself faced with a machine-gun redoubt with a garrison consisting of thirty-two N.C.O.'s and men and a large number of machine guns. The principal lesson of the November battle had been that such positions, when they could not be rushed under the barrage, must be "got round." These tactics were employed on this occasion, two platoons of "D" company under Sub-Lieutenant Blackmore going to the left of the strong point, and the remaining two platoons (Sub-Lieutenant Wilkes and Sub-Lieutenant Cowley) going to the right and keeping in touch with the Hood Battalion. That battalion, however, had lost direction temporarily, and when Commander Asquith took over command and brought them back to their alignment it was daylight, and touch could not be established with the rest of the Hawke Battalion. The dawn of February 4th thus found us with a gap in our line, and the enemy still in possession of a *point d'appui* in our first objective.

The early hours of the 4th February was spent in hard and continuous fighting, especially on the left, when Commander Shelton's company were persistently attacked, and in the centre, when continuous but unsuccessful attempts were made to close the gap in our line, and so force the enemy post to surrender.

The difficulty on the left was that, although verbal arrangements had been made for the co-operation of the Hawke and Nelson Battalions in forming our defensive flank, the plan had been apparently misunderstood, and the Nelson Battalion were not in position.

Commander Shelton writes:

Somewhere near 4 a.m., the enemy counter-attacked, and a number of them broke through on the left flank, which I discovered was absolutely in the air.

Luckily I had left a couple of Lewis guns in Puisieux Trench,

and these successfully dealt with the few men who had broken through. I realized, however, that the situation was rather
desperate, as if the enemy counter-attacked in force again the
chances were they would roll up my flank.

I sent down a runner with an urgent message to Battalion
Headquarters in the sunken road, requesting that men should
be sent up immediately to cover this flank. There was a gap of
about 400 yards. I waited for two hours, then sent down another. Nothing happened.

I sent off my last runner just before dawn. Still nothing happened.

It turned out afterwards that none of these runners arrived, as
they were knocked out on the way down by a sniping post operating on the open flank. This post, which caused a number of
casualties, was not located and captured until late in the afternoon, when one of two guns of the 189th Trench Mortar Battery came into action against it. In the meantime 'A' company
had reinforced 'B' and 'D', and so were not available for this very
important flank.

During the morning things were comparatively quiet— with
the exception of a good deal of shelling—but in the afternoon
the Germans counter-attacked again on 'C' company's front,
luckily not in great force, and we managed to drive them off.

The main trouble was caused by the sniping post, which succeeded in picking off any man who showed himself.

When evening came I realized that something had to be done,
so I decided to go down to Battalion Headquarters myself and
get hold of some men somehow. Taking Petty Officer Rosewarne with me, I started off. The shelling was very unpleasant,
but we managed to reach Battalion Headquarters— a little tin
shanty cut into the side of the sunken road. On arriving, the
Boche started to shell very heavily with 5.9's, enfilading the
entire road. One shell landed on top of the signallers' dugout
and knocked most of them out.

Battalion Headquarters was soon full of wounded. The M.O.
(Surgeon Padwick, R.N.) worked like a Trojan, and showed
great coolness and gallantry under very trying circumstances.
For this and other gallant acts he was awarded the D.S.O. .

The colonel said that he had no men for me, so Rosewarne
and I went out to try and find some. Luckily we came across

a Drake carrying party of about 100 men lying up on the side of the road. I ordered the officer in charge to drop most of the rations—with the exception of rum—and follow us up the line. The shelling seemed to have died down a little, and we started off.

On the way up we suffered seven casualties, two officers of the Drake and several of the men being killed.

We arrived eventually, and placed the men out along the unprotected flank, just in time to stave off another counterattack. The rum was more than useful, as the men were half-starved with the cold, the temperature being not far off zero. They had a thundering good tot, which put new life into them.

The achievement of "C" company in resisting the steady pressure of the enemy against an exposed flank for more than twenty-four hours was all the more remarkable because of the desperate conditions. The intense cold, the impossibility of effectual consolidation because of the frozen ground, and, above all, the fact that the men had been compelled by a piece of incredible folly to leave their overcoats behind on the evening of the 3rd, and had been alternately fighting and shivering in 10 degrees of frost ever since, must have made the position appear desperate to a less resolute leader.[3]

The situation of "B" and "D" companies in the centre of our line was, all this time, hardly less unfavourable. They were still cut off from the right of the brigade line by the enemy strong point already mentioned, which held out all through the 4th, and was the focussing-point of a general counter-attack at dusk. All through the day the existence of this strong point hypnotised the attention of the Brigade Headquarters, who, on the one hand denied vigorously that it existed, and, on the other hand, gave continuous instructions for its capture, apparently regardless of the fact that the tactics which had led "D" company of the Hawke to go round it in the initial advance instead of attempting to rush it by frontal attack followed on General Shute's wholly correct enunciation of the outstanding lesson of the earlier Battle of the Ancre. Happily, the loss of life which might have ensued if a direct assault on this position had been carried out on the afternoon of the 4th was avoided, "A" company being drawn into the defensive battle on either flank. Not, however, until the morning of

---

3. For his services on this occasion Commander Shelton was awarded the D.S.O., and P.O. Rosewarne (who was recommended for the V.C.) the D.C.M.

the 5th did the enveloping policy have its reward, when the strong point surrendered to Sub-lieutenant Bowerman, who throughout had played the chief part[4] (with Sub-Lieutenant Lyall) in the action fought by "B" company and "D" company on the flank of the Hawke line.

From this point the fighting died down, though only gradually, and on the evening of the 5th a real soldiers' battle,[5] in which the Hawke Battalion did everything that was asked of it and a little more, ended with a brigade relief. In the initial assault the impetuous and always cheerful commander of "D" company—Lieutenant E. W. Ellis—was killed, going forward too far in front of his company in the excitement of an initial and courageous success, and Sub-Lieutenants Blackmore and Wilkes and Cowley were wounded. In the fighting of the 4th, Sub-Lieutenant Collins of "A" company (who had first joined the battalion at Gallipoli) and Sub-Lieutenant A. J. Rorke ("C" company) were also killed. Ninety-one N.C.O.'s and men fell in the course of the three days' fighting, and Sub-Lieutenant Cowley and eighty-seven N.C.O.'s and men were wounded. Yet this price was paid for a definite tactical success, having a direct and immediate result. The next day Grandcourt was evacuated, and the German retreat had begun.

The patrols which made the first discovery of what at the time seemed a decisive event, and was in any case one of the first importance, were from the Howe Battalion, but the Hawke Battalion may claim some share of the credit, for they went out under orders from Commander Ramsay Fairfax, and were commanded by Sub-Lieutenants A. M. Graham and H. M. Bunce, former N.C.O.'s of the public schools ("D") company of the Hawke.

From the time of the relief of the Hawke and Hood Battalions events moved swiftly. The marines entered Grandcourt on the 6th February, the H.A.C. took Baillescourt Farm (a position on the left bank of the Ancre beyond that reached by the Hawke and Hood in the battle of 3rd to 5th February) on the 7th, the Bedfords extended our gains on the left of the divisional front on the nth, and on the 17th another decisive advance was made by the Howe and Marine Battalions, advancing from the position won by the Hawke on the 3rd February to capture the enemy position on the ridge beyond.

---

4. All the "D" company officers became casualties very early in the engagement.
5. In addition to P.O. Rosewarne, L. S. Panton was awarded the D.C.M., and the following received the Military Medal: P.O. C. T. Hall, L. S. Ker, A.B. O'Connor, A.B. Baldwin, A.B. Baker, A.B. Brutnell, Pte. Maughan, and A.B. H. G. Williamson. Sub-Lieutenants Blackmore, Lyall, and Rackham were awarded the M.C.

This last advance was of importance because, while the ground so lay that the capture of Puisieux and River Trenches protected the Beaucourt Valley from direct observation and gave us command of the Ancre Valley even beyond Grandcourt, we did not ourselves command a view to our left front of more than 300 yards. The advance of the 17th took us to the edge of what was really a narrow plateau, and gave us observation of the enemy gun positions and communications with their front as far north as Serre. With this success the first battle of the Somme, begun in July, 1916, was over, and the enemy retreat over the whole area of those operations began at once.

During these later operations (when Commander Shelton was in command of the battalion, Colonel Whiteman being on leave) the Hawke Battalion was suffering severely from an epidemic of sickness, which, coming on the top of serious losses, meant that it was relegated to "odd jobs" in support for carrying parties and such-like. Sub-Lieutenant Bowerman, Lieutenant Matthews, Sub-Lieutenant Laughton, and Sub-Lieutenant Cookson were among those evacuated sick; there were actually only five company officers fit for duty on February 17th. About that time a thaw set in. The result, however, was only to change the conditions, not to improve them, except for troops sufficiently far behind the lines to be in huts or billets. The price of victory in the Somme country was a progressive discomfort, as one left farther and farther behind the virgin lands never reached by the enemy, and plunged forward into the ever-broadening belt of devastated country.

Of these conditions the battalion had a sorry experience throughout February and the beginning of March.

From the 10th February till the 16th (after only two days at Engelbelmer, once regarded as the borderland of hardship, now, in the changed conditions, as the refinement of luxurious ease) the battalion were in the old second and third German lines of the November battle, employed on fatigues and carrying parties, with intervals when they were under orders, in the best Gallipoli style, to move forward to Berlin at an hour, half an hour, even fifteen minutes' notice. Then on the 16th they went forward to the German positions which they had captured on February 4th, and supplied carrying parties throughout the fighting of the 17th, and also reinforcements for the defence of the positions captured by the Howe and the Royal Marines on that day. Here or hereabouts till the 19th, when they caught a glimpse of the robust and kindly personality of the new divisional commander (Major-General C. E. Lawrie, C.B.) against a fleeting background of civilization at Hedauville. Then, with a momentary rebirth of optimism, they moved to huts at Martinsart, only to move off in three days to a sea of derelict mud at Pozières with instructions to pitch tents.

At Pozières the Hawke Battalion headquarters, revitalized by the return of A. P. Herbert (he had been on leave during the February fighting), committed a serious breach of discipline by giving orders for the tents to be pitched on the few and admittedly irregularly situated dry spots. Field service regulations, however, were strong against any such proceeding, and the tents were hurriedly taken down and set up again at more seemly and disciplined intervals.

In these tents the battalion remained (resting) for a fortnight; the rest consisted in supplying working parties to the Canadians, who were hurriedly building light railways to enable the pursuit of the enemy (whose enforced retirement had been the confessed object of the operations on the Somme and Ancre since July, 1916) to be put in hand not less than a month after our final and decisive success. "Say, guy, you've got my outfit," was the usual form of address of the Canadian N.C.O.'s taking over from British officers the working parties supplied by the naval and other divisions at this time. Usually it was not his outfit, but someone else's, and the illicit acquisition of working parties, by all and sundry whose command of a suitable accent and idiom enabled them to pass to the untrained eye as lumbermen, was a feature of these days.

One of the Hawke officers who came out from Blandford at this time writes:

> The whole division was so employed, the tasks lasting six hours, with an hour's march with picks and shovels each way. It was then early March, and the division was said to be at rest. It was so cold under canvas, however, that the vigorous daily work was a godsend, as it was much too cold to sit about in camp and much too muddy to walk about in it, and the only alternative to work was to roll up in blankets and sleep.
>
> On these working parties I met many old friends, and one experienced some of those advantages we enjoyed in the division through not being subject to the Army pool which did more than anything to break up the *esprit de corps* of divisions as units. Wellwood of the Howe, Pound of the Drake, Grant-Dalton, and other contemporaries of Palace and Blandford days, all employed on the same task with us, brought us news of other units

in the division, and tales of their personal welfare since last we met. The Hessian and Regina Trenches and the Schwabian Redoubt were in the vicinity of our work, and we had time to inspect these positions, which had been such formidable objectives in the Somme battles.

The main road alongside which we lay was always congested with traffic to and from the front: tanks, caterpillar tractors, cars, guns, ambulances, motor pigeon-lofts, cavalry, mounted machine guns, pack animals, engineering outfits and pontoons, stretcher bearers and dispatch riders, and the infantry column of fours—muddied, battered, and cheeky coming down; grave and full of purpose going up. I thus received my initiation in gradual stages, and gained some knowledge of the atmosphere of war under very favourable conditions. In seeing the effect of high explosives on the battlefield, I marvelled that any could survive, but gained the salutary point of view that there is a large element of luck in the line, and a shell more or less did not matter provided one managed to dodge it.

This extract from a contemporary note by a Hawke officer who had just joined the battalion is interesting as a reminder that the heavy losses—wholly exceptional even at that place and time—sustained by the Naval Division between October, 1916, and March, 1917, were bringing out from Blandford the last, virtually, of those officers who had seen no previous active service with the division, and at the same time the remainder of those who, wounded earlier, were now fit again. Of these last there were, among Hawke officers, not very many; indeed, the return of Sub-Lieutenants Arnold Cooke and Bessel in February, of Lieutenant-Commander G. U. Price, the original commander of "B" company, and Sub-Lieutenant H. A. Burr in March, to be followed by Lieutenant W. Potts and Sub-Lieutenants R. S. Stewart and Tompkins in July, almost completes the list.

Of those who came out to the battalion for the first time in 1917 there were, however, very many, among them Lieutenant Langham Reed and Sub-Lieutenants Bartholomew, Stephenson, Wood, W. D. Watson (who succeeded Codner as transport officer when the affair of the beard finally developed into a crisis in July, 1917), H. W. Dickins, George Clark, N. F. Hill, and G. Sugden. Nor must we forget, belonging to neither category, Lieutenant F. W. Stear, once a chief petty officer (lent by the navy) of the Anson Battalion, promoted for his fine work on June 4th, 1915, and posted to the Hawke Battalion in June, 1917. The battalion never had a better company commander.

Battalion Headquarters, as appointed after the November battle, remained unaltered till after the fighting of May, 1917, round Gavrelle, but there were changes among the company commanders. Lieutenant-Commander Shelton went home in March to the Senior Officers' Course, and Geoffrey Price succeeded to the command of "C" company, and Lieutenant Ellis, killed on February 3rd, was succeeded in command of "D" by Lieutenant Melland, who had been second in command of "B" company in 1916. Lieutenant Matthews remained in command of "B" and Lieutenant Wolfe Barry of "A" company.

CHAPTER 9

# Anticlimax

On March 20th, 1917, the battalion finally left their tents in the Pozières mud (called by an ironic staff officer Spring Gardens Camp), and began their march to the green fields behind the Lens-Arras front. Halting on successive nights at Warloy, Pachevillers, Neuvilette, St. Biville, Bours, and Ligny-les-Aires, they reached their final destination at Belle Rive on March 26th.

Belle Rive was close to Bethune, on the La Bassee Canal, and the division had come into the XIIIth Corps area in reserve for the great attack, planned for April 9th, on the enemy positions on Vimy Ridge and south as far as eight miles beyond Arras. The XIIIth Corps were concentrated behind the extreme left of this fifteen-mile front, and even a little north of it. The intention was that they should push through to Lens, and extend the battle northwards as soon as Vimy had fallen and the enemy front to the south had broken.

What actually happened is a matter of history. In the centre of the line opposite Arras we were successful, and carried the three main enemy positions on the first day. The Canadian attack on Vimy Ridge was not, however, the triumphant success it was claimed to be, and on the extreme right of the attack, south of the Scarpe, the VIth Corps definitely failed. The situation of July 1st, 1916, had, in fact, repeated itself, and the enemy had held us on both flanks. In the circumstances, it was decided to proceed methodically with the capture of our original objectives, and to drop the attack on Lens.

With much flourish of trumpets the Naval Division was thus brought south, the move being announced as consequent on our unexpected success. Marching from Belle Rive, after twelve days' valuable rest and training, to Nœux-les-Mines, when they stood by for the first two days of the attack, the Hawke Battalion marched to Bethonsart, behind Arras, on April 12th. Here Colonel Whiteman, addressing the battalion drawn up on the village square deep in snow, announced on the authority of General Headquarters that "the Bosch was beaten." The war was to be won in three weeks, with the assistance of the French, the Italians, and the Russians. The commentary which lies before me of a listener to this audacious prophecy is not unworthy of Thucydides. "*We only knew what we were told, and believed what we wished for. Everyone felt confident of success.*"

The confidence was indeed justified as far as the battalion was concerned. They were rested and contented, and would give a good account of themselves. But the situation in Arras and in our front-line positions east of the city, to which the battalion moved on the 16th, was too familiar to savour of sudden or sweeping victory. Arras itself, to settle down later to its old state of comparative luxury and peace, was at this time painfully reminiscent of the hinterland of the Somme. The battalion's effort to march through it in column of route was unsuccessful. In that chaos of transport, excited staff officers in cars, military police, mud and debris from the intermittent bombardment the mere infantryman had to get along as best he could, which was in ones and twos, and slowly at that.

Survivors have, indeed, compared the conditions with those prevailing in the "rush hours" in London after the war. Beyond Arras were the captured German positions, well sited on the crest of a hill, but not for occupation by British infantry, who had pushed forward a mile and a half down the gentle slope which ran from these positions to Gavrelle, where the enemy were now concentrating their defence, well content with our advance, which gave us nearly 3,000 yards of communications in full view of their accurate and merciless artillery.

Nor was our line anything but precisely what the experienced officer expected. There were the familiar shell-holes, half-connected up with each other, and the support trench, handed over as "newly dug," which turned out to be a mere scratch in the mud; here, too, was the cold, the rain, the wind, and the snow which heralded every attack of this disastrous year.

The battalion's first task was to help the Nelson in digging and pushing forward. Then, on the 17th, to go into "the line" themselves, and dig and get forward. The assembly trenches for the Naval Division attack had to be 400 yards ahead of the posts taken over. "A" and "C" companies, with Lieutenant Wolfe Barry and Sub-Lieutenant Dickins in command (Geoffrey Price being behind the lines in charge of surplus battle personnel under the rule which insisted that at least one senior company commander should be kept in reserve), occupied the line, digging at night the new trenches, and then, on the 19th, occupying them.

The enemy shelling was extremely severe, particularly on the 18th and the 20th, and as the trenches were shallow and of course entirely without deep dugouts, things were as unpleasant as they could be. Lieutenant Wolfe Barry was gassed in the first bombardment, and Sub-Lieutenant Bessel took command of "A" company.

The conditions were almost painfully familiar.

One of the newly joined officers wrote:

On the night of the 16th,, we went to dig a line for the infantry to occupy close up to the enemy wire. This was my first working party under cover of darkness close to the line, and the quietness of the enemy was uncanny. The chief worry was chasing from pillar to post in obedience to ill-informed authority with a company of men in your wake in search of picks and shovels, and having finally found them in another place, navigating a course over the open ground to a rendezvous in the line in pitchy blackness from landmarks only momentarily revealed by the flash of guns or Verey lights.

On the evening of the 17th 'C' company relieved Major Wilkie and his company of Nelsons in the line. Little warning was given, and at 1 o'clock in the afternoon I set out with Hughes and P.O. Short to reconnoitre the road over the open. On the way up we passed an 18-pounder battery calibrating on the village, and watched the church spire fall. There were no communication trenches as yet to the line, and on reaching the Nelson Headquarters, housed in the concrete haystacks. Colonel Lewis told me that though runners had been to the front line by day, a party of more than two would invite trouble, as our movements from that point forward were well under enemy observation.

Selecting a fallen aeroplane as a rendezvous for 7 p.m., I sent Hughes back to bring up the company and meet me there at the appointed hour. P.O. Short and I reached the line by availing ourselves of the folds in the ground and what cover we could find, and dropped into the trench, rather as a surprise to its garrison. I arranged details of the relief with Major Wilkie, and left him with a joke about his promising beard, and got back to our aeroplane by 6.30 p.m. Then started the most anxious wait. With nightfall troops rose up in all directions—carrying parties, ration parties, and burial parties—but no sign of our company at the rendezvous. Hour after hour we waited, asking passers-by, too concerned with their own difficulties to heed anything but the obstacles in their path, if they had seen any Hawkes; but with 'Out of touch in rear,' 'Step short in front,' 'Wire on the right,' or 'Mind the shell-hole,' they passed along and out of sight.

After about four hours, hearing a rumour from some Nelson stragglers that Wilkie's company had left the line, we concluded that Hughes had got the company up, and that the Nelson relief had been made. The area had emptied as the relief had passed, and without guides P.O. Short and I essayed to join our company in the line. The task was beyond us. We had made the same journey that afternoon, but with the fall of night the line of trees along the Point du Jour road, which had been our guide in an otherwise featureless landscape, no longer served. We appear to have moved in circles.

After some hours of stumbling into deep holes and tearing ourselves on wire we decided to wait for dawn. We had had no food or drink since breakfast, and my P.O. was shaken with a fit of ague. He was a fine type of man, intelligent and plucky, but this groping about in the damp mists for too long had brought back his fever, and he was feeling pretty low when the first streak of dawn revealed our situation not a quarter of a mile from the company's position in the line. The absolute quiet of the front had deceived us.

Hughes had missed the aeroplane, but, meeting a Nelson guide, had wisely carried on and effected the relief.

We were in a shallow trench not more than waist high, and as yet not continuous—the trench we had dug a few nights before on our night working party: the kick-off trench for the impending operations—and about 11 o'clock on the morning of the 18th we were subjected to an intensive shelling from 5.9s and 12-inch. The splendour of the day was our undoing. After a very cold night in cramped positions in the earth the sun was too powerful to resist, and very soon movement above the surface and the fresh-turned earth advertised the fact of our advent.

Well, there was nothing to do but sit tight. Obviously, the enemy had no intention of attacking us at that place, as he lay snug behind acres of wire and his long-prepared defensive system. He knew we were to attack, as our sustained preparations had advertised, but that morning's work was merely routine work on his part on finding new targets, and we might well have been spared it! However, to sit tight was the only thing—foolish, unintelligent, extravagant, and all that, but to which no alternative existed—just bad luck. . . . We worked up and down our line, skipping out of one incomplete trench into another, and doing what one could to keep the men going. Hughes had gone down gassed, and also C.P.O. Todd. P.O. Short, my companion of the night, had gone down with fever, and I had four men killed by 3 p.m. and numerous small casualties. Mick Maloney agreed to stand fast on the right of our line where we joined the Hoods, and I went to the left, where we touched the Bedford flank, and, each looking after his end, we awaited events.

In the evening I was ordered to send back a party to B.H.Q., about 2,000 yards in rear, to draw picks and shovels with which to repair my trench. Mick moved off with thirty men, leaving me alone with a half-garrisoned trench; no particular harm in that, except that if the assumption that Fritz would not attack us was sound, why garrison in daytime with a whole company subject to shell-fire casualties, and withdraw half a company just at the time when a patrol or patrolling enemy force might have made an inquisitive sortie into our position? These thoughts, doubtless not too well reasoned and partly the outcome of the strafe of the preceding day, were, however, in my mind, and I spent an anxious night keeping an alert front with men very wearied of the day, and no officer or N.C.O. help to share the job with me. . . .

April 19th passed uneventfully in the brilliant sun and light shelling. Towards sunset, at stand to, we noted a large party of enemy approaching us from Oppy and the direction of Oppy Wood. They were out of rifle range, but were advancing steadily towards us in massed formation. On focussing them in my glasses, I found they were not armed, and apparently without equipment. I went along to the left, and found the Bedfords uncertain what action to take. We knew the artillery had good

155

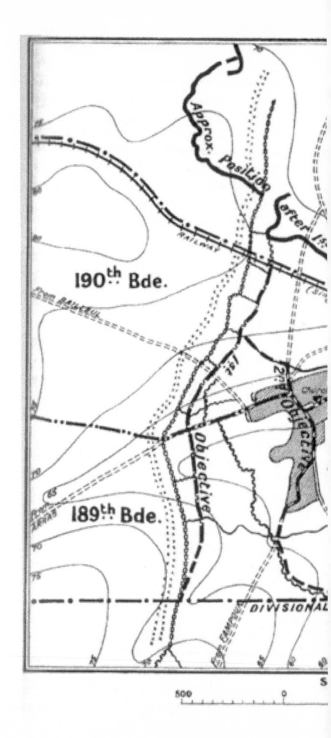

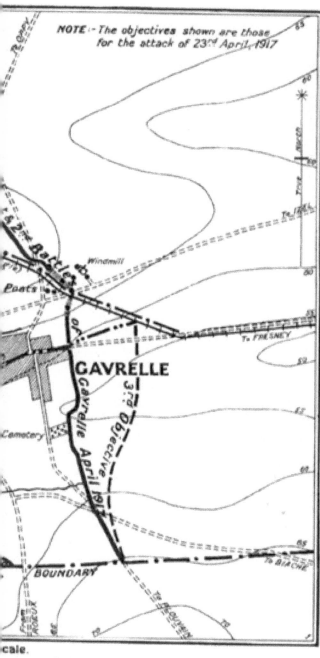

NOTE:—The objectives shown are those for the attack of 23rd April 1917

Windmill

Posts

GAVRELLE

Cemetery

Gavrelle April 1917

3rd Objective

To FRESNEY

To BIACHE

BOUNDARY

Scale.

500    1000

observation on this front, so decided to hold our fire unless our own guns opened on them with shrapnel. Everything remained quiet, and presently the information was passed along that they were a large gang of civilians impressed to work on strengthening the defences of the system, and must not be taken as a target!

This account, concealing nothing, reflects at once the conditions at the time, and the spirit in which they were met. It was 1915 over again, but with a difference. As the price of our losses, the Hawke Battalion was beginning all over again, but not quite from the beginning either of hope or enthusiasm. The war was taking its course, and the days had gone by when subalterns hoped to change it. It was 1917.

After two days behind the lines the Hawke Battalion moved forward on the evening of April 22nd to their assembly position for the battle of April 23rd, in which the divisional objective was Gavrelle.

The battalion was in brigade reserve; this was a very different task in France to what it had been in Gallipoli, when we had waited in our rest camp or in Achibaba Nullah with nothing but the flies to fight, and had gone up to the line, when the orders at last came, with the knowledge that all the fighting must be over, else the one and only reserve battalion would not be leaving camp. Men were cheaper at Arras, and the reserve battalion on this occasion only gave the assaulting troops five minutes' start. Then "B" company (Lieutenant Matthews in command, with Sub-Lieutenant Dodds and Sub-Lieutenant Elphick to do the donkey work) moved forward.

Five minutes is not long, and the company, laden with S.A.A., sandbags, bombs, picks, and shovels, found itself engaged in a comic opera battle, dealing with their fists, shovels, or anything that came handy with strange Germans, who might or might not be prisoners of war, as they emerged from dugouts which, at any rate, none of the attacking troops appeared to have occupied. Some of these Germans were benign old gentlemen with spectacles and long brown beards, who asked in evident anxiety to be directed to the prisoners-of-war cage; others required firmer handling, and one group actually turned a machine gun on one of "B" company's platoons, who had to rush the position. In the first German trench no sign could be found of the company commander, so Sub-Lieutenant Dodds took his party forward through the village, and delivered his miscellaneous stores to Commander Asquith, found characteristically in the front of our position discussing the situation with Stern-dale Bennett of the Drake.

Here, about midday, "B" company were joined by Battalion Headquarters, whose ceremonial entry was, however watched with no little interest by the enemy. Both Colonel Whiteman and his adjutant became casualties, and Lieutenant-Commander Lockwood took over the battalion for the remainder of the operations; Rackham succeeded Herbert as adjutant. The loss of the Colonel and Adjutant was a commentary on the futility of convention. Asquith of the Hood and Sterndale Bennett of the Drake, fighting through the whole morning, escaped scathless. The Hawke Headquarters, coming forward as such, were instantly observed. The incident had, moreover, a tragic climax, for Colonel Whiteman, making his way back again to the dressing station, was again, and this time fatally, wounded.

Farther on the right, behind the Drake Battalion, were "A" company, who had gone forward under Sub-Lieutenants Bessel and Stephenson. They had much the same experience in their first advance, but an easier time later, since the captured dugouts on the right of the enemy's position were deeper and stronger. The result was that, when, in the evening and throughout the next day, the German artillery deluged the village with high explosive (leading eventually to a strong counter-attack in the afternoon), this company suffered little damage. "B" company, on the other hand, lost nearly half their effectives.

All this time "C" company had been busy carrying trench-mortar ammunition (Sub-Lieutenant Dickins and sixty men), R.E. stores (Sub-Lieutenant Maloney and thirty men), and machine-gun ammunition (Sub-Lieutenant Cookson and thirty men). "D" company remained in reserve till late on the 24th, when they went up into the line to reinforce the Drake Battalion. Before this they had lost their company commander, Lieutenant Melland, who had survived the first landing at Gallipoli with the Anson Battalion on April 25th, 1915, only to be killed by a chance shot behind the fighting line. Sub-Lieutenant H. A. Burr, a N.C.O. of the old "D" company, promoted on Gallipoli, who had only just rejoined the battalion, was killed on the way up to the line.

Sad as these losses were, the miracle was that, working amid the shells and flying debris for two days, never far from the front line, and often in it, and sustaining on the second day the severest bombardment so far experienced by the battalion, the casualties were so slight. The action had, indeed, been triumphantly successful, and, though the credit must be given in large measure to the Nelson, Hood, and Drake, who had carried the successive enemy positions, the Hawke Battalion had materially helped.

It was cruel work. Carrying parties have no barrage, no time table, no routine, and usually no adequate orders. To stumble along blindly amid the debris looking for trouble (for where there is no trouble there is no need of bombs and S.A.A.) is the whole duty of these unfortunates. And every officer is on his own. Organised action is impossible. You need not go on, but you do. Every yard of the way seems a mile, and every mile successfully negotiated means only the most indefinite of reprieves. No wonder that details are missing from the records of these troubled hours, yet this account of the march down after relief (at 1 a.m. on April 25th) is vivid enough, and recalls the spirit of these days of swift reaction, when everything was good or bad, black or white, and the grey dawn of peace was distant.

The diarist writes:

On the way down I found, Maloney very sorrowful at the loss of his servant, who fell at his side, and together we carried on down to the candle factory with our platoons, following in any old order, friends greeting one another as if they had been separated for years. Presently we saw the glow of the galley fire. Could ever an old cooking cart, standing in a wet field, more perfectly embody the comforts and happiness of hearth and home? Old Joe Watson, all ready to feed the men, with his honest 'Leave it all to me, sir; I'll see none of my men go short,' standing within the glow of the coal, his sooty face illuminated with welcome for everyone, and trying to keep order round his dixies with the nimbleness of his tongue and, if necessary, the weight of his hand. 'What, Stiffie, you turned up again? What's Fritz doing to overlook your fat body for his corpse factory?' etc.

Then Old McCombie: 'May I shake your hand, sir? Very glad to have you safe back. Buses are ready as soon as you like to say the word, sir. Yes. Huts, sir, at Equaves; been busy all the time, me and Petty, getting in the blankets. You heard the colonel was 'it, sir, and Mr. 'Erbert; but they say the Hawkes done fine, and put the wind up Fritz proper. P.O. Peckham has a little bit of something for the officers. Will you step along, sir? I'll go and see what them lads is chewing the fat about.'

Then a long run over quiet roads, avenued with trees and camouflaged with netting. In the brilliant moonlight of early morning we arrive at Equaves Huts. Rolled in blankets, I slept on the floor till well into the next afternoon, when Jack Bates of the Black Watch took me off to the village to toast his luck at Gresham Hill.

★★★★★★

Of the next months there is little to tell, except that they were peaceful and on the whole pleasant. Commander B. H. Ellis (formerly of the Anson Battalion) succeeded Colonel Whiteman in command, and when Lockwood left in June to take up an Admiralty appointment, Lieutenant-Commander Shelton became second in command. B. B. Rackham was confirmed in his appointment as adjutant, and Lyell became Lewis-gun officer. Beyond this nothing of "military importance" occurred, except the inevitable changes among company commanders, Lieutenant Potts getting command of "A" company, Sub-Lieutenant Stephenson of "B," and Lieutenant Stear of "D." Lieutenant-Commander Price remained in command of "C" company till he went home for the Senior Officers' Course in September, when Lieutenant Dickins succeeded him.

But in other respects the period, spent mainly on digging the Red Line—the main corps defence line well behind Gavrelle, the capture of which was to have opened up such a vast field for strategic enterprise—and latterly in front of Oppy Wood, was a memorable one. It was the last period of prolonged ease and tolerable comfort which the division was to experience. One of the company commanders writes:

> I remember nothing of any importance that happened, except that Geoffrey Price stole the best armchair from the Arras Club.

It was a pleasanter memory than any which the battalion had taken from the Ancre.

Immediately after the Gavrelle battle the battalion moved back for rest and reorganisation to La Compté, one of those green and smiling villages behind the lines which knew in passing so many tens of thousands of soldiers, being but a day's march from the firing line, yet never knew the sound of a shell. So much for the distinctiveness of modern war. In no other war could such peace have reigned within a stone's-throw of half a million of fighting men.

The period of rest was unexpectedly curtailed, but only because, on May 4th, it was definitely decided to discontinue the Arras offensive. No battle, no rest, was the staff doctrine at this time, and the Hawke Battalion, with the rest of the division (in which many of the battalions were in even more need of time for reorganisation), was brought back to Roclincourt for nightly work on the Red Line. The whole battalion was thus employed, usually from 10 p.m. to 4 a.m., with an hour and a quarter's march each way, and this routine continued till May 20th, when the Hawke moved to a new camp (at St. Catherine) and took up work on the forward communications in the Gavrelle sector.

On June 1st there was a change of scene and work, and the Hawke went into the line on the extreme left of the divisional sector in front of Oppy. Here there was no satisfactory front line and no adequate communications, but the battalion had only a week in the line, during which they suffered a raid from the enemy on one of their bombing posts (in which the enemy captured a prisoner, but lost six men killed) and dug a new front line. Then, after a short time in support, they were relieved, for more work on the forward communications. The reason for this was that there was to be a new attack on the front to the left of Gavrelle by the 5th and 31st Divisions. And so we find the Hawke Battalion for another ten days occupied in training by day and digging by night. Then, on the 22nd June, they went back to Roclincourt for serious training, which continued till July 4th.

From this time till September the Hawke Battalion were in the line in support or in reserve in the Gavrelle–Oppy sector. The front, irregular and unsatisfactory when first taken over, was gradually straightened out and pushed forward, and our patrols became very bold and vigorous, P.O. Hilton of "B" company getting special commendation for a series of daylight patrols in the neighbourhood of the Gavrelle Windmill. The enemy seemed, indeed, to become more and more listless and unready, and raids carried out by the Howe and Anson Battalions in July and early September were highly successful. The only troubles all this time were the spasmodic gas shelling (which accounted for a good many of the officers and men invalided at this time, including Sub-Lieutenants Stewart, Ross, Elphick, and Wilson), and a peremptory order from brigade that Codner should cease to act as transport officer—an order which happily coincided with the concession of six months' leave for officers continuously on active service for more than two years. Codner was succeeded, for the period of his leave, by Sub-Lieutenant Wilson.

Generally, the conditions experienced were pleasant, by the comparative standards of those days. The weeks spent out of the line were not peaceful, as they had been in the Souchez sector, but the definite halt which had been called to the offensive on this front, the systematic digging of properly planned defences and communications under arrangements which allowed adequate rest for the men before going back to the line, and, above all, the weather, which was warm and tolerably dry till the end of August, made it possible to establish a regular routine of work, rest, and food.

Incidentally the work done by the Naval Division behind the lines at this time was not wasted. When the great German offensive was at its height in 1918, the Arras front was one of the few portions of our line which did not give way, and this fact was one of the decisive turning-points of the war in its closing stages on the western front.

On September 29th the Naval Division was relieved, and the Hawke moved north to the devastating wilderness of Passchendaele. Behind the lines, at the XVIIIth Corps school at Volkrinkhove, where the acting company commanders of the battalion (Stevenson, Potts, Dickins, and Stear) stopped on their way to the line for three days' pious exhortation, there was an atmosphere of optimism. There was also some excellent instruction by no less vivacious a personality than our own Colonel Levy, who had in the early days of the war given to the Naval Division such a remarkably sound course of instruction in the disciplining and leading of untrained troops.

"Everything is easy if you think for yourselves and use your brains, and if you don't use your brains you're no more use in war than in peace." That was the root principle of Colonel Levy's teaching, and at the XVIIIth Corps School it set in a clear light the intricacies of the new tactical methods called forth by the enemy's "pill-box" defences. This was the serious business of the course, and admirably done. The comic relief was provided, with equal foresight, by the corps commander, who came round at intervals to expatiate on "my battle," which he was fighting over the telephone wires with an inexhaustible energy, which "you gentlemen" would do excellently well to imitate; and by the C.R.A., who "could not express his unbounded astonishment at the grit of the temporary officer."

This C.R.A. was incidentally under the curious delusion that all temporary officers were clerks, and that all clerks were bank clerks—a hideous truth which he was so good as to tone down by referring to

# Operations of Royal Naval Division,

## October – November 1917,

### Scale of Yards

500     0     500     1000

━━━━━ Front line taken over from 9th Division.
━ ━ ━ "     " after attack on 26th October.
•••••• "     "     "     " 30th     "
+ + + + + "     " handed over to 1st Division on 5th November.

Heights in metres.

Poelcapelle

Hinton Farm
Moray House
DIVISIONAL
From POELCAPELLE
Fracas Farm
Beek Houses
Lekkerboterbeek
Oxford House
Terrier Farm
Hut
Berks Houses
Banff House
Bray Farm
County Roads
Cemetery
Burns House
Vacher Farm
Inch Houses
York Farm
Winchester Fm
Stoke Farm
Wellington
Adler Farm
Cemetery

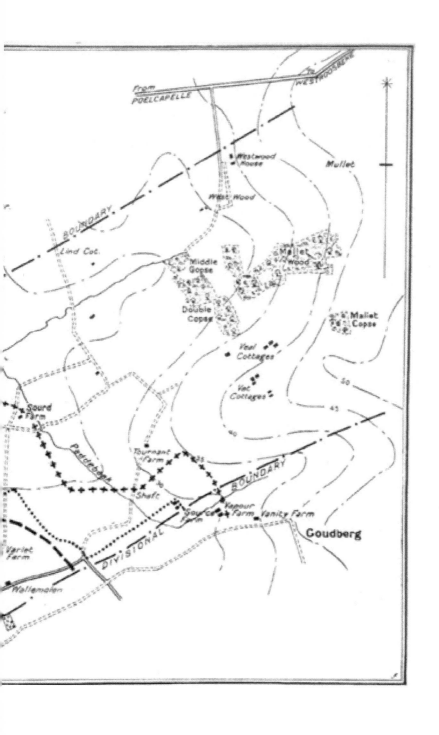

us all indiscriminately as "bankers."

The first camp of the Hawke battalion in the Flanders area was Brake Camp, near Poperinghe, and here they waited till they were joined by the four company commanders from Volkrinkhove. These same officers, primed with real enthusiasm and quite a little knowledge, looked forward to a few days of training with their companies, but it was the 188th and 190th Brigades who were destined, as it happened, for the first of the Division's advances, and the Hawke, Hood, Drake, and Nelson Battalions were moved forward at once for three weeks' work on the forward communications between the Steenbek and our gun and infantry positions round Langemark.

The move from Brake Camp took the battalion suddenly and with little warning into a new atmosphere, markedly contrasting with that of Volkrinkhove. Their new camp was a map reference—an open field of mud and shell-holes, with water 18 inches below the surface. It was raining hard, and the corps organisation, vibrating with efficiency a few miles farther back, proved here unequal to the task of providing bivouac sheets. Not yet, however, were the battalions' spirits wholly damped, and as soon as dusk fell a neighbouring and unguarded dump provided a ceaseless storehouse from which to draw corrugated iron, timber, duckboards, tar felting, and sandbags. The inefficiency of the staff work had its compensations, for no one ever commented on the methods which alone enabled the Hawke and other battalions to face the work of the next three weeks. As it was, a new camp came into being, and Zouave Dump became only a memory, though men and lorries would approach the site for some days, and then pass sadly by. Another wrong map reference, no doubt!

But after this the battalion had shot its bolt. Men were cheaper than timber on this front, and a prodigal War Office was never stinting of supplies. It was possible, with enough initiative, to keep the men dry in their camp, but it was not possible to keep them alive on night work in the forward area. The situation on the Flanders front at this time was simply deplorable. Neither our own infantry nor the enemy had any defined positions, and communication trenches were nonexistent. All that could be said was that between the artillery of the two armies were an indefinite number of posts occupied precariously by the infantry.

Round the gun positions and behind them the situation was even worse. On the front taken over by the Naval Division (and it was the same elsewhere) there were only two lines of communication

166

for men, material, and ammunition, and the real battle—a battle for actual life—was concerned with the maintenance of these precarious duckboards, and with the carrying and passage of supplies. With the successive advances—small in extent, but, relatively to the condition of the ground, very considerable—the duckboard tracks stretched farther and farther forward. Their position was inevitably known to the enemy, and even when they were intact only a proportion of the men and supplies which passed along them filtered through to the gun or infantry positions. But they were never intact, for by day and night the ceaseless artillery war was directed to their destruction.

One of the Hawke officers who was working on the maintenance of these perilous but vital communications writes:

Indiscriminate shelling was carried out to keep the ground liquid for several feet, and prevent the dykes and streams settling into permanent courses, and by bombing and shelling to prevent engineering material from reaching the gun positions.

Our task, then, was a pretty tough one—fighting against his gunnery and aeroplanes with beech-planking, pick, shovel, and pump. We strove to construct and maintain an artery upon which the life of a sustained action could depend. A more strenuous battle and nerve strain, I am told, than the actual show on October 23rd, when out of the hell behind the company emerged into a quiet morass where shelling was limited by the obscurity of the front-line positions, and the ignorance at the batteries of the location of friend and foe.

As far as my own company was concerned, I took up, at first, 100 men and all my officers, but very quickly realised that our progress would be limited to the amount of timber available each day. I pointed out the fallacy of taking 100 under fire, if fifty could do all that was required, and Commander Ellis granted the company this valuable concession, which afforded alternate days on for men and officers. But even with this reduced number the work of preparation exceeded the rate of supply; day after day, on arriving on the ground, we would find the track which the previous day's work had left firm and ready to receive the planks ploughed up with shells, strewn with broken limbers, dead or foundered mules, dumps of 18-pound shells, and all the litter and debris of the hours of darkness, when the teams proceeding to the batteries had reached the end of the planking and floundered into the mud, sinking deeper and deeper until they had to be abandoned.

Our day's work always started with shooting certain animals abandoned in the mud, and one day as many as twelve had to be dispatched close to the Mont de Hybou before we could proceed with our proper business.

The task, theoretically, was simple. To make a firm track, with ditches on either side at a gradient to carry off the water, and to lay planks upon it, presents no difficulty. But to do this, when each day's work is undone by night, is as unprofitable as Penelope's stitching. Every day some fresh problem presented itself. Shelling had diverted the water into a new channel perhaps, or Lieutenant Keeping, of our own field artillery, had ripped up our yesterday's planking to keep their 18-pounders from sinking out of sight. Another morning an incendiary bomb had burnt a big hole in the timber of the road, or a tank had squelched the foundations from under and submerged the track beneath the water. And all the time casualties. Casualties on the way up, casualties on the way down, casualties while at work!

I cannot add anything to this description, which reflects the actual day-to-day experiences of all companies of the battalion at this time, whether their actual task was on the maintenance of duckboard tracks, or as carrying parties or more ordinary working parties. The plain fact was that we were attempting an offensive under impossible conditions. The sacrifices exacted were obviously beyond any attainable reward. The trouble lay, in fact, just in that word "obviously." Not a song could be heard on the march anywhere on the Flanders front in October, 1917. The moral of the troops was amazingly high. Everything they were asked to do was done to the utmost of their power, but they had seen too much to be in any doubt as to the outcome.

The first engagement fought by the Naval Division was on October 26th, when the 188th Brigade, with the Hood and Hawke Battalion in support, attempted to carry the line of the Paddebeek and the enemy positions east of it. The ground across which the advance was attempted was the marsh land at the foot of the western slope of the famous ridge, which lay diagonally to our front, and along which the Canadian Corps had made a series of gallant and partially successful advances, outstripping the 9th Division, who had previously been in the Naval Division's place on the Canadians' left. The purpose of the

PASSCHENDAELE

188th Brigade's attack was, of course, to carry our line forward to the north of the ridge, and so help the Canadians to continue their own advance.

The story of the attack, which the Hawke Battalion watched from the support position throughout the ceaseless rain of the 26th, cannot be told here. It is enough to say that after hours of desperate fighting, maintained with the utmost resolution, the 188th Brigade (reinforced at 8 a.m. by Commander Asquith and the Hood Battalion) had to be content with an advance of some 300 to 400 yards, including five of the enemy strong points. Even the line of the Paddebeek was not reached, much less the high ground beyond it. And on our side of the stream the enemy still held, at dusk, Source Trench, Sourd Farm, Banff Houses, Bray Farm, and Berks Houses.

The last three posts had been reached and held earlier in the day, but it had not been found possible in daylight to consolidate them. At 8 p.m., however, the Hawke Battalion took over the left of the brigade front, and under cover of darkness at once advanced and reoccupied them. "C" company, under Sub-Lieutenant Bartholomew, were responsible for this enterprise, which at least prevented their reoccupation by the enemy. This small exploit was of importance as showing that the system of defence in depth by small and isolated posts was by no means impenetrable once the darkness gave immunity from machine-gun fire to the slow-moving infantryman. The Hood Battalion on the right had a similar experience, and the lesson, as we shall see, was not lost on their skilful and far-sighted commander.

Perhaps, however, the corps commander was well satisfied with the progress of "my battle." Certain it is that it was decided on the 30th to send the 190th Brigade to the attack under precisely the same conditions and against the same objective as those governing the daylight attack of the 26th. This time the Drake and Nelson supplied the reserves, and the Hawke and Hood were behind the line. The failure was almost complete, the Artists Rifles and the Bedfords in particular suffering disastrous losses from an intensive barrage put down on their assembly positions at the precise moment of the attack. A little success was, indeed, achieved by the K.S.L.I, on the extreme right of the divisional front, but when the Hawke took over their old sector on the left, on the night of the 31st October, they found Banff House once more abandoned. Nowhere had any advance been made.

The 189th Brigade were now to take their turn of active operations. The authorities still insisted that the Paddebeek crossing must be secured, and gave November 6th as the final date. This time, however, the choice of method was left by Divisional Headquarters to the battalions concerned, who proceeded, on the very next night (November 1st), to put into execution a different scheme, productive of equally different results.

For the origin and explanation of these operations we must go back to that tragic morning of October 26th, when the Hood Battalion, from our old front line, watched the pitiful slaughter of the men of the 188th Brigade, struggling vainly in the mud to find each other and their objectives. Commander Asquith had watched an even earlier attack (by the 9th Division) over the same ground with the same disastrous result, and his conclusion, after experiencing the conditions himself, was definite. Absolute mobility, prior reconnaissance, surprise, and personal leading by senior officers were the indispensable elements of success against the enemy's new system. These conditions could not be secured so long as the normal tactics of attack at dawn under a barrage were persisted in. The ease with which, on the occasion of the relief of the 188th Brigade on the evening of the 26th, the line handed over had been secured and extended, suggested, however, that night operations might provide a satisfactory solution.

The essential feature of the new tactics was prior reconnaissance, followed by a surprise attack, and the night of the 31st October was, in the circumstances, devoted by the Hawke and Nelson Battalions to a thorough investigation of the enemy positions, and no immediate attempt was made to restore the line.

The next evening (November 1st), at 6.10 p.m., operations began. While the Nelson Battalion on the left attacked Source Trench, the Hawke Battalion, whose front-line company ("D" company under Lieutenant Stear) held a line of posts from the Shaft to the neighbourhood of Banff House, attacked an important enemy stronghold, nameless on the map, but close in on their left front.

The actual attack was carried out by Sub-Lieutenant Perry with one and a half platoons, which advanced in three detachments directed against the front and the flanks of the position. In the darkness there was no danger from the enemy machine guns; the situation was far too obscure for either side to risk firing without a target. Movement was safe, and the parties made their way forward through the mud in good order until they came up against the enemy's wire. Here the centre party halted, while the others worked round the flanks and rushed in with bombs. Surprised on both sides, the enemy surrendered; nine men and a machine gun were captured, and a number more killed or wounded.

Immediately, Lieutenant Stear advanced his whole line 150 yards beyond the captured post, and was fortunate enough, as the result of this move, to make a further capture in the shape of an enemy ration party.

The net result of this simple and almost bloodless operation was an advance of nearly 200 yards over the same ground which the attacks of the 26th and 30th October had without success attempted to cross in daylight under a barrage.

The Nelson Battalion were equally successful, and now only Sourd Farm stood between us and the line of the Paddebeek.

The Hawke Battalion were relieved by the Drake on the night of the 2nd to 3rd November, and this battalion, in conjunction with the Hood, reached the brigade's objective early on the morning of the 4th.

★★★★★★★

Shortly after these successes the Hawke Battalion was relieved, and marched to Rubruck for a fortnight behind the lines. The conditions even there, except for the absence of danger, were deplorably bad, and no serious training was possible.

Chance, however, intervened. The daring gamble of Cambrai had failed at the eleventh hour, and the shattered divisions holding on in the first days of December to a mere fragment of our gains, and in some places driven back behind our original lines, needed reinforcement. On December 6th, just as the Hawke Battalion was preparing to move back to the Passchendaele sector, the orders came for the division to move to the Cambrai front.

As it happened, "C" company of the Hawke were the advance party for the 189th Brigade, and left at once on December 8th.

Sub-Lieutenant Dickins, the company commander wrote:

We entrained with other details of the brigade, and after a twenty-hour journey detrained at midnight at Bapaume railhead. Bapaume, the goal of our fighting in the early spring. How impressive it lay, deserted in the bright moonlight, with only a point-duty man at the cross-road with his lantern in his. hand to direct us on the way and dispel the illusion that we were trespassing in no-man's-land.

Through the deserted town we went, our heavy boots on the

*pavé* calling echoes from the hollow walls. The moonbeams, playing tricks with the shadows among the towering masonry, produced a feeling of melodrama which recalled to my mind Brangwyn's impressions of the ruins of Messina.

Turning to the left at the water-point, we set off along the Haplincourt road, and, soon leaving the town behind, we started up a song. The chief,[1] setting the pace, started up with his song *'If you want to find the corporal,'* and the men, now come to a country lane and freed from the restraint of the ruined city, like school-boys released from church, carried the answering chorus down the ranks. *'We saw him, we saw him, drinking all the buckshee rum; we saw him drinking all the buckshee rum.'*

Happily we strode along, kilometre after kilometre, with an occasional halt for me to ascertain from Bartholomew if they were all in touch in rear. . . .

The free air of the uplands was already dispelling the gloom, of our sojourn in Flanders, and we maintained a fine pace, and sang many times all the songs we knew.

The next day the battalion joined us, and soon we were moving up to Fins, Equancourt, and Metz, and those villages on the borders of Havrincourt Wood, which were to become very familiar to us before long.

Came the day when we were to make our reconnaissance of the approaches to the front, and Commanders Asquith, Ellis, and Beak, with the company officers of the Drake, Hood, and Hawke Battalions, set off early.

Keeping Boer Copse on our left and Beaucamp Well on the right, we struck the Hindenburg defences on the Highland Ridge. Great belts of rusted wire entanglements ran across the tawny-grass-lands, and in this vast empty land, where larks sang and no shell-holes or broken material lay to suggest a recent battlefield, we seemed to have come to a land of peace from the shell-shattered salient at Ypres.

But this impression was by no means a lasting one. Such calm as there was, was the calm before the storm, and more senior officers would have welcomed more of the conventional equipment of a battlefield, if this could have included well-sited trenches and trustworthy communications, as well as a few more men and guns.

---

1. *Anglice,* Company Sergeant-Major.

The position on Welsh Ridge which the Naval Division were to take over had been improvised to form a defensive flank to that portion of our line on the Flesquières Ridge which presented the residue of our Cambrai gains.

The position was relatively clean and fresh, but it was proportionately precarious. Yet it was vital. If it fell, the four miles of the Hindenburg line which we held on the Flesquières Ridge must fall also, and how far the retirement might spread few dared to prophesy. This was the mood of the corps staffs, which impressed itself not too favourably on the battalion commanders who took over from the division already on the spot.

On December 15th the Hawke Battalion moved into the line on Welsh Ridge, with the 190th Brigade on their left and the Nelson on their right. The 189th Brigade line was, roughly, the northern half of the crest of Welsh Ridge, the southern half being held by the 188th Brigade. The ridge faced almost due east; the northern end, where our line bent sharply round to join the Flesquières Ridge positions garrisoned by the Army division on our left, was held by the 190th Brigade.

The local conditions were of the kind the correspondents described at the time as obscure, and now as culpably unsatisfactory. No wire, disconnected trenches, derelict tanks, and a general atmosphere of muddle and insecurity. The task of the division was to construct out of nothing an organised and defensible position.

The weather changed from the dry freshness which had so invigorated the first arrivals from Flanders to bitter cold, and the conditions of January and February, 1917, were repeated, with the one vital exception that we were now facing, after a succession of victories, a victorious enemy. The preparation of successive defensive positions farther and farther back was the only task now regarded by the staff as urgent.

Yet the immediate problem for the Hawke Battalion was to knock their particular little corner of Welsh Ridge into defensible shape; to dig a new front line on the forward slope; to strengthen a main line of resistance on the crest; to patrol constantly for warning of the expected attack; and to keep down the enemy snipers, whose activity was, as ever, an infallible sign of heightened moral.

All this was done, only just done, when, on December 30th, the Germans launched their very strong attack. The Hawke and Nelson were behind the line at the start, but not for long. "B" and "D" com-

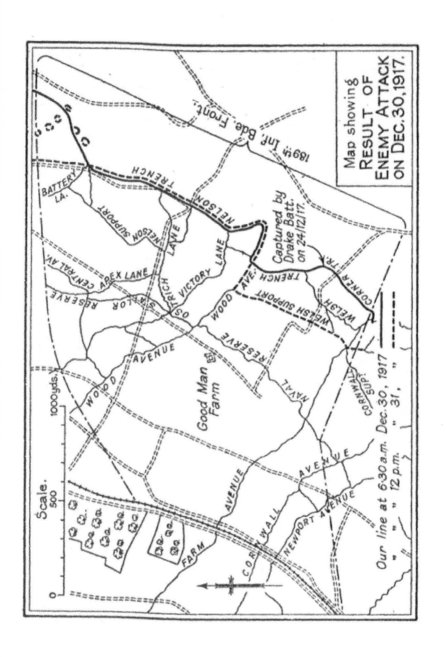

Map showing
RESULT OF
ENEMY ATTACK
ON DEC. 30, 1917.

189th Inf. Bde. Front.

BATTERY LA.

NELSON TRENCH

NELSON SUPPORT

APEX LANE

CENTRAL AV.

SAILOR RESERVE

OSTRICH LANE

VICTORY LANE

WOOD AVE.

WELSH SUPPORT

Captured by
Drake Batt.
on 24/12/17.

TRENCH

CORNER TR.

WOOD AVENUE

Good Man Farm

RESERVE

NAVAL RESERVE

WOOD

AVENUE

FARM AVENUE

CORNWALL

CORNWALL SUPT.

AVENUE

NEWPORT AVENUE

Scale.
1000yds.
500
0

Our line at 6.30 a.m. Dec. 30, 1917
"     "    12 p.m.    "  30,   "
"     "            "  31,   "

panies were thrown into the line on the left of the brigade line to reinforce the Hood Battalion at the point of junction with the 190th Brigade, and fought there in the second line (Eagle Trench) throughout the day. In the early hours of the 31st the garrison were burnt out of position, and retired to Sunken Road. At about 9 a.m. the enemy, attempting to exploit their success, put down a barrage and came over in force, but Lieutenant Stear, rising to an urgent occasion, took his mixed force over the top and met the enemy in the open with the bayonet. For five minutes the fighting continued, and then the enemy broke and were driven back beyond their earlier gains, so vigorously were they followed up, notably by Lieutenant Stear himself and Sub-Lieutenant Wilson of the same company, who unfortunately died of the wounds received in this brilliant and successful engagement in which he had played a considerable part. Both he and Lieutenant Stear received the Military Cross for their services.

By 9.30 a.m. on the 31st "C" company were also in the line in Battery Lane, and repelled a slight attack made against their left flank. The arduous work, however, of "A" and "C" companies had been the provision of carrying parties from Highland Ridge to the front line throughout the previous day. The fighting here had been heavy and continuous, and it had not been till dark on the 30th that, as the result of a fine counterattack by the Anson and Nelson, the vital crest of the ridge (part of which had been lost in the first attack) was once more safe in our hands.

The enemy orders, a copy of which was found after the attack, warned their storm troops "to expect a desperate resistance from the Naval Division." The division certainly in this engagement earned the compliment paid to them, for a vital position had been held against very superior numbers, and despite an initial success which might well have disorganised a defensive system by no means complete and only thinly manned.

In the light of this success, which "B" company's counterattack had materially assisted, the Hawke Battalion looked forward with greater confidence to the defensive fighting which was clearly in store for them in 1918.

# CHAPTER 10

# 1918: The First Phase

No year of the war had begun so ominously.

In 1915 a great adventure was only beginning. 1916 had found us contemplating the evacuation of Gallipoli, but the war was only beginning, and the "break through" was still the secret hope of all. 1917 had opened with much talk of "the turn of the tide," and had actually witnessed a German retreat. Now, in 1918, with weakened resources and no reinforcements behind us, we were facing a strong and pugnacious enemy.

It is true that the attack of December 30th had only cost us, in ground, a few advanced posts, but the significant features were quite different. The enemy were in strength and had shown themselves resolute, brave, and skilful, while behind our own lines were disorganisation, confusion, and an undercurrent of pessimism. Perhaps no one had expected the Naval Division to hold the Flesquières salient if it were seriously attacked. The result of holding it, with eighteen miles of devastated country behind the front line, was that rations were poor, communications vile, and accommodation for the battalions in support as wholly lacking as for those in the line. The enemy provided a further obstacle to decent campaigning by continuous shelling, which spared neither the front, the support, nor the reserve positions. Their obvious effort to damage our moral was, indeed, the only stimulus that kept up the battalion's spirits in these difficult days.

On January 5th the Hawke was relieved by a battalion of the 56th Brigade of the 19th Division (who had taken over the 190th Brigade front two days before), and retired to the support position behind the Hood and Drake on Highland Ridge. Here they were joined by Geoffrey Price, fresh from the Senior Officers' Course, and appointed second in command. Price brought back with him not only the latest

Aldershot tricks, which were not always applicable, but a mixed bag of books and Grand Marnier which formed a connecting link with half-forgotten days in Gallipoli, when the Hawke Battalion didn't even pretend to be conventional. Of the Grand Marnier, as of so much that was good, only the memory remains, but a copy of George Street's *Ghosts of Piccadilly*, given to one of the company commanders on January 7th, still remains with a note on the fly-leaf faithfully recalling the memorable conditions of an interval of rest.

> On the Cambrai front. . . . Frozen water, wet wood, no matches, and no gear has left us unwashed for ten days.
> Sandbagging for a handkerchief. Socks worn out. Chins unshaved. Bed, a sandbag on a muddy floor. Pillow, a steel helmet. No news from the world, and eighteen miles of despoiled and unpopulated country in rear. Perpetual gunfire. Casualties from shells, frostbite, and fever.
> Men exhausted; rations poor. Dark nights, and very long. Trenches old and fallen in; no accommodation for the men.

And these were the conditions at a point where the enemy offensive was expected to fall with the fullest force, and where our organisation of supplies and our provision for the comfort and safety of the front-line troops might have been expected to be complete. On January 9th, when the Hawke went back to the line, there were 10 degrees of frost at night followed by a thaw, and the opposing armies carried on the necessary routine, facing each other in the open, much as we had faced the Turks at Suvla in the blizzard of November, 1915. The communication trenches with the front line, Battery Lane, and the neighbouring trenches were 4 feet deep in half-frozen slush; the front line was in even worse condition.

To make the best of a bad job was the only wisdom, and records of this and the two following days tell only of the supply of hot food three times a day to the whole battalion. Luckily the enemy watched this outburst of philanthropic activity unmoved, and, thanks to it, the battalion, being relieved by the 190th Brigade, were little the worse for their experiences.

After a week at Equancourt in huts (an arrangement only come to with difficulty, and after a blunt refusal to put up with the ploughed field offered to them for their accommodation at Havrincourt), the Hawke returned to the line on the 19th, remaining in reserve for two nights before they relieved the Nelson Battalion in their old sector on

January 21st.

This was the last time that they were to occupy Welsh Ridge, the scene of one of the Naval Division's most successful, though inconspicuous, achievements, from which the Hawke Battalion had emerged with less loss than their share in an active defence might have suggested. On January 22nd they were relieved by the 2nd H.L.I. (19th Division), and moved back to work behind the lines.

Already, when at Equancourt, they had had to supply men to work on the Metz defences—a reserve system some eight miles behind the front line which was now being hurriedly completed, though it had appeared many months before on corps and army maps. Now, and until February 13th, the Hawke, like other battalions, had to supply men by the hundred every day to cope with the eleventh-hour zeal for defensive preparations.

Not until the middle of February was this part of their task completed, and then, having held and consolidated Welsh Ridge, and having put the defensive positions behind the Flesquières salient into something approaching order, the Naval Division had to go back into a fresh part of the line to wait for the German attack.

It will be remembered that Welsh Ridge, which had been the divisional sector in December and January, was a hastily improvised position linking up that part of the Hindenburg lines which we had captured in the Cambrai attack in November, and held against the enemy counter-attack at the beginning of December, with the new line to which we had been driven back In December by the enemy's "break-through" south of Marcoing. The result was that the sector north of Welsh Ridge ran almost at right angles to that ridge, and was very different in character.

The front-line system, which ran through Flesquières, consisted of an outpost line, and, as the line of resistance, the former Hindenburg support line. Behind lay what was called the intermediate system of defence, consisting Of the former Hindenburg front line, and still farther behind was a "second system," consisting of our own original front line.

These three systems were now to be the scene of the Naval Division's activities, and on February 27th they began the relief of the 47th Division. This division had eight battalions in the front-line system and four in the intermediate system on a total frontage of 6,000 yards; the second system was garrisoned, while the 47th Division were in the line, by troops of a reserve division. Now, each brigade of the

Naval Division had to contribute one of their three battalions[1] to the garrisoning of the second system (with their headquarters in Trescault or Havrincourt Wood), and with their other two battalions they had to relieve a four-battalion brigade of the 47th Division in the two forward systems.

This was the beginning of the thinning out process, due partly to the arbitrary refusal of the available reinforcements by the Government at home, and partly to the belief that the shock of the German offensive would be best met by an elastic defence backed up with strong reserves available for powerful counterattacks. Had the enemy, after carrying our forward systems, waited for a further organised attack, the policy might have succeeded, though it is open to question whether, even with our available resources, we could not have held at least the intermediate position if it had been defended with the usual resolution. As it was, the issue of events showed that, without much closer control of a fluctuating battle by the corps and army staffs, and without greater mobility, the reliance on counter-attack divisions was futile. It is easier to begin than to end a retreat against a skilful enemy.

Meanwhile, the "thinning out" tactics threw a very heavy burden on the battalions destined to meet the first shock of the German advance; of these, the Hawke Battalion was clearly one.

The new tactics meant, indeed, a revolutionary change, and a most unpleasant one. With all three brigades of the division in the line simultaneously, there was no chance of rest, and the German shelling covered each of the three positions occupied by battalions in normal rotation. The extreme length of the sectors allotted to individual battalions ("C" company of the Hawke under a sub-lieutenant relieved a whole battalion at nearly full strength) meant that even the solace of intercompany reliefs was impossible. Again, the depth of the battalion and brigade positions meant that any sort of close control was impossible. The subaltern in the front line found himself with treble the responsibility, little or no rest, no reinforcements to replace casualties, and no local reserve. The same applied with even greater force to the battalion commander.

---

1. It was just now that the reduction of brigades from four to three battalions had taken place. The change was effected in the Naval Brigades by the disbandment of the Howe and Nelson Battalions, and in the 190th Brigade by the withdrawal of the 5th K.S.L.I.; the Howe and Nelson personnel were temporarily formed into an entrenching battalion.

To complete the picture one must remember the constant shelling, and the constant warnings of impending disaster which rained down from the over-anxious staffs. It was always tomorrow that the great attack was coming; the next night was always the critical night for wiring, for patrols, for every active measure which might ease the responsibility, be it by ever so little, of those behind the lines.

Commander Ellis had rejoined the battalion from English leave at the beginning of February, and at the beginning of March a number of other changes took place, notable among them being the return of Sub-Lieutenant Blackmore, who became assistant Adjutant, and of G. H. Inman, who took over "D" company. Bartholomew succeeded Dickins (now Lewis-gun officer) in command of "C" company, and "A" and "B" companies were under Lieutenant-Commander Wainwright and Lieutenant Dodds.

From now onward, however, changes occurred from day to day, and no record can hope to be complete. From the end of February the battalion, whether in the front-line system, in unseen trench and unseen support (the official name for old Hindenburg front line), and in Ribecourt (where one company of the Hawke was stationed when in support), or in reserve at Trescault, was subjected to constant casualties and almost continuous "gassing." On March 1st, for instance, Trescault Ridge was intensively bombarded for five hours; on March 8th the front-line system was shelled with 5.9's for even longer, Sub-Lieutenant Maloney being killed while temporarily in command of "A" company. On March 12th the battalion was in support, and "C" company in Ribecourt lost four officers and 135 men. "D" company the next day, in the same place, lost three officers and 127 men—all gassed.

These casualties were not replaced, but the feverish calls of the staff for more and more wiring (in front of positions which were abandoned later under explicit orders long before they were attacked) continued. Between the 15th and the 18th the battalion, working on the defences round Ribecourt, where every breath in the open was a risky affair, lost over 200 officers and men. On the 19th the remnants moved into the front line in relief of the Drake, to meet on this occasion the authentic German attack.

Just before they went up they received much-needed reinforcements to the number of 170 men from the entrenching battalion, which had been formed when the Howe and Nelson were disbanded. This battalion was now disbanded in its turn, and the reinforcements enabled Commander Ellis to reform "C" company, which had been completely wiped out. Lieutenant Beaumont, formerly of the Nelson Battalion, was given command.

Of the old officers of the battalion, only Commander Ellis, Geoffrey Price, Rackham, Blackmore, and Smith (signalling officer) at headquarters, Lieutenant-Commander Wainright ("A" company) Lieutenant Dodds ("B" company), Sub-Lieutenant Perry ("D" company) remained by March 18th.

On March 21st the storm broke. To meet it, the Hawke Battalion had, excluding the transport and other details, eight officers and about 380 men, including Battalion Headquarters, now necessarily well behind the line. On the same front, three weeks before the attack, there had been nearly 2,000 officers and men.

Lieutenant-Commander Blackmore writes:

The retreat was for many of us a period of new experiences, most of them unpleasant, but some not lacking in humour. We had frequently been short of food in Gallipoli, but it remained for this lively week in France to teach us the reality of hunger, and not till then had we been compelled to slake a very real thirst with green water, as we did with that from the shell holes of the desolate Somme battlefield, without thought of discipline or consequences.

And I find it impossible to express what I felt on that last desperate day, when I looked across the shattered area and saw the trees beyond the valley of the Ancre. That seemingly simple sight heartened me, and must surely have heartened those others. One wonders if the determined counter-attacks made at Mesnil and in Aveluy Wood could have been so successful at any point in the barren waste just beyond.

But this was at the end when the worst was known. At the beginning one's imagination conjured up vague and far-reaching possibilities. The written warnings of the impending attack had lost some of their effectiveness, so often had we received them, but from the frantic energy with which our strong position had been made well-nigh impregnable, no doubt had been left as to its probable severity. When we voluntarily gave up our position on the evening of March 22nd, my thoughts reverted to our march through Sedd-el-Bahr, and I experienced again an extreme melancholy at the evacuation of ground won at such tragic cost.

LIEUT. C. S. CODNER, M.C., TRANSPORT OFFICER,
HAWKE BATTALION

On the night of March 20th to 21st, Geoffrey Price and Blackmore made their usual tour of the line, returning to headquarters about 2.30 a.m.

Blackmore's narrative continues:

I have no recollection of having on that occasion discussed with any seriousness the probability of attack at daybreak, nor when we looked out over that dark and peaceful no-man's-land of having visualized the feverish activity which we knew later must have been taking place. Company officers we had found undismayed, the men unmoved, and we turned in with scarcely a passing reference to the future, but at 4.45 that morning I found myself on my feet almost before the first shell had burst. Another minute, and the whole of headquarters was alive; the attack had come at long last.

For some time we had been interested in Smith's pigeons—that final means of communication, the maintenance of which must have proved so costly. But a few minutes of that hurricane bombardment sufficed to cut every wire forwards and to the rear, and then it was that we saw Smith appear out of the dug-out with his precious pigeons, and we watched with somewhat ironic humour his triumphant expression turn to one of dismay. It was too misty for pigeons to be of any service.

Preparations for the attack had been learnt almost by heart; the disposition of the men was carried out automatically, and we waited with varying degrees of anticipation for those developments which were to be expected, while the men, as far as we could see them, endured the heaviest bombardment which any of them had experienced with quite surprising fortitude. Runners began to arrive, and from the usual conflicting reports it slowly became clear that, in all essentials, our line had held.

The first waves of the attack had, indeed, found no gap on the Naval Division front, and the shock which broke our line to north and south, and threatened the allied cause with disaster, yielded the enemy here only a few posts in our outpost line at the junction of the 190th Brigade and "C" company of the Hawke Battalion. Here Sub-Lieutenant Perry and some sixty men were cut off and killed or captured, but the main line of resistance was not even reached, and "A" company, who held the right of the Hawke outpost line, lost hardly a post.

The point of entry on to the Hawke line was the extreme apex of the Flesquières salient—itself a miniature salient—and so local was the success, and so easily was it held in check, that no one, except the officers in the front line, were aware till noon that any ground had been lost. When the news came down to Brigade Headquarters, the usual arrangements for a counter-attack were put in hand. These were cancelled on instructions from Divisional Headquarters, but so normal was the situation that a battalion relief was carried through, the Drake taking over the front-line sector from the Hawke at 8.30 p.m. The Hawke, now barely up to the strength of a company, moved back to the intermediate system in front of Ribecourt.

That night, most unaccountably at the time, the Drakes were withdrawn, and the next day the Hawke spent watching the enemy creeping cautiously through the evacuated position. They examined with interest those solitary old tanks, empty and shell-pitted, which had for so long borne witness to that earlier attack stopped temporarily on the ridge on which they rested. Such gunners as were left amused themselves by dispersing the groups of the more curious and more venturesome of the enemy who clustered round the tanks from time to time. A day of expectancy passed with the recital of the amazing rumours which now began to circulate. A fresh and more highly-coloured supply of these were issued with rations, which reached the battalion just prior to orders for immediate withdrawal to the Metz defences, more secure in name than in fact.

It was at Ribecourt, on March 22nd, while the enemy were sweeping round on both flanks of the Naval Battalions, that it was found that no cross had been put up in Ribecourt Cemetery to mark Maloney's grave. The cross, which was already made, was carried out in front of our lines by an officer and six volunteers from "C" company for nearly a mile. The last two or three hundred yards to the cemetery were enfiladed by machine-gun fire, but one man with a spade ran on to dig a hole in the ground, and then the officer and an N.C.O. followed with the cross. Their self-imposed task accomplished, they returned, and the same evening the battalion was moved back to Neuville, the intermediate position being abandoned. The main body of the division fell back a shorter distance to the second (Trescault) system, and so the Hawke, well covered and still unperturbed, could spend the night in huts and tents. In the morning they manned the Neuville trenches to cover a further retirement in which they, with a company of the Hood, were to act as rear-guard to the division. Here the enemy

185

shelling was more severe, but, comparatively, at any rate, peace reigned, and it was under no pressure from anyone save the Corps staff that the Hawke withdrew later in the morning and marched back through the last prepared line of resistance (the Green Line through Ytres) to Bus, where they formed the brigade reserve. On their way, the battalion was fortunate enough to find a large canteen at Ytres entirely deserted by the staff in charge, and the needs of officers and men for food and drink and tobacco were supplied by the most primitive and pleasantest of all methods known to military art.

To quote again from Commander Blackmore's vivid story:

There were huts at Bus which augured well for the men, and it was hoped to give them a good rest. Indeed, immediately on arrival they were billeted in them and prepared to sleep, but in the early afternoon these huts were heavily bombarded, and it became necessary to put most of the men into a trench which encircled the west and north-west of the village. It was astonishing that there were no casualties.

In reconnoitring the area soon after arrival, I saw what was to me perhaps the most tragically remarkable, if gruesome, sight I had seen in the war. At the south-west corner of the village I came upon a complete battery of four of our '18-pounders,' which had been in action, but were now smashed, with our dead gunners lying almost in their proper places, and in rear a nearly full complement of dead horses. It could only have been the work of an aeroplane, but there was no large hole indicating the explosion of a heavy bomb, nor did the bodies show any sign of having been badly knocked about; it may have been gas.

We were filled with misgiving that we should have been shelled so promptly, and our suspicions were later strengthened by the report that the transport had been shelled out of Rocquigny, due west of Bus, which indicated a deep advance into the British line to our south. When, in the evening, a liaison officer called on the C.O., and it was learned that a complete brigade had pulled out of the line twenty-four hours too soon, and that we were to be prepared for eventualities from the existence of this gap to our south, the critical position in which we found ourselves was readily appreciated.

Such was our confidence, however, that this crisis was to be reserved for the morrow that we left our entire kit, except the usual fighting essentials, on the wire beds in some cellars where we hoped to sleep, and stood in groups in the courtyard of the house discussing the situation. It was now night, and I cannot say what prompted me to wander out of the gates and down the road. It was there I heard some Germans talking quietly to one another. I was so dumbfounded that I thought at first it was some of our own people joking, but it was unmistakable, and I hurried back with my warning.

No one would believe me, of course, but the precaution was taken of placing the men still with us in a rough position of defence, and of sending a runner to those in the trenches. As if in confirmation of my warning, the Germans then commenced to call to one another, and an overwrought Lewis gunner, lying prone immediately behind us, started blazing away down the road. It naturally startled us, but fortunately Rackham and I, who had been standing on the edge of the road with our backs to it, stepped forward instead of backwards. A hurried discussion took place. The Germans were in Bus, and we were but a handful in an unknown village in a wood, and, further, our being in front of the rest of the battalion rendered the remainder useless. We determined to withdraw to the trench, and this we did without difficulty. It was only later, when it became so cold, that we realized that we had lost our kit and our mess gear—an unpleasing discovery.

The men in the trench had been quickly sorted into their own units, and it was then we discovered the absence of the doctor, an American, who was known to have been resting in the cellars. Concluding that he had not been warned, it was decided we should send him a message, and volunteers were forthcoming at once. At the second attempt he was reached, but he declined to leave, maintaining it was his duty to stay where he was.

At this time an old dump halfway between the trench and the village, which had evidently been smouldering, burst into flame, and in this eerie light a curious passage of arms took place. In succession, three parties were sent forward into the village in the faint hope of being able to drive out the enemy. The C.O. himself took the first one into the right-hand corner, and a little later, after a rapid exchange of shots, we could hear the Bosches running for their lives, shrieking '*Kamerade*,' as they were chased by our men. But considerable cross-fire told us that this was possibly an isolated post, and some anxiety was felt for the safety of the C.O. A party prepared to go to

their help, but before they had left the others were safely back. The second raiding party was taken into the village itself, but could make no headway, and a third effort was equally unsuccessful. But, at any rate, we were satisfied that the village was occupied, and that it was not merely the work of local patrols. Later, in accordance with their invariable practice, they pushed their machine guns forward on the flanks, and we had the unusual experience of watching the flight of their stream of bullets, for those they were using were of the 'tracer' variety.

On the next morning (March 23rd) our position was more clear, and it appeared that the enemy were immediately in front of us, and also on our right flank—that is, to the south.

Not to put too fine a point on it, the whole sweep of country on the right was open to the enemy as far as the eye could reach, and enemy attacks were actually coming from the south. The result was that the presence of the rest of the 189th Brigade in the Green Line, due east of Bus (the Green Line, of course, ran north and south), was no protection to the Hawke Battalion, nor indeed to the rear-guard battalion of the 190th Brigade at Lechelle. Equally exposed were the Brigade Headquarters of the 189th Brigade (now commanded by the brave and genial Brigadier-General Du Pree) at Rocquigny. Instead, the covering force in the Green Line were themselves in the gravest danger.

At midnight, indeed, the situation there had been actually desperate, and it was only saved by the initiative of the battalion commanders of the Drake, the Artists Rifles, and the Bedfords, who swung round to form a defensive flank along the Ytres-Bus road, so that they, too, like the Hawke Battalion, could face south and meet the rapidly developing threat to their line of retreat. To meet the same danger from this quarter the 7th Fusiliers were also withdrawn by General Hutchison from Lechelle to the Bus-Rocquigny road early in the morning of the 24th.

It now remained to extricate the division from a position which could not grow better, and must grow worse in the absence of those vigorous counter-attacks for which so much security had been sacrificed.

The 17th Division was undoubtedly available; they were resting, covered by the Naval Division, north-west of Barastre. Why they were not sent forward in the direction of Combles and Lesbœufs to pivot on the right flank of the Naval Division and break the enemy's outflanking movement is a mystery. All hope, however, of successful counter-attack had obviously been abandoned, and at 5 a.m. orders were issued by the Vth Corps to the Naval Division (orders which could not possibly reach the fighting battalions) to fall back on to an undefined position in rear. The line Barastre-Rocquigny (the enemy were already in Rocquigny) was to be held by the 17th Division (who never got the orders), and by the 47th Division (which had fallen back long ago to an undefined position farther west).

So much for the contribution of the Corps staff towards saving a critical situation. Happily, General Lawrie and his brigade and battalion commanders, all of whom were careful to keep in close personal touch with the fighting troops, were quite capable of looking after themselves.

The six battalion commanders in the Green Line decided at 7 a.m. on the 24th to withdraw, a decision which was immediately carried out by the 188th and 190th Brigades, the 189th Brigade acting by agreement as a rear-guard. The three Brigadiers, after a conference with General Lawrie, had already ordered a retirement north of Bus towards Barastre, and though their orders only reached one brigade, and then not till 8 a.m., the retirement from the Green Line conformed exactly to the orders given. The rear-guard battalions (Anson, Hawke, and 7th Fusiliers) were ordered by their respective Brigadiers to stand fast till the other battalions of their brigades had passed behind them. Then the whole division was to rendezvous at the sugar factory near Le Transloy.

So it was that on the morning of the 24th the Hawke Battalion, still in their trenches north-west of Bus, while they engaged the enemy in Bus and the outskirts with rifle and Lewis-gunfire, saw endless parties, companies, platoons, even sections of the division marching round behind them northwest from Ytres and Bertincourt, fired at continuously, but making ordered and steady progress from the danger zone. To their front, the situation spelt an ever-increasing menace as the skyline showed up the enemy patrols coming across from the south in ever-increasing numbers. There was, however, a screen of machine guns at Lesbœufs, which prevented any immediate repetition

at Bus of the outflanking of the division at Ytres, and the only immediate danger to the Hawke Battalion was from the troops to their immediate front. Yet few who manned the trenches that morning, facing
an alert enemy inspired by success, expected to get away unscathed.
Behind their position was a steep bank, over which any retirement
must be only too easy a target, and for the rear-guard battalion to the
rear-guard brigade the outlook was none too bright.

At last, about noon, the last of the Hood and Drake had retired
into comparative safety, and Commander Ellis had to face his problem.
His decision, simple and sensible, was to withdraw in single file under
cover of his Lewis guns, and he was astoundingly successful; the little
battalion, now not much more than 200 strong, got away with barely
a casualty.

At Le Transloy, where the Naval Division was to re-form, they
were covered for the first and only time on the retreat by the 2nd and
17th Divisions, and the battalions had two hours' halt and the chance
of looting an opportunely situated ration dump. At about 3 p.m., however, it was learnt that the 2nd and 17th Divisions were falling back.
The corps, spoken to on the telephone, had no suggestions to offer, and it was decided, in the circumstances, that the Naval Division
should make for High Wood, and ultimately for the Thiepval Plateau.
Thus began a once famous march in parade order across the flank of
the advancing enemy, with the 7th Royal Fusiliers as a flank guard,
and the rest of the division in close order, the brigades marching parallel to each other in column of route at 1,000 yards interval.

Philip Gibbs at the time wrote:[2]

> They marched in parade order, with perfect discipline, throw-
> ing out flanking guards with machine guns, and so these men,
> weakened by losses, but strong in spirit, went across the Somme
> battlefield it was a great sight under the sky, and one that should
> be pictured in history . . . these men who had been thirty-six
> days in the line held themselves straight, and whistled to the
> tramp of their feet.

Commander Blackmore continues:

> Very casual shelling, and a few enemy aeroplanes were all that
> troubled us on that striking journey, excepting always the terri-
> ble monotony of the battered country. High Wood was reached

2. *Daily Chronicle*, April 1st, 1918.

at nightfall, and happily, almost at the moment that a Drake Lewis gun was mounted at the corner of the wood, and while the rest of us were endeavouring to take up a position of some sort in this unknown country, the first Verey light of the first enemy patrol went up, and was greeted with a burst of fire from the Drake. A slight pause, a second Verey light, and a further burst of fire, and the Germans believed this historic position to be held in force and withdrew, it is concluded, pending the preparation of an organised attack for the morning. This was a matter of fundamental importance, and had been but a question of a few minutes.

There were some infantry about here, but as usual they retired as soon as the Naval Division put in an appearance. But this did not worry us. Realising that the troops were secure for a brief time, the brigadier and the commanding officers were able to take stock of the position, and issue the necessary orders for its occupation. While they were away an excited cry had been raised, 'The *Uhlans* are on us!' This was succeeded by a tremendous scramble amongst the men, who were then sitting about while waiting, and by conflicting and haphazard orders of 'Man the road in rear' and 'Forward to the ridge.' Fortunately, before the confusion had been made worse by the effort to carry out either of these orders, the '*Uhlans*' were indeed upon us in the shape of a hard-galloping battery of guns passing through us to the rear. In that dim light, and at a time when the nerves of us all were just becoming somewhat ragged, these batteries, thundering past, were certainly an awesome sight. In a minute, however, calm prevailed, and shortly afterwards the C.O.'s returned with the dispositions completed.

An uncomfortable and consequently miserable night followed. Cold, hunger, and the unconscious anxiety of the forthcoming attack enabled one to sleep only in fits and starts in the shell-holes we occupied. Before it was light I wandered round our 'line,' and on my way back found a very dilapidated mackintosh at least three sizes too big for me. With the lesson of the two previous nights, I hung on to that mac throughout our many vicissitudes, and, indeed, used it for quite a time after I had replenished my kit. But I also found, which was perhaps more important, a half-carton of jam and a few hard (ration) biscuits, and though, when shared amongst us, it provided a very small addition to our meagre meal, it was at least something. How much, I wonder, would we have given for a cup of tea?

With the advent of dawn heavy fire was opened by their machine guns, pushed well forward as usual, and this fire swept the ridge continuously, making observation difficult and dangerous. Some casualties were suffered, and amongst those killed was an officer who had joined us with a small party of reinforcements during the night. Arriving in a cap, a steel helmet had been found for him, and he was in the act of putting this on when he was hit in the head. We had anticipated an immediate attack, but in this we were mistaken, and it was not until nearer 10 o'clock that the attack developed. Had the memory of High Wood imbued the enemy with caution?

In the meantime we were vouchsafed a wonderful, if disturbing sight, for by the light of day, in whichever direction we looked, we could see nothing but those hunched, grey-coated figures moving slowly in our direction. Only too conscious of the absence of any artillery support, fully aware that they were themselves but a handful, our men remained impassive, and quietly awaited the oncoming of that horde.

The troops on the left, owing to a misunderstanding, withdrew and left an ominous gap. It was here that the Sergeant-Major maintained the fine traditions of the regular soldier, for with his steel helmet in his hand, unconcerned by that stream of bullets, he waved those men who were scattered slightly in rear, in the nature of local supports, forward to the gap.

But a tragedy now cast a gloom over the remnant of the battalion, for the C.O., moving from point to point on the ridge in the search for the best place for observation, was struck in the neck by a bullet and seriously wounded. (Subsequently, to our universal grief, he succumbed to his wounds.) Stretcher-bearers and other volunteers, undeterred by the exposed position, worked their way forward to the shell-hole in which he lay, and made him as comfortable as possible. There was little time to be lost, and it was decided that an endeavour should be made to evacuate him before the attack, and an old blanket was procured and passed under him. Four volunteers, crouching at the corners, raised themselves at a given signal, and, clear cut on the skyline, carried our wounded C.O. to the rear. For a moment the hail of bullets continued, but when the enemy realized what was happening the firing ceased, and there was not another shot until the party had withdrawn behind the ridge. Unexpected as it was, this gallantry much impressed all ranks.

Other and more pressing matters now occupied our minds. Their protective machine-gun fire was so effective that reply on our part was almost impossible, and owing to the haphazard nature of the observation we were able to make a good deal of uncertainty existed as to the proximity of the enemy. In addition, there had been no further word from brigade, and Geoffrey Price, then in command, was not at all clear what had been decided the previous night.

Great difficulty was also being experienced in maintaining touch with our very extended and irregular 'line,' the actual position of which was, indeed, unknown, I think, to anyone. With these many and varied difficulties our prospects were certainly gloomy. Later, it was rumoured that we were to withdraw from such an untenable position. This was, however, an equally unpleasing prospect, for there are few more dangerous or more distasteful operations than that of getting away from an enemy who is really close to you.

After what seemed an eternity orders did actually reach us to the effect that we were to withdraw, ten at a time, and rejoin at Martinpuich. Somehow or other this was passed round the troops, and in small groups and in turn they left the line and made their way to the rear in various directions. And we were not a minute too soon. Rackham and I saw the last leave, and as we turned to find Price we saw the Germans cutting round behind us on the High Wood flank. Hoping the others had already left, we turned and made our way to the rear, bearing to the right, and began an exciting journey.

The country here was very undulating, and as we passed over the ridges, so we came under the machine-gun fire, and remained a good target until we had descended into the dip beyond, where we waited a moment before the next venture. It was in one of these pieces of dead ground that we came up with the line orderly-room clerk—I forget his name—who joined us. In this withdrawal we suffered, alas! a good many casualties, and in passing over one of the ridges side by side our clerk was shot dead between us. Satisfying ourselves that he was beyond help, we took his case of papers and pushed on. Here and there, scattered thinly over the countryside, the remnants of the battalion could be seen pressing in the general direction of Martinpuich. Later, we caught up with the sergeant-major, who had been hit in the foot, and, helping him as best we could, we slowly made our way through the ruins of Martinpuich and beyond to the sugar factory on the Albert-Bapaume road at Courcellette, where by degrees the units gathered.

When Rackham and I arrived we saw Price, and heard that he and Spoonley had jumped into a kind of sunken road at High Wood almost on top of three Germans, who, crying 'Kamerade,' promptly fired upon them. Replying suitably (to the cry, not the fire), they made a dive for it, and, it was thought at first, escaped being hit. Later, however, Price had felt a kind of stiffening, and Rackham, having taken him to a neighbouring sheltered spot, examined him, and discovered a deep flesh wound which would make sitting down an uncomfortable business for some time! For fear of blood-poisoning we persuaded him to go, and shortly afterwards he was walking down that long straight road to Albert. We learned later that he had only just missed being caught by enemy troops advancing to cut the road.

Drawn up along the side of the road was a motorcycle machine-gun squad, which, being more fleet than the infantry, or more valuable, or perhaps it was merely habit, withdrew also to Albert shortly after our arrival. While waiting and resting the divisional general arrived in a car, and got out in an endeavour to cheer us with the news that he had a fresh brigade on the Thiepval Ridge in our rear. After a short parley with the brigadier and a word with many of the men he went on to Albert, taking the wounded sergeant-major with him, and he, too, narrowly escaped being caught there.

I expect most of us thought it would have been more satisfactory if the fresh brigade had been in front of us, especially as the enemy now began to appear on the outskirts of Martinpuich, some half a mile away. We were quickly seen, the road here being on the top of the ridge, and stray shots were fired in our direction, but on this occasion we had the satisfaction of replying, and their farther advance was held up for a considerable time. The general was doubtless satisfied, if only from our utter isolation and insignificant numbers, that any sort of defence of the position was out of the question, for the enemy later appearing well round both flanks, he gave the order to withdraw farther west to the Ancre. Perched on his horse, he was an excellent mark for the enemy, and as he moved off with us he ordered the men to keep away from him.

*En route* we passed the fresh brigade on the ridge. I was chased by an anxious battalion officer, who asked if we were not going to stop there with them. I fear my reply was a little pointed, and I referred him to the brigade major, who was just behind (or it may have been the staff captain), from whom, however, he received still less satisfaction. Reaching Thiepval, we were ordered to occupy some old trenches in a semicircle round the Mill Road across the Ancre, and as before very long our old enemy again approached us, we wondered what had happened to that fresh brigade. Some firing was exchanged, but obviously they merely wished to obtain contact with us, for so we remained in close touch, and, as if by tacit consent, we left one another alone. Hopelessly fatigued, hungry, without the prospect of food—this was the third night there had been no issue of rations—and cold, the troops snatched a brief and mealless rest.

Rackham, Smith, Spoonley, and myself were, I think, the only officers, and with some sixty odd men were all that were left of the battalion, but later that night Edwards joined us with a few men, and finding he was the senior officer, Rackham gladly handed over command to him. But this inactivity did not last long. We had previously seen another division withdrawing in one long line down the farther bank of the Ancre, and this may have governed the decision to withdraw across Mill Bridge and, after destroying the bridge (it was but a plank one), to occupy the railway line alongside the river. This was successfully accomplished by 5 a.m., and we took up our position on the left at Mesnil in the same trenches as had been occupied by the division in 1916.

This coincidence was, for the moment, lost sight of in a far more important occurrence, for, on passing through Hamel, we each received a tin of 'Maconachie' and a ration of oatmeal, and early that cold morning, the attack not being pressed, we had our first meal for a long time, and a hot one at that. Rest, taken in snatches, it is true, with this meal, put new life into us, and, in consequence, a more lively interest was taken in consolidating, in a rough-and-ready fashion, the position we had taken up.

We had so long been without artillery that a solitary gun, which went into action behind us, created a mild sensation. Firing at the many groups of the enemy to be seen on the Thiepval Ridge and along the valley of the Ancre, it did quite useful work, but it was not long before its position was discovered by the Bosche, who promptly brought a battery to bear upon it, with more discomfort to us, however, than to the gunners.

On March 26th the battalion were relieved by the 12th Division (another of the mysterious counter-attack divisions) at 10 p.m., and went back to Engelbelmer, a march which must have revived many curious memories for those few who had gone back along the same route from the same trenches after the great victory of November 13th, 1916. The promise of rest—neither officers nor men had had their boots off for six days—was vastly welcome, but in the middle of their first meal the battalion was suddenly called out to spend the night on outpost duty outside the village, the enemy having broken through the 12th Division's lines. The alarm subsided with the dawn, but the next two days were spent in standing by, while the situation on the front changed alarmingly from hour to hour, and the Hamel trenches, a virtually unassailable position, were unaccountably lost. An isolated enemy patrol even ventured as far as Engelbelmer, and was captured by the Hawke sentries. Thanks, however, to two brilliant exploits by the 188th and 190th Brigades, the enemy were definitely held in front of Mesnil, and on a line running through Aveluy Wood. On the 30th the crisis was over, and the Hawke Battalion marched back to Hedauville, when Commander Jones reported and assumed command, only to be wounded the same afternoon.

At Hedauville they expected, and with every reason, a decent interval for rest and reorganisation, but, like their new commanding officer, they found the situation less peaceful than it might have been. Indeed, the showing of the division in the line, who had already lost Hamel, had made it necessary to send the 2nd Division, which, like the Naval Division, had fought its way back with every credit from the Flesquières salient, to take their place. The 17th Division would not be refitted before April 15th, and it would not have been reasonable to expect the 2nd Division to remain in the line for the whole three weeks which were in question. In the circumstances the Hawke Battalion was warned to be ready to move back from Hedauville to

THIEPVAL RIDGE, MARCH, 1918

Mesnil on the 5th April.

To bring the battalion up to something approaching a normal establishment, Lieutenant-Commander W. Arblaster, of the Hood, was given temporary command, with Major K. C. H. Warner, of the 8th Kent Cyclist Battalion, as second in command. This released Lieutenant Edwards to command "D" company. Sub-Lieutenant Beaumont remained in command of "C," and Sub-Lieutenant Dodds rejoined to take over his original ("B") company. At the same time the battalion was reinforced by a considerable detachment of Royal Welch Fusiliers, with five officers (Lieutenant H. Hughes Jones, Lieutenant B. C. Farrant, Lieutenant D. O. Davies, Lieutenant J. S. Laing, and Second Lieutenant D. Vaughan), as well as by a number of men from miscellaneous units of the division, who had been collected at centres behind the lines from the flotsam and jetsam of the widespread and disorganised retreat.

The task of absorbing these drafts, far more numerous than the relics of the battalion itself, was no light one, but it was enormously helped by the enthusiasm and energy of the Welch Fusilier officers in what cannot have been the particularly inspiriting task of subordinating their own *esprit de corps,* and in some cases their individual seniority, to the needs of an efficient reorganisation.

The success which attended the efforts of everyone concerned had only one attendant drawback, that, in the pressure of such urgent work, no recommendations for officers, N.C.O.'s, or men in connection with the difficult and well-sustained fighting of the previous weeks were submitted.

The 3rd, 4th, and 5th April was spent in organising the platoons (three only to each company, in view of the shortage of platoon commanders and N.C.O.'s), and in issuing iron rations, field dressings, and ammunition. Then, on the 6th, the battalion marched to Engelbelmer, and on the night of the 6th to 7th took over the trenches on Mesnil Ridge from the Artists Rifles.

The condition of the trenches, which had been left undrained and untended since they were last occupied by the battalion in November, 1916, was deplorable, but the reward of three weeks' hard fighting was found in the complete immunity with which, in broad daylight, it was possible to walk outside the line in full view of the Thiepval and Hamel Ridges. The enemy had, indeed, been momentarily fought to a standstill. It was very different a few weeks later, but by that time both sides had been reinforced, and supplies of engineers' material were becoming once more available. In these early April days there was nothing of the kind, and the conditions had reverted, as far as externals were concerned, to the primitive conditions experienced on the Aisne in 1914.

The battalion did two spells in the line (with three days' rest at Engelbelmer) before their turn came for a real fortnight's rest near Toutencourt, where a rifle range, real generals available for inspections, and a troop of Follies, brought back the memory of happier and less anxious days.

This was, indeed, another period of transition. The days of bitter defensive fighting were over, and the experience gained was soon to be turned to account. Much of the credit for what was to follow should, however, be given to Commander Ellis, the fine leader who just at this time lay dying at Wimereux.

Bernard Ellis had commanded during the darkest hours which the battalion had experienced, yet he had brought it, perhaps, to its highest point of efficiency. He had established a fighting tradition among the junior officers and among the rank and file for which their earlier experiences had provided, inevitably, no foundation. He came to the battalion with the reputation of a strict disciplinarian, but he knew no distinction between discipline and fighting efficiency, and on the last point the battalion soon learnt not only to accept but to value his judgment. It was in this way that the period of his command laid the foundations of the successes which the battalion was to win in the final advance. If battalion headquarters represented still, and to the end, an earlier vintage, Stephenson, Dodds, Wainright, and, indeed, almost all those who were to lead companies and platoons in the days to come, had gained these first active experiences under Ellis's leadership.

Of the petty officers and men the tale is a little different, and the break in continuity more complete. As far as the rank and file are concerned, very few of the original company remained with the battalion. There were happy exceptions. C.P.O. Malpress stayed to the end to add a touch of humour to the monotony of distributing rations at a time when there were, for whole weeks together, enough to go round. Thanks to P.O. Steele, the Hawke Battalion Headquarters were destined to have a sufficiency to eat and drink to the day of the Armistice, and thereafter, if rumour speaks truthfully, a considerable surplus; while the orderly room remained in the safe keeping of P.O. Peckham, that staunch ally of adjutants, who continued to deal with harassing returns with his accustomed *sang froid* until the time came for him to put his own name on the list for demobilization.

Amongst other ratings of the battalion at this time who were to remain, more or less, until the end were C.P.O. L. E. Caldwell, Battalion Sergeant-Major; C.P.O. J. Mitchell, of "A" company, who, after the Armistice, not only became a "star "performer in the battalion boxing competitions, but invariably led the way in those long cross-country runs; and C.P.O.'s McCombie and Jennings, of "C" and "D" companies. P.O. Rosewarne, who rejoined a little later, was to prove as invaluable to the sports officer (Sub-Lieutenant G. H. N. Inman) in assisting to arrange boxing competitions and football matches as he was in maintaining the prestige of the battalion when, as he frequently did, he represented it in inter-unit competitions. There were, too, C.P.O. Barrie, the Police Sergeant; A.B. H. G. Archdale, the runner; P.O. Marsh, the Sergeant Cook; P.O. Snowdon, the Gas N.C.O., and worthy member of the football team, which won the divisional cup in 1917; the Battalion Cobbler, P.O. Mustard; and P.O. Gibson, of "B" company.

Of the others death, wounds, and sickness had taken, by May, 1918, a heavy toll. Their names find mention only too seldom in this or any other written record, yet they had played, perhaps, the chief part. On their achievements had been founded the tradition which was to help the reorganised battalion, with less than a dozen experienced officers and some 600 raw recruits, to their final and even astonishing successes

# CHAPTER 11

# The Advance to Victory

The difference between the feelings of those in France and those at home took on, in the summer of 1918, a novel colour. For once pessimism was the prerogative of the civilian, and a definite growth of confidence was noticeable in France. The Hawke Battalion, which returned to the old Hamel sector on May 8th, provided no exception. Commander Jones (who had commanded the Anson at Gallipoli and the Nelson at Passchendaele) had, as we have seen, succeeded Commander Ellis, and Lieutenant-Commander Lockwood came back opportunely to his old post as second in command. This was on April 12th, and enabled Lieutenant-Commander Arblaster and Major Roberts to rejoin their units.

Blackmore was formally appointed adjutant, a singular fact about the appointment being that he was the one adjutant of the Hawke who, prior to his appointment, had ever been inside an orderly room in England. Surgeon-Lieutenant Leake, R.N., was the new battalion M.O., and C.P.O. Coldwell the new regimental-sergeant-major, Codner returned to take on once more the arduous work of Transport Officer, and Day remained as quartermaster.[1] There were thus at headquarters three officers who had served with the battalion at Gallipoli, and these, with Commander Jones (who was actually the last of the original R.N.V.R. officer remaining with the division), provided a remarkable link with the past.

The company commanders, Stephenson (who rejoined early in May), Dodds, Beaumont, and Edwards, represented a new post-Beau-

---

1. Other headquarters officers were Sub-Lieutenant W. J. McCann (Signalling Officer), Lieutenant D. D. Davies, R.W.F. (Assistant Adjutant), Sub-Lieutenant W. D. Watson (Assistant Transport Officer), and Sub-Lieutenant F. V. Wood (Intelligence Officer).

court generation, but had seen much equally stern fighting. The platoon commanders were the new factor, the product for the most part of the Cadet battalions at home, but with long records of service in many instances as N.C.O.'s. The exceptions were the Welch Fusilier officers, who remained with the battalion till invalided as the result of wounds or sickness, and one or two of the older officers (among them Sub-Lieutenant George Clarke, Sub-Lieutenant Woodgate, Sub-Lieutenant Strickland, Sub-Lieutenant E. J. B. Lloyd, and Sub-Lieutenant Cockburn) who rejoined the Hawke after the retreat or were transferred from the Nelson or Howe battalions.

The rank and file of the reorganised battalion was inevitably more experimental. Seventy-five *per cent*, were young and not very thoroughly trained recruits, and the presence of these was inevitably a source of some anxiety. Blandford had been forced some months before to adopt the rigid thirteen weeks' system of training recruits, which meant that no man under any circumstances ever went to the front wholly disciplined or wholly trained. In normal times these recruits had anything from three weeks to two months' further training at the "Divisional Wing" in France, and then joined up with a battalion sufficiently strong to absorb them almost one by one, and each into different platoons and even sections. Now, on the contrary, whole sections consisted of nothing but recruits. Except as officers, servants, company cooks, signallers, transport men, and N.C.O.'s, trained and experienced men were lacking except in so far as a few of them had rejoined with the latest drafts.

The months of May, June, and July, spent in the trenches opposite Hamel (till June 5th) and on the Auchonvillers Ridge (from June 20th to July 23rd), were, seen in retrospect, just weeks spent in marking time. To the numerous subalterns,[2] however, to whom these weeks were their first on active service as officers (though one and all of them had seen service abroad in the ranks), and to the still more numerous recruits, they were days of eager and anxious experience. To the senior officers they were days of hard and anxious preparation.

2. Among these were Sub-Lieutenants H. Cooper, J. Williams, S. C. Vokins, A. W. Withnell, A. A. Leighton, E. E. Wicks, F. C. Richardson, T. C. Wall, C. H. Darrell, J. V. C. Rudnick, W. Telfer, E. H. Smith, B. H. Salter, J. O. Harris, E; H. L. Millard, and W. E. Willison. Of these, J. O. Harris (an officer of brilliant promise who won the D.S.O. as a platoon commander in the battle for the Drocourt-Quéant line), W. L. Willison (who led "C" company with great distinction in the attack on Le Barque), A. A. Leighton, C. H. Darrell, and E. E. Wicks were to die within a few weeks in the final offensive.

HAWKE BATTALION OFFICERS, JUNE, 1918.

*Back Row*: Sub-Lieut. Millard, Sub-Lieut. Harris, Sub-Lieut. Telfer, Sub-Lieut. Woodgate, Sub-Lieut. Watson, Sub-Lieut. Voxins, Sub-Lieut. Farrant, Sub-Lieut. Wellison.

*Centre*: R.S.M. Coldwell, Lieut. Jones, R.W.F., Lieut. Cotter, R.N.V.R., Hon. Lieut. & Qr. Day, Sub-Lieut. Works, Sub-Lieut. Leighton. Sub-Lieut. Codner, Rev. McNutt, Sub-Lieut. Davies, R.W.F., Sub-Lieut. Strickland, Sub-Lieut. Rudnick, Sub-Lieut. Rue. *(French Inf.)*

*Sitting*: Sur.-Lieut. Leake, Lieut. Beaumont, R.N.V.R., Lieut. Stephenson, R.N.V.R., Lieut.-Com. Lockwood, Com. Jones, Lieut.-Com. Blackmore, Lieut. Edwards, R.N.V.R., Lieut. Dodds, R.N.R.

*Lying*: Sub-Lieut. Wood, Sub-Lieut. McCann.

The enemy showed during May and the beginning of June a very considerable activity, principally in shelling the conspicuous Mesnil Ridge and the dugouts behind the crest. The weather was, for once, ideally fine, and one enthusiastic but optimistic recruit wrote home to say that "he was fighting in his shirt sleeves," a description of a quiet period of trench routine which shows that the interval for training was not superfluous.

The description was, indeed, singularly inappropriate, since the line was held in depth, only one platoon of each company being in the "outpost" line—disconnected posts on the 1917 model, but a long way from the enemy—another in the old trench system, and the remaining two in those dugouts in Mesnil which had provided in November, 1916, the more luxurious accommodation for battalions out of the line.

The only active incident of this period was a successful raid carried out by "D" company of the Hawke, in conjunction with a company of Marines, on Hamel. The objective of "D" company was the railway embankment and the neighbouring posts, the Marines raiding the village itself on the left of the Hawke objective.

The Hawke platoons engaged were (from left to right) the 14th, 15th, and 16th under Sub-Lieutenants Telfer, Kelland, and Rudnick. The 13th Platoon (Sub-Lieutenant Williams) was in the outpost line, and a Lewis-gun section was detailed from "C" company (commanded on this occasion by Lieutenant Farrant) to fire down the Mesnil-Hamel road. The effect of this was to drive the enemy from our right towards the centre and left of the battalion objective.

The 16th Platoon in the circumstances met with no opposition, the enemy posts nearest to the railway being deserted. The 15th Platoon rushed the gully formed by the curve of the embankment, and the 14th climbed the embankment on the left. Here they met with considerable opposition, and were reinforced by the platoon from the gully, who had already captured two machine guns and an authentic sergeant-major.[3]

The fight on the embankment was protracted, and had reached no definite issue, though the enemy had been driven back some distance with a good deal of loss before the recall signal went up.

In the fighting the battalion lost Sub-Lieutenant Kelland and two men killed, and twelve men wounded. The loss to the enemy was at

---

3. One of these guns, with the sergeant-major, was captured by Sub-Lieutenant Telfer himself after a stand-up fight.

least eighteen men killed and an estimated thirty wounded. One prisoner and two machine guns were, as has been said, captured by the 15th Platoon.

The distinctive feature of the enterprise was the successful fight of the 14th Platoon, and the skilful withdrawal of this and the 15th Platoon by Sub-Lieutenant Telfer in the face of a still vigorous opposition. The raid was carried out by platoons composed mainly of recruits, under officers new to their work, and its success was not without importance for this reason. The reconstituted battalion was more than a match for the new opposition.

On June 5th the battalion moved off to Rubembré for three weeks' rest and intensive training. When next it was behind the lines—fifteen weeks later—the war was virtually finished; just now, however, there was no sign of any ending. The Germans were still on the offensive both in the north and the south, and the most that could be said was that the routine of trench warfare was slowly re-establishing itself over an ever-increasing length of the allied line.

Training in the circumstances followed the ordinary lines, save for a greater amount of leisure arranged to enable battalion and brigade sports to be held "under divisional arrangements." This type of preparation for scientific war may or may not have its advantages. Like all other devices of despairing staff officers seeking to determine the contest of blood and iron by some mysterious alchemy devised in the purer air of St. Omer, it reached on occasion ridiculous heights, recalling, indeed, the drill and discipline slogan of 1914, the bombing gospel of 1915, the raiding craze of 1916, and the patrolling mania of 1917. The spectacle of recruits at Aldershot playing ball in the barrack square under the supervision of skilled instructors was, indeed, sublime in its irrelevance to the tragic contest of empires now nearing its decision, and the diversions of Rubembré, more rational and better earned, must nevertheless on a sober view be in some measure disassociated from the dramatic events into which, after a short spell in the Auchonvillers sector, the Hawke Battalion found itself plunged at the end of July.

What is more to the point is the experience gained by the battalion in the trenches in July of a visible and positive demoralisation among the enemy. The reward of four years of hardship and suffering was for the first time actually in sight. Even the enemy artillery were inactive, and under our own bombardments their defences visibly crumbled away. A raid by the Drake Battalion on July 12th, in which, with the loss of one man of the raiding party, twenty-one prisoners and a machine gun were brought back in triumph and heavy losses in killed and wounded were inflicted, marked for the 189th Brigade the climax of their ascendancy. They were now to reap the fruits.

On July 20th, when the division were still in the line, it became known that General Foch's counter-stroke on the Marne had thrown the enemy back across the river, and on the 21st Château Thierry was retaken. The enemy was in retreat.

★★★★★★

The first battle of the concluding allied offensive had been directed against the enemy lodgement across the Marne. It was a preliminary operation, fought while the Naval Division were still in the line opposite Beaumont Hamel with no thought of an early close to the war. The first rumour of more dramatic events reached the division on August 8th in the form of unexpected orders to move to the Montigny area, just south of the Albert-Amiens road. On that day the Fourth Army, in conjunction with the French (whose actual advance began on the 9th), attacked the enemy salient south of Albert. The objective was, roughly, our old 1916 line, the possession of which would restore Montdidier and free the Paris-Amiens railway. By August 12th the objective had been gained, and the way was clear for the Second Battles of the Somme.

Marshal Foch's intention had been that the offensive should continue against the enemy front south of Albert, and it was with a view to protecting the flank of the further advance that the Naval Division had been moved south. As is now known, his plan, after discussion, was abandoned, and it was decided to turn the German positions west of the Somme by striking from above Albert southward in the direction of Bapaume. This meant an attack on a front extending further north even than Gommecourt (the northern limit of the attack of July 1st, 1916), and involved a few days' respite for the enemy.

In this offensive the Hawke Battalion was now to take part. Their move southward had taken them to Behencourt, and thence on August 5th to Halloy. On August 15th began the march north, through Vauchelles to Souastre, just behind Bucquoy, through which ran the 37th Division line. The intention was to attack from Bucquoy on the first day of the offensive in a southerly direction, to cut across the Albert-Bapaume road, and thus to turn the enemy positions south of Bucquoy through Hamel to the Somme itself. The purpose of the plan was, of course, to avoid a renewal of the frontal attack over the whole length of this fatal and familiar battleground. This plan spelt an important and fortunate modification in the old-fashioned tactics, and determined the share of the Hawke Battalion in the new battle; the Naval Division was to follow immediately behind the left brigade of the 37th Division when they attacked, and the 5th Division immediately behind the right brigade. The 37th Division were to halt on the first objective (the German front-line system); the Naval Division were to push on to the railway in front of Achiet-le-Grand, then to cross it, and to reach a line east of the village.

The railway was the objective of the 189th and 188th Brigades, and, rather unfortunately, as it happened, it was decided to reach this in two bounds, the first ending on an imaginary "Brown Line" a little east of Logeast Wood. This was some 2,000 yards beyond the final objective of the 37th Division, and about as far again from the railway. On the 189th Brigade front the Brown Line was to be attacked and held by the Hawke on the right (with their flank across the Bucquoy-Achiet-le-Grand road in touch with the 5th Division), and by two companies of the Drake on the left (in touch with the 188th Brigade). The Hood and the rest of the Drake were to go through to the railway.

The attack opened on August 21st at 4.55 a.m., and the Hawke Battalion (with the rest of the first line of the Naval Division) followed immediately behind. There was a dense mist, but, thanks to the skilful leading of the company commanders, direction was kept. Dodds with "B" company was on the right, Willison with "C" company in the centre, Wainright with "D" on the left, and Stephenson's "A" company in support.

The 37th Division took the front-line system with very little loss, and the Hawke Battalion followed behind them. The fighting on this day was of a novel character, companies advancing in lines of platoons, and meeting in the derelict and virtually undefended trench system with no hint of serious resistance. The enemy in every case at this first stage either retreated or surrendered.

When the Hawke came to advance on their own under the protection of a barrage, though not of the old intensive kind, but more in the nature of a desultory bombardment of potential enemy strong points, they met with literally no opposition, unless isolated prisoners, pathetically anxious to surrender, can be said to have infused an element of terror into the veiled and mysterious movement of this dawn of victory. How changed was the atmosphere from the cruel fighting of November, 1916, may best be gathered from a note written by "C" company platoon commander:[4]

> A number of prisoners, who showed little inclination to fight, several machine guns, and some artillery, were captured.

With the gain of the Brown Line and its consolidation the fighting was over for the Hawke Battalion. The battalions behind them passed through to an unknown event, shrouded in a still impenetrable mist, which lifted only to reveal their presence to the enemy's machine guns. Still, the advance had covered well over three miles from the time of starting, and when the Naval Division were relieved on the evening of August 22nd, Achiet-le-Grand, if not ours, was yet ours for the asking.

The guns had come up on the night of the first advance, and on the 23rd the tide of victory swept forward. No halt was to be called now or henceforward to a remorseless offensive directed by a new and confident imagination of a commander-in-chief to whom war was not a profession but an exercise of will.

The fighting of the 23rd drove the enemy back across the Arras-Achiet-le-Grand-Miraumont railway to a new line from Grevillers through Loupart Wood to Warlencourt, covering the Albert-Bapaume road. As long as the enemy held this line they could hold on to their positions between the Ancre and the Somme, and the main object of the offensive was thus still to be achieved. Failure, however, was not to be thought of. So, when on August 24th the New Zealand and 37th Divisions went forward again without much success, the Naval Division was ordered to take up the fighting on the right of the New Zealanders, and to advance through Loupart Wood (reported partially cleared) to the capture of Le Barque and Thilloy.

The Hawke Battalion had advanced in the morning of the 24th from its position in reserve to the neighbourhood of Logeast Wood. Late in the afternoon they were ordered to march to the western edge of Loupart Wood, and Commander Jones was given verbal orders that the battalion was to attack at 7.30 p.m. There were no maps and no orders, and on the road to the forming-up place, though no one knew precisely where this was, battalions of the Naval and other divisions, with their transport, were intermixed in considerable confusion. Time was pressing, and if the Hawke were to get forward at all it was clear that they would have to leave the shelter of the sunken road, which

---

4. Sub-Lieutenant Vokins, who gained the Military Cross for resolute leading in the fighting four days later on the outskirts of Thilloy.

was the safest line of approach, and go forward in the open.

Unfortunately, just as the battalion left the road, a flight of enemy aeroplanes came on the scene.

Lieutenant-Commander Blackman wrote:

> It was an exciting moment, for there were many planes, and they swooped upon us with heavy machine-gun fire and bombing, flying very low indeed. They were up and away again before anything could be done, and the casualties amongst the troops and horses there must have been very heavy, many bombs dropping into the crowded sunken roads. 'Brads'[5] was there, and his horse was so badly hit that he shot it. It was a fortunate escape for many of us, but I fear it unsettled many of our men, already disturbed by the uncertainty of the position. Moreover, we were not at our kicking-off place at the time when we should have been beginning the attack.

Even when, about 7.45 p.m., the battalion reached its destination and got in touch with Brigade Headquarters, it was found that no one knew exactly where the objectives were to be found. Even the position of the enemy's outpost line was unknown.

The obvious solution was a reconnaissance, and Brigadier-General Du Pree rode forward with Commander Jones and the commanding officers of the Hood and Drake Battalions to show them from his map the line of advance. Their reconnaissance, however, was unsuccessful, as they were unable to get any view of the objective.

It was in these difficult circumstances that the brigadier, on his own responsibility, but with the expressed approval of the battalion commanders, cancelled the order for the attack, and after notifying the units on the right and left (there was, of course, no time to get orders from the division), reported his action to Divisional Headquarters.

Later in the evening maps arrived, and orders to advance at 6 a.m. the next morning. The Hawke, Hood, and Drake Battalions, in line from left to right, formed the right of the attack as far as the Naval Division were concerned. Further to the right, the 47th Division were reported to have advanced and captured Warlencourt, but as a matter of fact this was not the case, and the right flank of the 189th Brigade was exposed. The original plan for the attack had provided against this possibility, two tanks having been ordered up on the previous evening

---

5. Our old friend, Surgeon Bradbury, D.S.O., R.N. (at this time Surgeon Lieutenant-Commander), who was commanding one of the Naval Division Field Ambulances.

specifically to clear the trenches on the right, which ran parallel to Loupart Wood, and formed the right divisional boundary. These tanks, unfortunately, had gone back when the attack was postponed and had not reappeared. It fell to the Drake, in the circumstances, to clear the trenches, should they be occupied; the space between the trenches and the edge of the wood was the frontage, roughly, of the Hood Battalion, and the Hawke Battalion was to advance through the wood itself.

Whether on the previous evening the enemy had been in occupation of the trenches which threatened so formidably the flank of our advance is uncertain. It became only too clear, however, that they were holding them effectively in the morning. The result was serious.

Through the middle of Loupart Wood, dividing the frontage of the Hawke Battalion, there was a road. To the left of this were "A" and "B" companies, and, partly because the wood here gave, in the prevailing mist, remarkably good cover from view, partly because not only the enemy machine guns, but also their artillery, were ranged on the nearer edge of the wood, these companies, with the exception of one platoon, went through the wood with slight losses. Very different was the fate of "C" and "D" companies, and of Battalion Headquarters. At the very beginning of the attack Commander Jones, most cheerful and considerate of commanding officers, who had survived Gallipoli, Passchendaele, and Welsh Ridge without a wound, was killed by a machine-gun bullet.

Under Lieutenant-Commander Wainright the advance continued, but half-way through the wood the two companies came to a clearing on which the enemy machine gunners concentrated their fire. The chief centre of resistance was an enemy machine-gun post southeast of the wood, and it was in attempting gallantly to rush this post that Commander Wainright was killed. Here, too, fell Sub-Lieutenant Willison and Sub-Lieutenant Darrell, with some twenty N.C.O.'s and men. The Hood also suffered heavily, and, but for a heavy mist, this battalion and the two Hawke companies must have been almost annihilated. As it was, their advance was, for the time being, definitely checked.

As has been said "A" and "B" companies, under Lieutenants Stephenson and Dodds, were making more rapid progress, and, partly thanks to the mist, had reached the Albert-Bapaume road with hardly a casualty. At the road they came across, at point-blank range, a large party of the enemy not holding any defensive position but clearly taken by surprise; these surrendered, assuming no doubt that their advance party, who were at this moment holding up the two right companies of the Hawke (and the Hood and Drake Battalions as well) with tragic success, had been overpowered. It was so foggy here that it was impossible to see more than ten paces ahead.

On crossing the road the two Hawke companies had, in accordance with their orders, to change direction and advance due east against Le Barque. This was done, and, still under cover of a thick mist, Le Barque itself—only a heap of ruins—was entered, and four machine-gun posts surprised. The surprise was mutual, but, as we had learnt to our cost on the Fifth Army front in March, the attacking force on the look-out for opposition has a decisive advantage over the defender ignorant of the imminence of attack.

The early morning sun, looming like a red disc through the mist, kept the two companies on their course, and they found themselves crossing the valley south-east of Ligny-Thilloy punctually and according to plan. Still stealing unawares on a somnolent enemy, they surprised in the hollow of the valley a battery of 5-9's, and captured the guns' crews without a shot being fired. This, however, was the last of their triumphs, for as they climbed the ridge at the far side of the valley the mist cleared, and the audacious adventure was revealed in its true and not too formidable character to a large force of Germans immediately in front. Two derelict trenches were hastily manned, but not before the enemy had opened up a heavy machine-gun fire and inflicted a good deal of loss.

Lights were put up to attract attention, but there was no response, and the position quickly became desperate, as the enemy put a barrage down on our improvised line, and began to creep round both flanks. Lieutenant Stephenson was wounded, and so also was Sub-Lieutenant Leighton, detached with a small party to endeavour to check the advance of the enemy from the north against our left. The endeavour failed, and Sub-Lieutenant Dodds, now in command of the two companies, extricated himself with Lieutenant Hughes Jones and some forty N.C.O.'s and men only with the utmost difficulty, leaving behind in the trenches Lieutenant Stephenson and a number of wounded men.

The enemy came on in line, excited and clearly suspicious of some deeply-laid plot. The wounded were, however, well cared for, being taken to a German Field Hospital only a little way off, which was, however, being hurriedly moved under the threat of the morning's fighting. The German Intelligence Officer at this hospital knew, as it

211

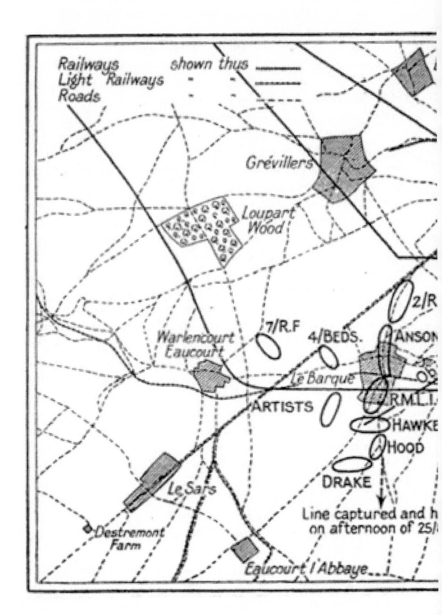

MAP ILLUSTRATING OPERATIONS OF THE

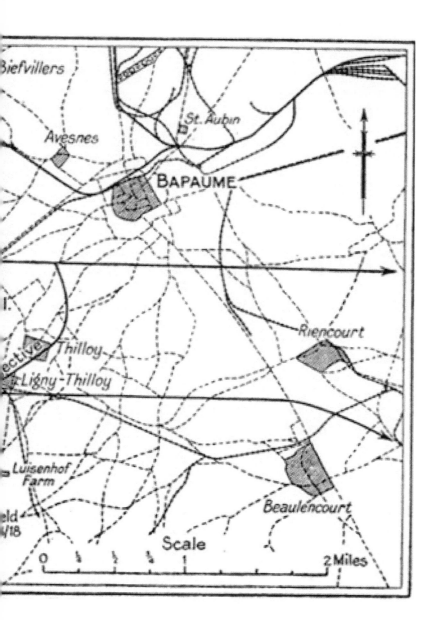

HAWKE BATTALION, AUGUST 25, 1918

turned out, of every move of the Naval Division through the summer, and, incidentally, complimented the division on its achievements throughout the war.

While these incidents were developing so unfavourably, the main body of the Hawke, with the Hood and Drake, remained for a long time held up at Loupart Wood. Not until 10.30 a.m. was the opposition overcome, and the survivors of the three battalions advanced across the Bapaume road to the "Yellow Cut."

Commander Blackmore, who had taken over command of the Hawke on the death of Lieutenant-Commander Wainright writes:

> The 'Yellow Cut,' was a deep ravine running parallel to our line of advance against Thilloy. The farther edge of the ravine actually commanded the village, and was for this reason being swept with very heavy machine-gun fire from guns beyond. Beak[6] and I and one or two others went ahead, and from the shelter of a dip on the forward slope of the ridge we could see into Thilloy on our left front, where there seemed to be considerable German activity. We realised that to advance farther would mean disastrous casualties, and possibly the wiping out of what remained of us. We were entirely on our own, with our flanks in the air, and we decided we should serve a more useful purpose by holding what we had got, which would make it more easy for those operating on our flanks, and we consequently pushed out posts on to the forward slope protecting the remainder in the cut. It was here, about noon, that we were joined by Dodds and the remainder of 'A' and 'B' companies. A little later, Sub-Lieutenant F. V. Wood took a patrol into the outskirts of Thilloy and found it occupied—indeed, we had ourselves seen the Bosche moving up. A counterattack was subsequently delivered from here, but our heavies, directed by planes, broke it up, and when the enemy attacked again our infantry had become established.

The new position was of importance; it isolated Bapaume from the south-east and enforced on the enemy a further and substantial withdrawal. In the circumstances, and despite the misfortunes of the early morning, the net result of the day's fighting was a definite victory.

The evening of August 25th marked the end of the active share of the Hawke Battalion in this operation. The next two days (August

---

6. Commander Beak, V.C., D.S.O., M.C., O.C. Drake Battalion.

26th and 27th) were not signalized by any further success, though many attacks were made by the 188th and 190th Brigade on Thilloy and Ligny-Thilloy, still in possession of the enemy.

The failure to drive out the enemy rear-guards by a frontal attack from their last strongholds covering Bapaume was represented, there is reason to think, by the late Sir George Harper, who was in command of the IVth Corps, as not particularly creditable to the fighting qualities of the infantry of the division, and a gallant though belated effort was made to arrange, even at the eleventh hour, for the break-up of the division. The attempt failed, and it is justifiable to suggest that the idea of meeting the desperate resistance of isolated rear-guards by old-fashioned and equally isolated frontal attacks was itself an unwise one. As so often, when the time came for an advance in a wider form two days later, the advanced posts, for which so much had been vainly sacrificed, fell without a shot being fired.

★★★★★★

On August 30th the Hawke Battalion, with the rest of the division, was transferred to Sir Charles Ferguson's XVIIth Corps, to take part in the new battle which had opened farther to the north on August 26th.

The immediate object of the second battles of Arras was to seize the northern end of the Hindenburg system and the Drocourt-Quéant system beyond it. To carry these systems was to drive a wedge between the new positions to which we were forcing the enemy to retire east of the Somme, and those to which the enemy was still clinging on the Lys. We should thus compel him to evacuate the Lys salient and to fall back in front of Cambrai to the lines of the Canal du Nord and the Canal de l'Éscaut. The plan was, in this event, to press on against the line of the canals, to seize Cambrai, and to drive the enemy back on Mauberge before he could extricate his forces in the south from the pressure of the Franco-American offensive.

This plan was fully carried out, and at its two most critical stages, the attack on the Drocourt-Quéant line and the attack on the Canal du Nord-Canal de l'Éscaut positions, the Hawke Battalion was actively engaged.

The attack on the Drocourt-Quéant line is notable in the history of the war, as of the Hawke Battalion, because it introduced a variation in the orthodox trench-to-trench attack actually as superior to that employed in the August offensives as those had been to the costly and ill-considered methods of 1916. The first step forward had been,

215

as we have seen, the attack by two divisions in depth, the second division to exploit the success of the first simultaneously with the capture of the enemy's front-line system. How this prevented those successive retirements to new and equally formidable prepared positions which had paralysed our 1916 attacks was seen in the fall of Bapaume within ten days of the opening of the second battles of the Somme. Now the lesson was applied with even greater success and on a larger scale.

The plan for carrying the Drocourt-Quéant line was based on the exploitation of the attack of the right division of the Canadian Corps by two British divisions of the XVIIth Corps, which were to follow the Canadian Division, cross the enemy lines in the Canadian Corps area, and sweep down from there into their own area behind what would, under the old methods, have been their first and probably their only objective. This was the old ideal of the advocates of the "breakthrough," logically thought out and now to be put to a triumphant test, unhampered by too many time-tables, barrages, and other checks and balances appropriate enough to the working of the British constitution but not to the handling of troops in the field.

The change was illustrated by the orders given to the Naval Division. When the situation had developed sufficiently, the divisional commander[7] was to get the order "Move." He was then to make his way forward through the Canadian and 57th Divisions, cut the Quéant-Cambrai railway, seize the high ground east of Quéant, and press on to Inchy.

When the battle opened at dawn on September 2nd, the Hawke Battalion, attached to the 188th Brigade, was in reserve in the neighbourhood of Henin. The order to "move" reached the division at 7.45 a.m. on that day, and the Hawke, following in the wake of the 188th Brigade, who were to lead the division's attack, moved first to the cemetery near Hendecourt (captured by the 57th Division only a few hours before), and thence, at about noon, to a position just west of Cagnicourt Wood. At 2 p.m., having reached the division's first objective across the Quéant-Cambrai railway, the 188th Brigade had the pardonable desire to relieve their own battalions with those of the 189th Brigade which were temporarily attached to them.

Commander Lockwood was now commanding the Hawke (with Sub-Lieutenant J. O. Harris as his adjutant, Lieutenant Blackmore being on leave), and he got orders to move forward to the sunken road

7. Major-General Blacklock, C.B., who succeeded Major-General Lawrie at this juncture.

in rear of the railway and to prepare to take over the captured position at nightfall.

Unhappily for the personal comfort of all parties, the days had gone by when fresh battalions could be used for such purposes. Having reached the first objective with the 188th Brigade, it was now for Commander Egerton[8] to reach and hold Inchy with the 189th. Commander Lockwood, in the circumstances, got fresh orders at 5 p.m. to march on Inchy in conjunction with the Hood Battalion, and when, at 6.20 p.m., the detailed orders had been duly cancelled, the advance began. This was the new warfare in which the objectives remained. It was only the plans for taking them which were subject to cancellation.

Commander Lockwood set about moving on Inchy by the simple manoeuvre of marching down the Inchy road, with "D" and "A" companies (Lieutenant Edwards and Lieutenant Flowitt in command) on the left of the road, with "C" and "B" companies (Lieutenant Beaumont and Lieutenant Biggs) on the right, and an advance guard in front. These dispositions provided the battalion with the first example in four years of fighting of the actual employment of an orthodox advance guard, and it is to the credit of the Crystal Palace authorities that this precaution, omitted by the Highland Brigade at Magersfontein, was remembered by Colonel Levey's disciples on the road to Inchy. This was fortunate, for the incident which disturbed with never-failing regularity our marches from Sydenham to Streatham (the advance guard being fired on by Colour-Sergeant Ashton with one round of blank and a rattle) had a remarkable though, of course, less impressive parallel at 7.30 p.m. on the Inchy road, when a German machine gun actually fired two rounds at the Hawke scouts before withdrawing.

No further opposition was encountered until, intersecting the Inchy road, the battalion came to the junction of the Buissy switch and the Hindenburg support line. From both these trenches machine guns opened in the gathering dusk on the Hawke advance guards. Detachments from the leading companies moved to the flanks to try and get behind the enemy, but they only encountered opposition on an even wider front. The sad fact was that the new warfare had at this junction run up against the old. The enemy were holding the trenches, and the trenches had to be captured before we could go any farther.

Wisely, Commander Lockwood decided to rest his battalion and

---

8. Temporarily commanding the 189th Brigade, *vice* Brigadier-General Du Pree.

to wait for daylight and the assistance of the Hood Battalion before making a formal attack. A nine miles' advance was sufficient for the day, and the Hawke found itself at any rate in the very front of the battle as it lay down to rest and watch on the night of the 2nd to 3rd September.

With the dawn, however, came the imperative need for action. The enemy still held the trenches, and if the XVIIth Corps was to be wholly successful, it must reach Inchy and the line of the Canal du Nord before the enemy's resistance had had time to harden. With the Hood on their left, the Hawke attacked at 9.30 a.m. on the 3rd September. There was, of course, about the desperate fighting that followed nothing of the old-fashioned trench-to-trench attack. We were not advancing against a continuous and carefully prepared position under a barrage; rather, it was an action between an advance guard and an isolated rear-guard which had chosen an abandoned trench system as the scene of its spasmodic but effective activities. The Hawke attacked with two companies ("B" on the left and "A" on the right), the other two being in support. Fighting, which soon involved all four companies, continued all the morning, but by 1.10 p.m. the trench system was finally cleared and we were in the village of Inchy, with none of the enemy nearer to us than the banks of the Canal du Nord.

Before advancing farther, Commander Lockwood was anxious to find out the position on his right flank, where the Drake were reported to be. He and Harris went forward at 2 p.m. on a reconnaissance, and after advancing a quarter of a mile to the south-east, saw the Drake advancing well away to the right against Tadpole Copse. There were, however, no signs of the enemy between himself and the Drake, and he sent back instructions to the rest of the battalion to come forward.

Before they had done so (actually only two officers and fifty men had arrived on the scene) orders came for the Hawke to capture the southernmost of the three bridge-heads across the canal. At once the Hawke Battalion Headquarters, with the small detachment available, went forward into the village. They were, however, held up by heavy machine-gun fire, and despite the assistance of the Marine Battalion and some cyclists they could make no headway. Deciding to bring up the rest o his battalion, Commander Lockwood went back to Brisbane Trench and from there organised a further attack.

The plan now was for two parties, each consisting of an officer and fifty men, to make their way by derelict trenches to two points, each roughly 500 yards to north and south of the bridgehead. It would then, it was hoped, fall to a converging attack. By 10 p.m. the right party (under Sub-Lieutenant Chapman) was only 300 yards from their objective, and the northern party (under Sub-Lieutenant Harry) not much more than that. But the intervening space could not be rushed by the forces available, and not till 7 a.m. on the 4th, when some fresh troops were available, was the position captured by Sub-Lieutenant Harris, who guided a fresh party personally to the assembly point and led the attack. Although the bridge-head could not be permanently held, the enemy posts were destroyed, and our line was established barely 100 yards west of the canal, in touch with the Drake, who had entered the outskirts of Mœuvres. On the evening of the 4th the Hawke were relieved by the Artists Rifles, and the objective which they had reached was safely consolidated by the time the Naval Division was relieved by the Guards Division three days later.

The battalion had barely had time to recover from their severe losses in front of Ligny-Thilloy, and now had again lost heavily. Lieutenant Biggs (who had succeeded Lieutenant Stephenson in command of "A" company), Sub-Lieutenant Strickland, Sub-Lieutenant Wicks, and Sub-Lieutenant Chapman, with some fifty N.C.O.'s and men, had been killed, and the wounded were nearly 300. The battalion was, however, to have ample time to absorb the new drafts, for they were taken out of the line to Somblin, and then to the neighbouring village of St. Leger till August 25th.

Lieutenant Flowitt (an officer of the former Nelson Battalion who had joined the Hawke just before the Drocourt-Quéant attack) remained in command of "A" company,[9] with Sub-Lieutenant George Clarke as second in command; Lieutenant Matthews came out from England to take over "B" company, and Lieutenants Beaumont and Edwards remained in command of "C" and "D" companies.

The headquarters establishment remained unchanged, and other officers who were available to take part in the remaining engagements were Second Lieutenant Hughes Jones whose share in every engagement in which he took part with the Hawke Battalion was a prominent one), Sub-Lieutenants J. O. Harris (who received the D.S.O.—a rare distinction for a platoon commander—for his fine work in the attack on the Canal du Nord bridgehead), F. C. Harry, J. B. Johnston,

9. Lieutenant Dodds had been wounded in the later stages of the engagement of August 25th.

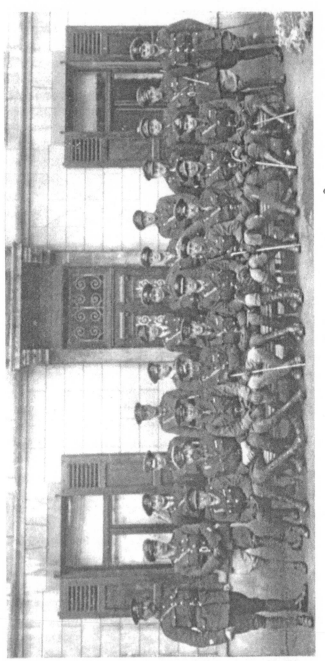

OFFICERS OF THE HAWKE BATTALION AT DOUR, 1918.

*Standing*: Sgt.-Major Hawker, Sub-lieut. Withnell, Sub-Lieut. Loveday, Sub-Lieut. Brough, Sub-Lieut. Watson, Sub-Lieut. Wood, Sub-Lieut. Nicoll, Sub-Lieut. Kellow, Sub-Lieut. West, Sub-Lieut. Inman, Sub-Lieut. Smith, Sub-Lieut. Rudnick, Sub-Lieut. Clarke, Sub-Lieut. Faulkner.

*Sitting*: Lieut. & Qr. Day, Sub-Lieut. Codner, Lieut. Valentine, Lieut. Flowitt, Lieut.-Com. Blackmore, Com. Shelton, Sub-Lieut. Woodgate, Sur.-Lieut. Leake, Lieut. Stear, Lieut. Rackham.

T. W. Reeve J. G. Todd, J. W. Orr, W. H. Warkwise, J. A. Woodgate (second in command "D" company), A. W. Withnell, A.. M. Valentine, M. Thomson, T. S. Cockburn, G. T. S. Ryan, C. Oubridge, P. A. Friend, G. F. Summers, and L. D. Harvey.

This bare chronicle of names may seem a poor substitute indeed for the proper appreciation of the scores of individual exploits which contributed to the battalion's achievements in the closing engagements now to be described. The fact is however, that battles against rear-guards deployed in great depth over a wide front (in the advance to the Canal du Nord the battalion actually covered nearly ten miles) cannot be spectacular. In the war of positions, where rapid and effective retreat is virtually impossible, the attacking force must get to close quarters with bomb and bayonet if they are to have even a chance of success, and individual skill and resource may well be the deciding factor. Now it was different. An advance was at least more like a route march than it was like the trench-to-trench attack of earlier days. The ability to keep direction steadily under spasmodic fire, to adopt a preconceived plan quickly to unexpected circumstances, to maintain communication with Battalion and Brigade Headquarters, to control platoons and sections without hampering their initiative these were the keys to success. These abilities are rare but they are not spectacular, and they cannot be described except by their results.

★★★★★★

On September 25th the Hawke Battalion returned to the Inchy-Mœuvres sector, which had been consolidated exactly as it had been handed over. The objective of the impending attack was a position 1,000 yards west of the Canal de l'Éscaut, to reach which the divisions engaged on this front had to carry (1) the line of the Canal du Nord immediately east of Mœuvres; (2) the Hindenburg support line, which lay behind the canal and roughly parallel to it; and (3) the high ground to the south-east between Anneux and Graincourt. These three successive objectives were to be captured by the Naval Division, and the attack was to begin at dawn on September 27th.

A frontal attack on the Hindenburg line was to be avoided. The division was to cross the canal on a narrow front, and after seizing high ground immediately beyond the canal, was to bomb down the Hindenburg line from north to south. Similarly, the attack on the Anneux-Graincourt position was to be launched from the left of the captured Hindenburg line. The canal defences and the Hindenburg support system were to be attacked by the 190th Brigade. The 188th

Brigade had to go on to attack the Anneux-Graincourt position, and the 189th Brigade (including, of course, the Hawke Battalion) was in divisional reserve. The 188th Brigade were to advance against their objective at 7.58 a.m., by which time the 190th Brigade were due to have captured the Hindenburg line. In rear of the 188th Brigade the Hawke Battalion had to move across the canal.

Roughly speaking, these expectations were fulfilled. At any rate, the Hawke Battalion moved forward from Mœuvres across the canal about 8 a.m., and found that, though spasmodic fighting was still going on in the Hindenburg line, the attack on Anneux and Graincourt had been punctually launched. Under cover of the Bourlon Ridge, Commander Lockwood waited with his battalion till midday, when the orders came to go forward in support of the right of the Anson, who were held up a mile short of the Anneux-Graincourt Ridge by an enemy detachment at the sugar factory on the Bapaume-Cambrai road.

For a time the Hawke waited in shell-holes, their line extending that of the Anson on the right and directed against Graincourt. The Drake were on the left of the Anson, with Anneux as their objective. "A" and "C" companies were to lead the Hawke attack.

At 2.15 p.m., under cover of an artillery bombardment, the whole line moved forward, and the Hawke and Anson captured the sugar factory. Here Commander Lockwood was severely hit as the Hawke Headquarters followed up the battalion, and the leading Hawke platoons were held up for a time in shell-holes, until a final attack led by Sub-Lieutenant Clarke and Lieutenant Hughes Jones in a most gallant and efficient manner carried the outskirts of the village. Without a moment's delay Sub-Lieutenant Clarke pushed forward, and not only captured the enemy trench system beyond the village, but also a battery of field guns. The result was to cut off the retreat of some 300 of the enemy. By 6.30 p.m., when the enemy counter-attacked, the 189th Brigade was organised in defence of the entire captured position from Graincourt to Anneux, and was able to beat off the enemy attack without difficulty.

When, at dawn on the 28th, the 57th Division went through our lines to secure the line of the Canal de l'Éscaut, it seemed that for the time the task of the Hawke was finished. Later in the morning, however, the battalion was ordered forward to co-operate in this difficult but all-important operation.

The Hawke Battalion found in the neighbourhood of the canal a

Hon. Lieut. and Quartermaster H. A. Day, M.C.;
Surgeon Lieut. Leake, M.C., R.N.; and Lieut. B. B.
Rackham, M.C. R.N.V.R.,at Dour, November, 1918

situation of incalculable and dangerous confusion. Parties of the 2nd Division, on the right of the 57th Division, were reported to be across the canal and the river; parties of the 57th Division had certainly crossed the canal (though it was feared that they had been cut off); but the enemy still held out in La Folie Wood, this side of the canal, on the left of what was now the Naval Division's front. To clear up the position and to force the crossings of the canal and river[10] was the task definitely assigned to the 189th Brigade at 4 p.m. on the 28th.

The Hood Battalion was directed by Brigadier-General Curling[11] to La Folie Wood, and the Drake Battalion on Cantignual Mill, where the enemy had retired from the canal, but held the river crossings in strength.

At the same time General Curling sent Captain Wright and Lieutenant-Commander Blackmore (who had taken command of the Hawke Battalion when Commander Lockwood was wounded) to reconnoitre another crossing to the south, where the river crosses the canal, and where there was a lock gate not wholly destroyed. This crossing was found to have been secured by the 2nd Division, and it was decided to bring "B" and "C" companies (Lieutenant Matthews and Lieutenant Beaumont) of the Hawke Battalion to this point, so that they might cross and join up with the Drake and Hood Battalions as soon as these battalions also could get across.

The situation, however, was not as satisfactory as these plans suggested. The Hood were fighting hard in Folie Wood, but were not, in the late afternoon of the 28th, doing much more than hold their own. Thanks largely to a brilliant feat of arms on the part of a leading seaman, the Drake had secured a slender foothold across the river opposite Cantignual Mill, but were held to the very edge of the river bank, and were unable in the daylight to reinforce the small garrison of the post they had established. And when Lieutenant-Commander Blackmore came back at 4.30 p.m. to the lower crossing, he found that even this bridge-head had been lost, the 2nd Division detachments having been driven back.

As the engineers were to attempt during the night to throw pontoon bridges across the river, he decided to wait till dawn, and then to send his whole battalion across, if possible, in several parties simultaneously. For this purpose "D" company also was brought forward dur-

---

10. It is important to remember that, whereas the Canal du Nord was dry, the Canal de l'Escaut, as well as the Escaut River, were not. 11. General Curling had taken over command of the 189th Brigade from Commander Egerton on September 3rd.

ing the night to the neighbourhood of the lock gates. "A" company, however, had been temporarily attached to the Drake Battalion, and was held by Commander Beak in reserve at Cantignual Mill.

During the night the efforts of the engineers were successful, and two pontoon bridges were put across the river to the north of the lock gates. Everything now turned on the courage and dash of the combined infantry attack.

The dawn was cold and misty, and in partial concealment the 5th and 6th Platoons of "B" company under Sub-Lieutenant Valentine with one platoon of "C" company under Sub-Lieutenant T. W. Reeve got across one of the pontoon bridges under heavy shell fire with few casualties, though Sub-Lieutenant Reeve was among the killed. The rest of the battalion, less "A" company, rushed the lock gates, and "A" company itself, crossing under Commander Beak's orders opposite Cantignual Mill, completed a triumphant operation by an advance of 3,000 yards to the ridge overlooking Niergnies and the environs of Cambrai.[12] Here at noon the line had been established when the Marines and R.I.R. came forward to relieve the victorious 189th Brigade.

On October 1st, after another small advance by the 188th and 190th Brigades, the whole division was relieved, and confidently expected a certainly well-earned rest. Indeed, the divisional commander was on his way back to England when he was recalled with orders to attack and capture Niergnies to secure the flank of the Third Army for their impending attack on the Beaurevoir line.

The difficulty had resulted from the decision not to bombard Cambrai, which made it hard to get forward immediately south of the city. During the first days of October the operations had flagged, and finally, on October 5th, the XVIIth Corps were informed that the immediate capture of Niergnies and its defences was of vital importance, and must be achieved.

The attack was to be carried out, like so many others, by the 188th and 189th Brigades, and by the night of October 7th to 8th they were in their assembly positions north-east of Rumilly, waiting confidently for the opening of the barrage.

The first objective, to be attacked by the R.I.R.[13] (on the right)

---

12. Sub-Lieutenant Clarke was largely responsible for this success.

13. The Irish Rifles had joined the 188th Brigade in May, 1918, when, as the result of heavy losses, the two Marine Battalions had been amalgamated. The brigade thus consisted of the Marine Battalion, the Anson Battalion, and the 2nd R.I.R.

and the Drake Battalion, was the enemy trench in front of Niergnies. The second objective, comprising the village and the enemy works immediately behind it, was to be attacked by the Royal Marines and the Hood.

The task of the Hawke Battalion was to safeguard the left flank of the attacking troops by seizing the high ground west of Niergnies.

The attack on Niergnies, in sharp contradistinction to the operations in which the Hawke had recently been engaged, was a purely local attack, with a limited objective, under a barrage. Like all such attacks it was costly, but unlike most of them, including two made on the 4th and 5th October by another division against the same objective, it was successful.

The attack made history because of the use by Germans in a vigorous counter-attack of captured British tanks, and still more because of the brilliant manner in which the situation, momentarily serious, was restored by Commander Buckle and Commander Pollock, who turned against the tanks the anti-tank guns and rifles which their battalion had captured a few minutes before. These events, however, did not happen on the Hawke front, where the battle proceeded according to time-table, though with serious losses, Lieutenant Cookson[14] (commanding "A" company), Sub-Lieutenant Harris, D.S.O. (commanding "B" company), Sub-Lieutenant Harry, and Sub-Lieutenant Johnston being among the killed in this, the last serious engagement fought by the Hawke Battalion.

As a matter of interest in this relation, I print below the operation orders.

"Hawke" Battalion Operation Orders for the Attack.
7th October, 1918.

1. Information.—The Third Army continues the attack at a date and hour to be notified later.

2. Intention.—The 63rd (R.N.) Division attacks on the right of the XVIIth Corps, and will be responsible for the protection of the left flank from the junction of the trench and railway at G.4.*b*. eastwards to the cross-roads at B.25.*c*.1.8.

The 99th Infantry Brigade, 2nd Division, VIth Corps, attacks on our right.

The 57th Division is responsible for the protection of the left flank from G.4.*b*. westwards.

---

14. Lieutenant Flowitt was on leave.

The attack will be carried out with the 188th Infantry Brigade on the right and the 189th Infantry Brigade on the left, The 190th Infantry Brigade is in reserve, and will move in support of the 188th Infantry Brigade.

3. Instructions—*(a) Move.*—The brigade will move to a position of assembly in the vicinity of the factory in L.6.*c.*, in accordance with orders which will be issued later.

*(b)* By 30 minutes to zero brigade will be formed up on a taped line running from G.10.*a.*1.9., to G.10.*d.*3.6., with "Hawke" Battalion on the left and "Drake" Battalion on right. "Hood "Battalion will be in rear of the "Drake" Battalion.

*(c) Dispositions.*— "Hawke "Battalion will form up on the line from G.10.*a.*1.9. to G. 10.*a.*65.25. Battalion will attack in two waves, "C" and "D" companies in the first wave, with "A" company in support to "C" company, and "B" company in support to "D" company in the second wave. Companies will attack in two lines with two platoons in each line. Distance to be maintained between lines will be 50 yards, and between waves 150 yards.

*(d) Objectives.*—Battalion objective will be the trench to the left of the "Drake "Battalion from G.5.*b.*7.8. to A.29.*d.*0.5., and the trench from A.29.*d.*0.1. to G.4.*b.*8.7. After capture objective will be consolidated in depth with three companies in the line ("A," "C," and "D" companies), and one company ("B" company) in reserve in the vicinity of Buerre Mill.

"D" company will hold from G.5.*b.*7.8. to the corner of the copse in A.29.*d.*0.5.; "C" company, on the arrival of "A" company, will hold from A.29.*d.*0.5. to road (inclusive) at A.29.*c.*6.2.; and "A" company will move up (see below) and occupy from road (exclusive) to railway at G.4.*b.*6.7. During the advance "B" company will be responsible for the "mopping up" of Buerre Mill, and "A" company will move forward and take up a position on the left of "C" company. Companies will find their own local supports, and principal tactical features will be organised for defence.

*(e) Communications and Liaison.*—Communication between companies and Battalion Headquarters will be maintained under arrangements to be made by the battalion signal officer. All means possible will be used—runner, visual, rockets, etc.—and it is of the utmost importance that information is got back as

soon as possible.

"Nil" information reports are of the greatest assistance when there is nothing of importance to report. The positions of Battalion Headquarters will be notified later.

Liaison will be maintained between companies by means of patrols, and flank companies will maintain liaison with the units on their flanks at all costs.

(f) *Contact Planes.*—Contact planes will call for flares at (a) zero plus two hours; (b) zero plus three and a half hours; (c) zero plus four and a half hours.

A counter-attack plane will be up from zero hour onwards.

(g) *Artillery.*—Six brigades of Field Artillery will form the barrage. Three brigades of Field Artillery will protect the left flank. Three brigades of heavy artillery will cover the attack. The barrage opens and dwells on the line G.17.*a*.8.8.-G.4.*c*.45.30.-G.3.*a*.9.4. for ten minutes, and then moves forward at the rate of 100 yards in three minutes. There will be a pause of thirty minutes east of the first objective. Thereafter the barrage moves at the rate of 100 yards in four minutes. On lifting off the first objective the barrage pivots on A.29.*d*. central and swings, so as to form a protective barrage round the second objective and left flank.

(h) *Machine Guns.*—The 63rd M.G. Battalion and two companies of 52nd M.G. Battalion will (a) provide an overhead barrage for the advance on first objective; (b) cover the left flank of our advance; (c) earmark two companies to cover the advance to second objective.

(i) *Tanks.*—Tanks will operate as detailed at the conference this morning.

R. Blackmore,[15]
Lieutenant and Adjutant.

By 5 p.m. on the 8th October all objectives were finally gained by all battalions.

Not only had a strongly defended position been abandoned by the enemy, with a loss in captured alone of 34 officers, 1,155 men, 81 machine guns, and 9 field guns, but the way was now open for the advance of the left of the Third Army. The next morning the whole

---

15. Lieutenant-Colonel Clutterbuck, R.M.L.I., had been appointed O.C. Hawke in succession to Commander Lockwood.

line south of Cambrai moved forward. By October 10th Cambrai had fallen, and the last of the enemy's prepared positions was definitely and finally broken.

# Conclusion

From the evening of October 8th, when the sharp but brief engagement at Niergnies was over, until the beginning of November, the Hawke Battalion rested in the neighbourhood of St. Pol. By the time the orders came for the battalion, with the rest of the Naval Division, to join the XXIInd Corps in Belgium the war was virtually over. Certainly nothing of military importance remains to be told. The pursuit of the enemy, in which the Hawke joined on November 8th, took the form not so much of a successful advance as of a constant endeavour on the part of our well-equipped and well-provisioned troops to overtake an enemy who was prepared to jettison anything and everything in a headlong flight. Actually, if the truth be told, the enemy got the better of the argument; at least, we never got so close as to force him to stand and fight.

However, the issue of the war was settled, and the extreme pressure put on the infantry in these last days to harry the enemy rear-guards was more political than military in its object. But if, for the soldier, as for the civilian, peace was the one remaining objective, the vigour of our pursuit had its effect in hastening, if only by a few days, the inevitable surrender of the enemy.

It was, indeed, characteristic of the thoroughness with which even at the eleventh hour this pursuit was carried out that, as late as 10.30 a.m. on November 11th, the Hawke Battalion should be reaching out towards a defined objective, the railway line west of the small village of Vellereille-le-sec. And here, on their objective, the Armistice found them.

It was a well-earned respite, and when, on the first evening of peace which they had known, the battalion billeted in the village before which they had come to rest, those few who had served with the battalion since its formation at the Crystal Palace must have looked, back with something akin to pride on their achievement.

The battalion had learnt in a hard school, had experienced defeat, and had now found peace in victory. But if the knowledge of men, cities, and fortune which it had gained in four years was greater by a good deal than men bred in the ways of peace learn in a score of years, the Armistice was only an incident in the career of men to whom the war was only an interlude. To the end they remained a battalion of amateurs, conforming more easily, as the years went on, but still with a mental reservation, to the ways of the army. At Dour the reservation became at times almost apparent, and as old friends came out from England to rejoin the battalion in its peaceful but hilarious autumn, the reaction from war and its customs became more marked.

An account of these months of reaction would be, however, out of place here, where we have only tried to tell soberly, but not too seriously, of the experiences of the battalion in war. For us who survive the experience of peace continues, and is more varied in London in 1925 than it was in Dour six years ago. The point of this story lies elsewhere.

The Hawke Battalion was one of the most definitely civilian units which took the field in the Great War. It fought long and arduously, but it never lost its civilian character. That was its almost unique quality. I can hardly hope that in pages devoted so exclusively to military operations I have succeeded in conveying throughout the appropriate atmosphere. But it persisted, for all that.

That this was so was in a large measure due to the enduring influence of the first commanding officer of the Hawke Battalion. The common-sense attitude which Colonel Wilson had ingrained into the battalion survived his period of command. We had no use for heroes. If only for this reason I have been chary of recording systematically decorations earned or awarded, still more so of distributing even the most discriminating praise to the individual achievements of officers and men. The battalion served as a whole and to the best of its ability in an essentially incongruous task, and in that spirit I have tried to write.

We had our share of decorations, and I do not want any word of mine to be understood as suggesting that they were not well deserved. But the war was not won by personal gallantry, and it was characteristic of the Hawke that their officers and men should have understood this fact well. There was work to be done in those years which required method, endurance, and common sense above everything else. The Hawke Battalion claims that it did its share of this work, and it claims nothing more.

Presentation of the King's Colour to the Hawke Battalion at Dour, 1919

# Afterword

### A Note on Literature and the War

The doings of a single battalion in a war now some years past cannot claim to be of historical importance. For those, however, who are personally interested, this story of other days may have recaptured a memory or two, and to the majority—to the critics, to the students of war in peace—the story may have had at least an academic interest as providing an indirect, though not a deliberate, criticism of some current writing about the war.

The stream of war literature grows in volume with the stability of the peace, and as prosperity increases may be expected to pour itself forth with increasing gusto. It is, indeed, admitted that the great war book has yet to be written, and by the "great war book" is meant, of course, the book which shall reveal to the future the littleness of the war contrasted with the greatness of the author. The admission that such a book in its ideal form is not yet written is a generous one from present-day critics, who, being authors first and critics only in the second intention, must, surely, have each written at least one book about the war. But if none of our critics claim that the really great war book has yet appeared, the praises they lavish on those published up to the present time are a sad reflection on our latter day standards of taste. For the literature of the war as it is assembled on our shelves is devastating in its perversion of values, and there seems to the plain man to be but little room for any culminating offence against artistic relevance.

The apparent fact is that the bulk of the war literature has been written by people who were either peculiarly unfortunate in their experiences, or regrettably peculiar in their reactions to them, and even the fine poems and letters begotten of the earliest days' activity have been superseded now in popular memory by the more profuse outpourings of less exact observers. The days when the war was a matter of serious concern were marked by some authentic and accurate studies of the home front, most notably by Mr. Bennett and Mr. Wells, and by some finer poems which have enriched our literature permanently. The writers of the introspective school were perhaps thrown for a time off their balance by the majestic impact of objective reality and the realists by their patriotic consciences. But the eclipse was only temporary.

Self-expression, simple if not pure, is a necessary form of self-indulgence for some types of the literary mind, and the scepticism and disillusion of a prolonged campaign, the despair of a few and the anguish of the many, provided a fertile soil in which to preach, by precept, if not by example, the artistic and ethical importance of the individual revolt against compelling necessity. For Rupert Brooke and Grenfell Hampstead soon substituted Osbert Sitwell and Sassoon. Wells and Bennett had a surer hold, because the civilian audience to whom they had appealed did not put on the full-dress uniform of disillusion till after the Armistice; also, no doubt, disaffection is harder to dissemble in prose than in verse. But the time came when even in prose the disciples of self-expression could safely tell the story of those interesting years in which their attention had been, as it now appeared, exclusively engaged in the study of their own reactions to those events which, but for their fidelity, might have interrupted irreparably the serious work of the suburbs.

The incursion of the egotist into the field of war literature would have been a small enough matter had it not been for the fact that some twenty millions of more or less educated people were standing about Europe and America after the war, wondering what it had all been about. When they read the outpourings of the ardent spirits to whom every parade had been a crisis of conscience, whose belief in the rights of the individual was insulted by the merest glimpse of a uniform, when they read of the long agony of soul which so many men of military age had, it seemed, experienced from August 4th, 1914, actually until 11 a.m. on November 1th, 1918, these same twenty millions inevitably sat up and took a little notice. Perhaps this was the truth about the war? Perhaps they had been in very fact only the blind and passive victims in a discreditable episode revolting to more honourable men ? Perhaps it was really the case that the brave men were those who had resisted the blandishments of the Chorus and evaded the sterner if less effectual provisions of the Military Service Acts ? Was it not at least plausible that the real heroes were those who fought, but without enthusiasm, especially as it seemed clear that these few alone could claim alike the favours which public opinion still reserves for those who fought and the blessings promised by the Prince of Peace to those who do not?

Amid such a universal scepticism the novelist and the essay writer reaped a glorious harvest, not only in readers, but in disciples. Every variety of honest doubter, from the man who was only afraid of being afraid and won the V.C., to the man who was only afraid of being killed and was shot for cowardice, figured as the true type of gallant and perfect knight in the different novels of the period. It was left, oddly enough, to an officer in the Hawke Battalion to beat all records with the closing sentence of an otherwise excellent and truthful story,[1] which tells of "the bravest man I ever knew," and how they shot him at dawn. He was not shot by the enemy.

But these sidelights on the "realities" of active service were as nothing to the devastating revelations of the mental and moral wreckage thrown back on the patient and heroic civilians by the cruel act of demobilisation. Personally, I returned home from the front by the front door, but the most cursory survey of the writings of Arnold Bennett, W. L. George, Stephen McKenna, Alec Waugh, Oliver Onions, even John Galsworthy, shows me that this was an unpardonable piece of eccentricity. The return "from five years of hell out there" to a home whose occupants were still occasionally sober and still practised an ostensible monogamy should have kindled a sense of intolerable grievance; after a month, drink and drugs should have claimed me, and a little later the falsification of accounts should have become second nature to me. In the sequel a series of liaisons with titled debutantes would have been interrupted only by death, big game shooting, a successful debut as a dramatist or poet, or an eleventh hour marriage designed to prove that "five years of hell" could deprive a gentleman of every shred of morality and yet leave him with a fuddled respect for the laws of legitimacy.

Had the post-war mind turned, by way of reaction from the excitements of battles, to a study of the real and tragic sorrows which war inflicts on legitimate non-combatants, it is certain that no soldier would raise a protest. Suffering is a part of man's lot, and arguments on the morality of war based on the personal suffering of individuals are as empty and sterile as most attempts to build out of the complexities

---

1. *The Secret Battle*, by A. P. Herbert.

of human life a social or political system which shall exorcise the evil while retaining the whole of the good which is in mankind. But the fact remains that too many of those who fought began by ignoring and ended by becoming almost indifferent to the sufferings of those at home, and any writer who had employed his gifts in giving permanence to this aspect of the universal tragedy would not have wasted his time.

It is not, however, of such a work still to be written that most men think when they speak of the great literature which the war will yet bring forth, but of some tremendous indictment of the catastrophic effects of war on the individuals who took part in it. The whole tendency of the later literature of the war is biased by this extraordinary obsession—extraordinary not only because it is supported by little evidence, but because it shows the extent to which the professionalization of literature has debased our standards of accuracy, decency, and perspective.

No doubt for many men of sedentary habits, not accustomed to the ordinary business of life, the war was a novel and bewildering experience. To the vast majority of all classes it spelt only an intensification of effort for an unusually compelling cause. Normal man is a social animal, who spends his life in peace as well as war in some form of corporate activity. Even the element of personal danger is familiar to an appreciable minority of men in their daily work. Only men strange to the practical work of the world and alien to physical risks, yet also by some peculiar complex unfitted for such work and reluctant to assume such risks, could see in active service that unbelievable and abhorrent *Chimaera* of suffering and degradation for which it passes by statement or implication in so much modern fiction. Shocking though it may appear, it is at least arguable that the agonies of soul depicted by these modern writers are not the torments of a superior sensibility, but only the exaggerated reaction of a too specialized civilization which produces whole classes who have lost the aptitude for practical activity.

Is it surprising that the loss of this aptitude should have proved paralyzing to creative art? The great literature of the war will surely not be written by the psychological by-products of an age of urban over-population, but by men who can understand with sympathy the conditions subject to which alone mankind can at once think and act effectively. These conditions are at once moral and psychological, and it is only by a close study of the true psychology of men in action as shown in the objective reality of their actions at the time that they can be understood. The concentration of literary energy on the peculiarities of those few men and women who reacted abnormally to the test of action is, seen in this light, a more serious matter than might at first sight appear. What men can achieve by corporate effort in war, they can achieve in peace. If the work of the world in peace is to be entrusted to those who, on the claimed ground of finer sensibility, failed to endure with at least a comparative stoicism the perils of war, the world in peace will be the loser. And if as a race we concentrate our educated sympathies on these rarer types, we may in time come to conform to them in the mass, with results disastrous to that slow progress of mankind towards a corporate morality wherein lies the only hope of lasting welfare upon earth.